John Marquart

600 Miscellaneous Valuable Receipts

Worth their Weight in Gold

John Marquart

600 Miscellaneous Valuable Receipts
Worth their Weight in Gold

ISBN/EAN: 9783337342869

Printed in Europe, USA, Canada, Australia, Japan

Cover: Foto ©Suzi / pixelio.de

More available books at **www.hansebooks.com**

600

MISCELLANEOUS VALUABLE

RECEIPTS,

WORTH THEIR WEIGHT IN GOLD.

A THIRTY YEARS' COLLECTION,

By JOHN MARQUART,

LEBANON, PA.

TO WHICH IS ADDED

TWO SIMPLE GAUGING TABLES,

TO ENABLE MERCHANTS TO TAKE INVENTORY OF THEIR STOCK.

LEBANON, PA.:
PUBLISHED BY CHRISTIAN HENRY.
C. P. PERRY, BINDER AND PRINTER, COR. **FOURTH & RACE,** PHILADA.
1860.

Entered according to Act of Congress, in the year 1860, by
CHRISTIAN HENRY,
in the Clerk's Office of the District Court of the United States for the Eastern District of Pennsylvania.

STEREOTYPED BY L. JOHNSON & CO.
PHILADELPHIA.

PREFACE.

The title of this work is "SIX HUNDRED MISCELLANEOUS VALUABLE RECEIPTS, WORTH THEIR WEIGHT IN GOLD." The indication of it will at once show to the reader what he may expect by procuring a copy of it; and, by perusing thoroughly the contents, he will be perfectly persuaded to have a copy of the same, let the cost be what it may; and that it will—what its title indicates—be worth its weight in gold. There should not be a family, young gentleman or lady, without a copy of this valuable book. It is not the great number of receipts that makes a book valuable; only the usefulness is appreciated. The reader is referred to the Index to find what he wants. The heading of each department is in alphabetical order, and he will see it commences with a B, Battery; C, Cakes and Pies; D, Diseases in human beings; &c. &c.; and each department is subdivided into an alphabetical order. For example: you have a sick horse; all you have to do is to look for the H in the index, and you will find at the heading of this department "Horse-diseases, cures for," and whatever the disease may be you can find under this head. Say you want a cure for the gripes in a horse: look for "Gripes, cure for," and the corresponding number will be 444, which, after you have found this number, will be what you want to cure the gripes with; and so on with every receipt you want to make use of, which is so simple that any school-boy who is able to read can find. The object of this book is to show in a clear and comprehensive manner how to use the within-mentioned receipts; and they are embodied in as little space and as simple language as possible, and include all the information derived from them. The compiler has been thirty years in collecting some of the "*Six Hundred Miscellaneous Valuable Receipts, worth their weight in gold,*" some of which never before appeared in print, and some have been collected from the very best of works treating on this subject. His aim has always been to include all the very best and most useful and valuable receipts. It is not deemed necessary to comment on the usefulness of the contents of this work, as all will have ample remuneration for the money laid out to possess a copy of it. In the performance of the task of collecting these "*Six Hundred Miscellaneous Valuable Receipts,*" the chief aim was to render this book as extensively useful as possible. It is confidently believed that it will form a course of useful science for the farmer, mechanic, merchant, tradesman and professional man, as well as the heads of families and their children; and it is also believed that there are few persons who will not find, on looking over its contents, some articles that will be useful and interesting to them. The receipts are so simple and plain that he who reads can understand.

Should any of the readers wish to make use of some one of the receipts, and have not the necessary scales or measures for the compounding of the same, he only has to copy it off and go to a druggist, who will at once compound the article for him. And any person that wishes to manufacture for wholesaling articles, and the quantity of the ingredients mentioned in the receipts is too large or too small, he, in either case, must make the ingredients in proportion to the quantity he intends to manufacture; and he must also be careful to get always the very best of ingredients, or he may not succeed in getting the articles desired.

The contents of this work, or heads of the different departments in the index, are as follows, to wit:—

Battery, galvanic, how to construct for gilding and silver-plating. Bedbug-poison, how to make. Brandy, how to imitate foreign, &c. Beverages, how to make. Blacking, how to make. Brass polish, how to make. Burning-fluid, how to make. Butter, rancid, how to cure. Cakes, how to bake. Cider, how to make and keep good. Cements, how to make. Cordials, how to make. Cow-diseases, cures for. Diseases in human beings, cures for. Dyeing, how to manage. Eggs, how to preserve. Extract of vanilla, how to make. Foul smell, how to destroy. Fish, how to keep fresh. Gilding edges of paper. Gin, Holland, how to imitate. Gloves, how to clean. Grease-spots, how to remove. Horse-diseases, cures for. Hams, how to cure. Ice-cream, how to make. Inks, writing, &c., how to make. Lard candles, how to make. Lime-water, how to make. Milk, how to preserve. Mildew, how to take out of linen. Painters, how to mix different colors to make different shades, &c. Perfumery, how to make. Pickle, how to make to cure meat. Printers' ink, how to make. Preserves, &c., how to make. Rectifying raw whiskey, how to put up stands. Rum, how to imitate. Sealing-wax, how to make. Sheep, cures for. Sugar, how to clarify, and how to boil coloring. Silk, how to clean. Silver, how to plate with, and German, how to make. Soldering without fire. Spirits, Jamaica, how to imitate. Swine, cures for. Syrup, simple, how to boil. Tinctures, how to make. Washing, how to save labor. Water-proof, how to make. Whitewash, brilliant, how to make. Wines, domestic, how to make, and foreign, how to imitate. Whiskey, Monongahela, &c., how to make. Yeast, how to make for distillers, &c.

To which is also added gauging regular-lying casks, which will enable any person to ascertain in a few minutes what number of gallons are contained in regular-shaped casks of different dimensions, when full or partly full, which is very handy to merchants in taking an inventory of their stock.

INDEX.

	Receipt
BATTERY, GALVANIC—To construct, for Gilding and Silver plating	488
BEDBUG-POISON	536
BRANDY—Blackberry, how to make. No. 1	311
Blackberry, " " No. 2	316
Bordeaux, to imitate	303
Cherry, how to make. No. 1	304
Cherry, " " No. 2	312
Cherry, " " No. 3	314
Cognac, to imitate. No. 1	293
Cognac, " " No. 2	294
Cognac, " " No. 3	295
Cognac, " " No. 4	296
Cognac, " " No. 5	301
Common, how to make	305
Domestic, " "	306
French, how to imitate. No. 1	297
French, " " No. 2	298
French, " " No. 3	307
French, " " No. 4	308
French, " " No. 5	309
Ginger, how to make	319
Lavender, " "	318
Peach, " "	310
Raspberry, " "	313
Rochelle, how to imitate. No. 1	300
Rochelle, " " No. 2	302
Rochelle, " " No. 3	317
Rose, how to make	315

INDEX.

	Receipt
BEVERAGES—Cottage Beer, how to make	86
Cream Beer, how to make	92
Gas, " " "	91
Ginger pleasant, how to make	94
Ginger Powder, " "	95
Ginger Imperial, " "	89
Ginger Beer, " "	88
Ginger Pop, " "	96
Mead	93
Mead, Sassafras	98
Spruce Beer	87
Spruce White	90
Pineapple-ade	99
Silver top	97
BLACKING—Harness, &c., how to make	560
Jet, for harness and boots	590
Japan, for leather	589
Liquid, how to make. No. 1	247
Liquid, " " No. 2	248
Oil paste, " " No. 1	50
Oil paste, " " No. 2	251
BRASS—Polish for	72
BURNING-FLUID, how to make	540
BUTTER—Bad, to improve	512
Rancid, to cure	511
To cure, that it will keep for years	513
CAKES AND PIES—Bread-cheese, how to bake	126
Buns, how to bake	133
Biscuits, " "	109
Cider, " "	111
Cream, " "	130
Cup, " "	113
Custard, without eggs	116
Frosting, how to	101
Ginger, how to bake	114
Green corn Omelet	522
Lemon, how to bake. No. 1	102
Lemon, " " No. 2	129
Lemon, white, how to bake	105
Lemon pies, " "	110

	Receipt
CAKES AND PIES—Mock mince pies	108
Muffins	131
Pound cake, plain, how to bake	127
Queen " " "	103
Rice " " "	128
Rusks, " " No. 1	107
Rusks, " " No. 2	132
Sponge cake, " "	104
Strasbourg " " "	106
Sugar " " "	112
CIDER—General Rules to make	266
How to make	262
How to manage	263
Observations on	265
Raisin, how to make	264
Rule for making good	267
To keep good for years	268
To keep good	269
CEMENTS—Crockery	508
Hard, for seams	509
Liquid	507
Water and fire proof	510
Which will get as hard as a stone	506
CORDIALS—Aniseed	253
Citron	254
Cinnamon	256
Cloves	258
Orange	257
Peppermint. No. 1	255
Peppermint. No. 2	261
Rose	260
Strawberry	259
Spirits, for beverage, to manufacture	252
COW-DISEASES—Cure for distemper in cattle	465
Flesh-wounds in cattle, tincture for	559
Frenzy, or inflammation of the brain	482
Garget in cows	447
Hoven or blown in cattle, cure for	479
Hoven in cattle, Mr. Gowen's simple remedy	432½
Method to cure the frenzy	483

INDEX.

	Receipt
Cow-Diseases—Paunching	484
Pleura Pneumonia in cattle, cure for	556
Purging drink	480
Red-water in cattle, to cure	468
Scouring, in cattle, " "	469
Scouring	558
Swelled cattle with green food, cure for	470
Tar-water for cattle	466
Worms or bots in cattle or horses	557
Yellows or jaundice in cattle, cure for	481
Diseases in Human Beings, Cures for—	
Balsam-de-Malda, how to make	6
Balsam Locatellis, how to make	35
Bitters, German, " "	36
Blood-spitting, cure for	553
Burning and scalding, cure for	15
Burns and scalds, " " No. 1	19
Burns and scalds, " " No. 2	20
Burns, liniment for	34
Cancer, cure for. No. 1	69
Cancer, " " No. 2	70
Cancer, " " No. 3	71
Cerate, simple, how to make	30
Chilblain, frost-bitten, cure for	14
Colds, cure for	75
Consumption, cure for	59
Corns, certain cure for	535
Corns, cure for	9
Cough, " "	45
Cough-drops	41
Cough-drops, Dr. Monroe's	43
Cough-Mixture. No. 1	42
Cough-Syrup	545
Cough-drops. No. 2	550
Cramp in the stomach, cure for	40
Croup, cure for	66
Diarrhœa, " "	64
Dyspepsia, " "	44
Dropsy, " "	51
Dysentery, " " No. 1	68

INDEX.

	Receipt
DISEASES IN HUMAN BODIES, CURE FOR—Dysentery. No. 2..	526
Dysentery, cure for. No. 3	527
Dysentery and bloody flux	528
Epilepsy, cure for	580
Erysipelas, " "	596
Eye-water, how to make	55
Eye-water or Collyrium	56
Eye-water or Vitriolic Collyrium	57
Felon, certain cure for	67
Giddiness, cure for	31
Godfrey's Cordial, how to make	32
Gravel, Turkish cure	525
Headache, bilious or sick, cure for	587
Hooping-cough, Dr. Barton's remedy	571
Liver-complaint, cure for	58
Lip-salve	85
Lockjaw, cure for	495
Life Tincture (a German medicine)	33
Liniment, children's sore throat	26
Mad dog bite, Dr. Stoy's cure	1
Mother-drops, Dr. Stoy's	4
Mother-drops, simple	5
Mortification powders, Dr. Stoy's	2
Nails on toes, ingrowing	76
Nipples, sore, ointment for	531
No. 6 Medicine, how to make	7
Ointment to draw splinter out of the flesh	47
Paregoric elixir, how to make	61
Peppermint-essence, how to make	8
Piles, certain cure for	549
Piles, a mild aperient for	567
Piles, a cure for	532
Piles, liniment	28
Piles, ointment for. No. 1	29
Piles, ointment " No. 2	498
Piles, ointment " No. 3	530
Piles, simple cure	12
Purifying the blood	60
Quinsy, cure for	552
Rheumatism, cure for. No. 1	52

DISEASES IN HUMAN BODIES, CURE FOR— Receipt
 Rheumatism, cure for. No. 2................................ 53
 Rheumatism, "   " No. 3................................ 73
 Rheumatism, "   " No. 4................................ 496
 Rheumatic Gout, cure for. No. 1........................... 497
 Rheumatic Gout, "   " No. 2............................ 529
 Rheumatism, inflammatory, remedy for.................. 534
 Rheumatism, liniment.. 561
 Rheumatism, simple cure.. 562
 Salt Rheum or Scurvy, cure for............................... 544
 Scabby heads on children, cure for......................... 16
 Scarlet Fever, cure for.. 62
 Salt, medical use of... 65
 Sleepless, how to make a tea for............................. 17
 Smallpox, cure for... 63
 Smallpox, "   " 533
 Sun-stroke, "   " 551
 Summer-complaint, cure for................................... 37
 Summer-complaint, Blackberry Syrup for................ 39
 Swelling from bruises, to prevent........................... 27
 Swinney, cure for. No. 1....................................... 24
 Swinney, "   " No. 2.. 25
 Tetter, "   " No. 1... 21
 Tetter, "   " No. 2... 22
 Tetter, Ringworm, Swinney, and Rheumatism........... 23
 Toothache-drops... 546
 Toothache-preventive.. 600
 Vermifuge, Hamilton's celebrated.......................... 54
 White Swelling, cure for.. 74
 Whitlow.. 554
 Worms, Dr. Stoy's simple cure for........................... 2
DYEING—Aluming... 160
 Black, on silk... 167
 Black, inclining to purple, on wool and silk............... 185
 Black, inclining to brown, "   " 186
 Black jet, on woollen... 187
 Black, on cotton... 208
 Blue-black, on silk.. 168
 Blue, Prussian, on woollen..................................... 188
 Blue vat, for silk and woollen................................. 214

	Receipt
DYEING—Blue, on silk	166
Brown, on silk	163
Brown, on silk dress	175
Brown, on woollen cloth, or cloth of any description	181
Brown, on the red cast	182
Brown, inclining to snuff	184
Buff, on cotton	201
Brown, on cotton	204
Crimson, on silk	179
Dove, on silk	177
Drab, on cotton	205
Drab, on silk	176
Drab, on wool	191
Dye-liquors, preparing	161
Fancy dyeing, on cotton, various shades	198
Flesh, on silk	180
General remarks	159
Gloss on silk, a fine	209
Gloss on silk	201
Gray, on silk	171
Green, on silk	164
Green, on wool	189
Green, on cotton	200
Indigo, Sulphate, how to make	165
Indigo, vat for cotton, how to set	213
Lilac, on wool	190
Maroon, on silk	169
Olive, on silk	173
Olive-brown	183
Orange, on silk	170
Orange, on wool	197
Orange, annetto on cotton	202
Pink, on silk	162
Purple, on cotton	207
Red, on cotton	203
Red, on wool	192
Slate, on cotton	206
Slate, on silk	172
Slate, on woollen	195
Stone, on silk	174

	Receipt
DYEING—Tin Liquor, No. 1, how to make	193
Tin Liquor, No. 2, " "	194
Tin Liquor, for pinks, scarlet, crimson, &c.	211
Tin Liquor, for scarlet and crimson, on silk	212
Yellow, Turmeric	199
Yellow, on silk	178
Yellow, on woollen	196
Black, on leather	222
Blue, "	221
Purple, "	224
Red, Turkey, on leather	217
Red, on leather	218
Shades, different, on leather	223
Yellow, on leather	219
Yellow, on leather	220
Blue, on straw	216
Red, "	215
EGGS—Preserving, to keep. No. 1	514
Preserving, " No. 2	515
Preserving, " No. 3	516
EXTRACT—Vanilla	539
FOUL SMELL—To destroy	504
FISH—Fresh, how to keep	523
GILDING—Edges of paper	491
GIN—Holland, how to imitate. No. 1	277
Holland, " " No. 2	278
Holland, " " No. 3	279
Holland, " " No. 4	280
Holland, " " No. 5	281
Country, how to make	282
GLOVES—French Kid, how to clean	591
How to clean	592
GREASE—Spots to remove, a liquid for	10
Spots to remove from woollen cloth	11
HORSE-DISEASES—Abscess, cure for	361
Adhesive Plaster, and sewing	354
Alterative Balls, for surfeit, mange, &c.	435
Anbury, or wart	362
Anodyne medicine	449
Appetite, loss of	364

	Receipt
HORSE-DISEASES—Astringent drink, after looseness	427
Astringent balls, for profuse staling	436
Bandage	355
Bladder, Inflamed	365
Bleeding, to stop	353
Bleeding in general	420
Bleeding, to stop, a paste for	461
Blood-Spavin	366
Blue water, for wounds, how to make	48
Bone-Spavin	368
Bots	369
Bowels, inflammation of	372
Broken knees	376
Broken wind	374
Burns and Scalds	377
Canker	378
Canker, liniment for	379
Canker in the mouth, mixture for	464
Capped Hocks	380
Cold	381
Composition, for sand-cracks	410
Convulsions	382
Convulsions, clyster for	443
Cough	383
Cough-drink, for horses	428
Corns	384
Curb	385
Cracked Heels	386
Diabetes	389
Diabetes, balls for	390
Drink, to check over-purging	426
Drink, for an inflammatory fever	431
Drink, for worms	439
Eyes	391
Eye-Water, No. 1	392
Eye-Water, No. 2	457
Farcy	394
Farcy, cure for	395
Fever-Balls	429
Film, or cataract	393

	Receipt
HORSE-DISEASES—Food and Regimen	360
Fulness of blood	421
Foundered Feet	397
Grease	396
Gripes	387
Gripes, draught for. No. 1	388
Gripes, " No. 2	445
Gripes, cure for	444
Gripes, further treatment	446
Gripes, white ball for	447
Hoof-bound	398
Horse-Powder, how to make	13
Horse, how to make him drink freely	487
Inflammation of the lungs	458
Lameness	453
Lampass	399
Laudanum draught	448
Laxity	400
Laxative and diaphoretic powder	422
Lungs, inflammation of	401
Mallenders	402
Mange	403
Mange, liniment for	456
Mange, ointment for	455
Mercurial ball, for worms	438
Molten Grease	404
Ointment	357
Ointment, Blistering	367
Ointment, Green	358
Paste-balls, for broken wind	375
Pectoral balls, for broken wind	434
Physic	424
Poll-Evil	405
Powerful mixture, for fever	430
Purging	423
Purgative balls	425
Purging-balls, for jaundice	432
Purging-balls, for worms	440
Quitter	470
Restorative balls after jaundice	433

	Receipt
HORSE-DISEASES—Restorative, for profuse staling	437
Ringbone	408
Sallenders	412
Salve, how to make for wounds	49
Sand-crack	409
Scratched Heels, ointment for	462
Sitfasts	411
Sores and Bruises	356
Sore Backs, cure for	485
Sprains, bracing mixture for	460
Sprains, embrocation for	459
Sprains, &c., lotion for	486
Staggers	363
Staggers, balls for	442
Strains	413
Strains in different parts, an astringent embrocation for	463
Stomach-drink after expulsion of the worms	441
Strangury	414
Strangles	415
Surfeit, or bad coat	451
Suppurating poultice	406
Treatment	373
Thrush	416
Thrush in feet, cure for	454
Treatment according to appearance of the part	359
Urine-balls	452
Vives	417
When on a journey	450
Wind-gall	418
Worms	370
Worms, remedy for	371
Wounds	419
Wounds, ointment for	46
Wounds in cattle, farrier's cure	352
HAMS—To cure, without pickle	519
ICE-CREAM—How to make	134
INKS—Black writing, how to make	136
Black writing, cheap	137
Blue " No. 1	38
Blue " No. 2	143

	Receipt
INKS—Green writing	570
Indelible, how to make	139
Japan black writing	135
Red writing. No. 1	141
Red writing. No. 2	142
LARD CANDLES—How to make	505
LIME-WATER—How to make	18
MILK—How to preserve any length of time	115
How to preserve	568
MILDEW—How to take out of linen	577
PAINTERS—Colours, how to make different shades	225
Colours used, different names for	226
Linseed-oil, how to prepare, for boiling varnish	228
Linseed-oil, how to boil, for painting	229
Oils, different kinds used in painting	227
Paint, outside, cheap	575
PERFUMERY, &c.—Black Teeth, remedy for	83
Cologne, how to make	82
Cologne, superior article	541
Cologne	537
Gums and Teeth, how to clean	84
Hair-Oil	574
Hair-Oil, common	78
Hair-Oil, excellent	79
Hair-Grease, or ox-marrow imitated	80
Hair-Oil, how to make	77
Hair-restorative	543
Lotion for Freckles	547
Otto of Roses, how to make	588
Pomatum, ox-marrow	542
Pomade against baldness	564
Preventing hair falling out	538
Soap, Shaving, how to make	572
Soap, " best invented	573
Tooth-Powder, rose	81
Tooth-Powder	548
PICKLE—To cure Hams, Pork, and Beef	517
T. B. Hamilton's receipt	518
PRINTERS' INK—How to make	138
Printing-Ink, excellent	597

	Receipt
PRESERVES, &c.—Barberries, how to make	123
Blackberry-Jam	520
Cherries, how to preserve	124
Cucumber-Catsup, how to make	503
Currants, how to preserve	125
Fruit, how to keep fresh	500
Fruit and Vegetables, how to preserve	501
How to keep	117
Peaches, how to preserve	119
Plums, elegant green	118
Plums, magnum-bonum	120
Quinces, how to preserve	121
Raspberry-Jam	122
Tomato-Catsup, how to make. No. 1	499
Tomato-Catsup, " " No. 2	502
RAZOR-STROP-POWDER	578
RATS—Poison, how to make	586
RECTIFYING—Raw whiskey, stand, how to put up	270
RUM—Jamaica, how to imitate. No. 1	283
Jamaica, " " No. 2	284
Jamaica, " " No. 3	292
New England, " " No. 1	287
New England, " " No. 2	288
St. Croix, " " No. 1	289
St. Croix, " " No. 2	290
SEALING-WAX—Red, how to make	593
Black, " " No. 1	594
Black, " " No. 2	595
SHEEP—Foot-rot, cure for. No. 1	473
Foot-rot, " No. 2	474
Foot-rot, " No. 3	475
Foot-rot, prevention and cure	476
Maggots in	478
Scab, cure for	477
SUGAR-COLOURING—How to boil	343
How to clarify	100
SILK—Stained by corrosive or sharp liquors, how to clean	598
SILVER—How to write in	599
Articles, how to clean	576
Copper, how to	563

	Receipt
SILVER—German. No. 1	581
German. No. 2	582
German. No. 3	583
German. No. 4	584
German. No. 5	585
By heat	492
Plating fluid, galvanism simplified	489
Silvering of metal	565
Solution, for plating copper, brass, &c	490
SOLDERING—Iron or any other metal without fire	566
SPIRITS—Jamaica, how to imitate	286
Pure, how to make	345
Pure, how to make by distillation	346
SWINE—Cholera, how to cure with alum	569
Common diseases, how to cure	579
Measles, how to cure	471
Rupture in	472
SYRUP—Simple, how to make	344
TINCTURES—Allspice, how to make	323
Cardamom-seed	321
Catechu	291
Cinnamon	320
Cloves	326
Japonica	299
Kino	285
Red Sanders	325
Rhatany	322
Saffron	323
VARNISHES—Amber	236
Copal, how to boil. No. 1	230
Copal, " " No. 2	231
Copal, gold colour	232
Copal, to dissolve, in fixed oil	235
Harness, how to make for	240
Iron and Steel, how to make for	524
Leather, how to make for	241
Leather, how to boil	243
Linseed-Oil	237
Seed-lac	233
Shellac	234

	Receipt
VARNISHES—Sheet Iron	250
Straw and Chip Hats	249
Turpentine	238
White, hard	239
VINEGAR—Cider, how to make	154
Common, " "	146
Currant, " "	151
Elderberry, " "	156
Gooseberry, " "	150
German, " "	157
How to make. No. 1	143½
How to make. No. 2	144
How to make. No. 3	145
How to make. No. 4	147
Primrose, how to make	152
Raisin	153
Raspberry	350
Sugar	149
Wine	148
How to strengthen	155
How to sharpen, or increase sharpness	158
VENICE TURPENTINE—How to make	242
WASHING—Occupying one hour	493
Another receipt	494
WATER-PROOF—Leather, how to make	245
Leather preservative	246
Shoes and Boots, how to make	244
WHITEWASH—Brilliant	555
WINES—Apple, how to make	342
Blackberry, " "	521
British Champagne	351
Bottling	338
Cider	340
Claret, how to imitate	333
Currant	339
Cypress	341
Fining	337
Lisbon, how to imitate	331
Madeira, " " No. 1	329
Madeira, " " No. 2	330

	Receipt
WINES—Malaga, how to imitate	332
Port, " " No. 1	327
Port, " " No. 2	328
Racking	336
Sherry, how to imitate	334
Teneriffe, " "	335
WHISKEY—Apple, how to imitate	273
Bourbon, " "	274
Irish, " "	275
Monongahela, how to make. No. 1	271
Monongahela, " " No. 2	271½
Scotch, how to imitate	276
Wheat " "	272
YEAST—Distillers' and Brewers', how to make, with hops	347
How to make another	348
Beer, how to make, with	349

600

MISCELLANEOUS VALUABLE RECEIPTS.

No. 1.

Doctor Stoy's Cure for the Bite of a Mad Dog.

TAKE 1 ounce of red chicken-weed, (gathered and dried in the shade during the month of June,) put it into 1 quart of strong (or brewers') beer, boil it down to 1 pint. Strain the tea through a clean linen cloth, then stir into the tea 1 ounce theriac so that it will be well mixed. The theriac is not to be boiled.

Dose.—For a man with a strong constitution, one half-pint taken in the morning, sober, and the next morning the other half-pint, also sober.

The patient ought to fast three hours after he has taken the medicine; then he can eat bread and butter, or bread and molasses, for at least a week or ten days; he must not eat any pork, nor any fish or water-fowls, and must not drink any water. He can drink any kind of tea, and he must not get angry or overheat himself for two weeks.

For a person of a weak constitution, make 3 doses out of the above-prepared quantity, and also for children in proportion. 3 doses will be sufficient for a cure.

For animals, the medicine must be doubled; and its food, water and wheat bran, to be given warm.

No. 2.

Doctor Stoy's Simple Cure for Worms.

Take ½ pound fresh butter, unsalted.
2 ounces of garlic, cut fine.

Put the garlic into a pint of warm water, then strain it into the butter; put it on hot coals, and mix it well through.

No. 3.

Doctor Stoy's Mortification-Powder, to prevent Lockjaw.

Take ¼ pound gunpowder.
¼ pound brimstone.
½ pound alum.
1 ounce charcoal.

Pulverize the above ingredients in a mortar, and mix thoroughly.

Dose.—For a strong constitution, take as much as will lie on a ten-cent piece, in a small teaspoonful of strong vinegar.

N.B.—The charcoal is only used in case of wounds, to dry them up.

No. 4.

Doctor Stoy's celebrated Mother-Drops.

Take 1 ounce opium.
1 ounce castor.
1 ounce saffron.
1 ounce maple-seed.
1 quart Lisbon wine.

Mix all the above ingredients, and distil in the sun or a warm stove for three weeks.

Dose.—For adults, from 20 to 30 drops, twice a

day, and for children from 5 to 10 drops, twice a day.

No. 5.

Simple Valuable Mother-Drops.

Take ½ ounce ether.
½ ounce laudanum.
½ ounce essence of peppermint.

Mix the above ingredients in a vial, and shake it well, when it will be ready for use.

Dose.—One teaspoonful, or 60 drops, for adults. If one dose does not allay the pains in half an hour, take another. To children, give in proportion to their age.

No. 6.

How to make good Balsam-de-Malda.

Take 3 ounces powdered benzoin.
2 ounces balsam of Peru.
½ ounce hepatic aloes in powder.
1 quart rectified spirits of wine.

Put all the above ingredients into a bottle, and digest them in the sun or near a stove for a week or two; then strain the balsam. Or you may use it by taking the clear from the top as you want.

This balsam, or rather tincture, is applied externally to heal recent wounds and bruises. It is likewise employed internally to remove coughs, asthmas, and other complaints of the breast. It is said to ease the colic, cleanse the kidneys, and to heal internal ulcers, &c.

Dose.—For adults, from 20 to 60 drops; for children in proportion.

No. 7.

How to make No. 6. Thompsonian Medicine.

Take 1 ounce Cayenne pepper.
½ ounce cloves, bruised.
¼ ounce Russian castor.
¼ ounce mace, bruised.
1 quart brandy.

Put all into a bottle, and distil in the sun or near a warm stove for two weeks, when it will be ready; you can strain it, if you think proper, or pour the clear off as you use it.

Dose.—One teaspoonful, in 1 gill or half teacupful of warm water sweetened with sugar, for adults. For children, mix more water, and give in proportion.

No. 8.

To make good Essence of Peppermint.

Take 1 pint spirits of wine, (alcohol.)
¼ ounce oil of mint.

Mix and shake it well; let it stand a day, and, if not clear, filter it through paper. Add a little turmeric, to colour.

No. 9.

A cure for Corns.

Take nightshade-berries; boil them in hog's lard, and anoint the corn with the salve. It will not fail to cure.

No. 10.
To make a liquid to remove Grease-spots out of Woollen Cloth.

Take 1 quart spirits of wine, (alcohol.)
     12 drops winter-green.
     1 gill beef-gall.
     6 cents' worth lavender.

And a little alkanet, to colour, if you wish. Mix.

No. 11.
Another, to clean Woollen Cloth.

Take equal parts spirits of hartshorn and ether. Or ox-gall mixed with it makes it better.

No. 12.
A certain and simple cure for Piles.

Take 3 cigars; rub them fine.
     1 handful the inner bark of elder.
     1 gill hog's lard.

Boil all the above ingredients together, and, after it becomes cool, anoint the part a few times a day.

No. 13.
How to make Horse-Powder.

Take ½ pound fœnugreek-seed in powder.
     ½ pound flour of sulphur.
     ½ pound antimony, powdered.
     ½ pound cream of tartar.
     ½ pound saltpetre, powdered.

Mix all the above ingredients thoroughly.

Dose.—1 tablespoonful three times a week, mixed with their feed; and if the animal is sick, give every day.

No. 14.

A simple cure for Chilblain, (Frost-bitten.)

Take alum, and dissolve in warm water, and apply it to the affected part.

No. 15.

A cure for Burning or Scalding.

Take sweet oil, mix into it pulverized red chalk and white lead. Then take a feather and anoint the affected part. With children you must be careful that they do not scratch at the sore, or else it will leave a mark.

No. 16.

A cure for Scabby Heads on Children.

Take 1 pound pickled pork.
1 pound cabbage.

Boil the above the same as you would for eating; then skim it off, and wash the head with the liquid.

No. 17.

How to make a Tea for a Sleepless person to Sleep.

Make a tea of Jerusalem oak, which grows in the woods, and drink it, as you would any other tea, before going to bed.

No. 18.

How to make Lime-Water.

Take ½ pound of unslaked lime; put it in an earthen pot; pour 2 or 3 quarts of pure water on it; cover the pot; let it stand one day; skim off the top, and take the clear water for use. To keep it any length of time, put it in bottles and seal them.

No. 19.

A cure for Burns and Scalds. No. 1.

Mix in a bottle 3 ounces of olive-oil and 4 ounces of lime-water. Apply the mixture to the part burned five or six times a day, with a feather. Linseed-oil is equally as good.

No. 20.

Another cure for Burns and Scalds. No. 2.

Spread clarified honey upon a linen rag, and apply it to the burn immediately, and it will relieve the pain instantly and heal the sore in a very short time.

No. 21.

A cure for Tetter. No. 1.

Take as much mustard as will make into a salve mixed with honey; spread it on a rag, and lay it on the sore for 24 hours. If the sore is not dead, make new salve, and lay it on 3 or 4 hours longer.

Then take the inside of elder-bark and stew it in lard; put in beeswax enough to make a salve; set it by until it gets cold. This is to heal the sore. Don't let the sore get wet.

Then take mullein and boil it in water, and wash with after the wound is healed. This is to harden the tender skin again.

No. 22.

Another cure for Tetter. No. 2.

Take one ounce of sulphuret of potash. Obtain it from a druggist. Put the sulphuret into a large glass bottle, and pour on it a quart of cold water, (soft;) stop it tightly, and leave it to dissolve. Care must be taken to keep it closely corked. To use it, pour a little into a cup, and, dipping in it a soft sponge, bathe the eruption with it five or six times a day. Persist, and in most cases it will soon effect a cure. Should the tetter reappear in cold weather, immediately apply the solution.

No. 23.

A never-failing Salve for the cure of Tetter, Ringworm, Swinney, and Rheumatism.

Take 3 fresh eggs.
¼ pound fresh butter, unsalted.
½ gill oil of spike.
½ gill oil of stone.

Take the eggs and break them in an earthen pot, and whip them up with a pine-wood shovel; melt the butter on coal; don't let it boil; then pour the butter on the eggs; stir them; then mix it with the oil of stone and spike; mix it well; then it is ready for use. Make it the third day after new moon, and it must be the first time used. Rub the diseased part with the salve at a warm stove, or in the sun in summer.

For horses, take double portions to prepare the salve.

For children of 12 years of age, take 2 eggs and half the quantity of the other articles.

No. 24.

A cure for the Swinney. No. 1.

Take 1 pint spirits of turpentine.
1 tablespoonful cream of tartar, pulverized.
1 large teaspoonful pulverized frankincense.

Mix all the ingredients together in a bottle, and let it stand in the sun four or five days, and shake it well; then ready. Take a feather and grease the diseased part.

No. 25.

Another cure for the Swinney. No. 2.

Take 1 ounce oil of spike.
1 ounce oil of stone.
1 ounce oil of juniper.

Mix all the above oils together; take a feather and anoint the diseased part.

No. 26.

A Liniment for Children's Sore Throat.

Mix two parts of sweet oil and one part of spirits of hartshorn.

No. 27.

To prevent Swelling from Bruises.

Apply at once a cloth five or six folds in thickness, dipped in cold water, and when it grows warm renew the wetting.

No. 28.

A Liniment for Piles.

Take 2 ounces emollient ointment.
½ ounce laudanum.

Mix these ingredients with the yolk of an egg, and work them well together, and then anoint the diseased part or sore.

No. 29.

Ointment for Piles. No. 1.

Take 1 scruple powdered opium.
2 scruples flour of sulphur.
1 ounce simple cerate.

Keep the affected part well anointed; be prudent in your diet; don't eat too much; keep in pure air; have abundance of exercise, &c.

With strict regard to these directions, the dreadful complaint we have alluded to will depart and give you no more affliction.

No. 30.

To make Simple Cerate.

Take 1 pound white wax.
4 pounds lard or mutton-suet.

Melt them with a gentle heat, and stir it well until cool.

N.B.—Yellow wax will answer the same purpose.

No. 31.

A cure for Giddiness.

Take 2 ounces Epsom salts.
1 ounce senna.
1 pint wine.

Distil in the sun or a warm stove a few days. (Ready.)

Dose.—Take as much as will physic you thoroughly the first day, and after that take as much as will physic you once a day: take it in the morning, sober. This cured a case of seven years' standing.

No. 32.

To make Godfrey's Cordial.

Dissolve ½ ounce opium and one drachm oil of sassafras in two ounces spirits of wine, (alcohol.) Now mix 4 pounds of molasses with 1 gallon of boiling water; when cold, mix the other ingredients with it. (Ready.)

It will soothe the pains in children.

No. 33.

To make Life Tincture. (A German Medicine.)

Take 1 quart good whiskey.
- 9 drachms aloes.
- 1 drachm zedora-root, bruised.
- 1 drachm agaric, bruised.
- 1 drachm saffron.
- 1 drachm gentian-root, bruised.
- 1 drachm myrrh.
- 1 drachm nutmeg, bruised.
- 2 drachms rhubarb.

Distil in the sun or a warm stove a few days, then it is fit for use.

Dose.—For adults, 1 teaspoonful (or 60 drops) in sugar.

No. 34.

Liniment for Burns.

Take equal parts of Florence oil, or fresh-drawn linseed-oil, and lime-water; shake them well together in a wide-mouthed bottle so as to form a liniment.

This is found to be an exceedingly proper application for recent scalds or burns. It may either be spread upon a cloth, or the parts affected may be anointed with it two or three times a day.

No. 35.

Locatelli's Balsam.

Take 1 pint olive-oil.
½ pound Strasbourg turpentine.
½ pound yellow wax.
6 drachms red saunders, pulv.

Melt the wax with part of the oil over a gentle fire; then add the remaining part of the oil and the turpentine; afterward mix in the saunders, and keep stirring them together till the balsam is cold.

This balsam is recommended in erosions of the intestines, dysentery, hæmorrhages, internal bruises, and in complaints of the breast. The dose when taken internally is from 2 scruples to 2 drachms for adults.

No. 36.

To make German Bitters.

Take ¼ pound gentian-root.
2 ounces bitter orange-peel.
½ ounce chamomile-flowers.
cinnamon and cloves as much as you wish.
1 quart whiskey.
2 ounces red saunders.

Put all together in a bottle, and distil in the sun or near a warm stove for one week. *Dose.*—1 tablespoonful in the evening before going to bed; take it clear, or in water. It strengthens the stomach and gives vigor to the system, and is an excellent remedy for dyspeptic people. I received the above recipe thirty years ago.

No. 37.

A cure for Summer Complaint.

Take ¾ teaspoonful pulverized rhubarb.
1 teaspoonful magnesia.

Put it into a teacupful of boiling water; let it stand until it is cold; stir it well. Then add 2 teaspoonfuls of good brandy, and sweeten it with loaf sugar.

Dose.—For a child 1 to 3 years old, 1 teaspoonful five or six times a day.

How to prepare food: Take a handful of flour; tie it into a clean cloth; boil it three hours; after it is cold, take off the crust, and take the hard white substance and pulverize it; put into it a sufficient quantity of milk to make it thin; let it boil one or two minutes; stir it well with a piece of cinnamon-stick, and sweeten it with sugar.

No. 38.

To make Blue Ink.   No. 1.

Take 1 ounce best Prussian blue.
1½ ounce oxalic acid.
1 pint water.

Let it dissolve, when it will be ready for use.

No. 39.

To make Blackberry-Syrup, for Summer Complaint.

Take 2 quarts blackberry-juice.
1 pound loaf sugar.
½ ounce nutmeg, grated.
½ ounce ground cinnamon.
¼ ounce cloves, ground.
¼ ounce allspice, ground.

Boil the above ingredients together; when cold, add 1 pint fourth-proof brandy. *Dose.*—From 1 teaspoonful to 1 wineglassful, according to the age of the patient, as often as will be necessary to effect a cure.

No. 40.

A cure for Cramp in the Stomach.

Warm water, sweetened with molasses or brown sugar, taken freely, will in many cases remove cramp in the stomach when opium and other remedies have failed.

No. 41.

Cough-Drops.

Take tincture of bloodroot, syrup of ipecacuanha, syrup of squill, tincture of balsam of Tolu, and paregoric, of each 1 ounce. Mix. This is used in all severe coughs from colds. It is a valuable mixture. *Dose.*—½ to 1 drachm, whenever the cough is severe.

No. 42.

No. 1 Cough-Mixture.

Take ½ ounce paregoric.
1 ounce syrup of squill.
2 drachms antimonial wine.
6 ounces water.

Dose.—2 teaspoonfuls every 15 minutes until the cough abates.

No. 43.

Dr. Monroe's Cough-Drops.

Take 4 drachms paregoric, 2 drachms sulphuric ether, 2 drachms tincture of Tolu. Mix. Take a teaspoonful night and morning, or when the cough is troublesome.

No. 44.

A cure for the Dyspepsia.

Take 1 ounce pulverized rhubarb.
    1 ounce caraway-seed.
    1 tablespoonful grated orange-peel.

Put these into a decanter with 1 pint of best brandy, shake it well together, and keep in a warm place. *Dose.*—1 tablespoonful in the morning, fasting, and at night going to bed. Shake the mixture well before taking it.

No. 45.

A cure for Cough.

Take ½ pint honey.
    3 tablespoonfuls elecampane-root, pulv.
    3 tablespoonfuls ginger.
    1 pint vinegar.

Put all the above in a jug, and make a paste of flour or chop-stuff, and shut the jug close up with this paste; and then, when you put your bread in the oven, put this jug in also, and leave it in the oven until you take the bread out; then it is ready for use. *Dose.*—1 teaspoonful two or three times a day, and as you can stand it.

No. 46.

To make an Ointment to heal Wounds in Horses.

Put into a well-glazed earthen vessel 2 ounces beeswax and 2 ounces rosin. When this is melted, put in ½ pound hog's lard; to this put 4 ounces turpentine; keep stirring all the time with a clean stick. When all is well mixed, stir in 1 ounce of pulverized verdigris; be careful that it don't boil over: it ought to be a coal fire. Strain it through a coarse cloth, and preserve it in a gallipot. This ointment is very good for old and recent wounds, whether in flesh or hoof; also galled backs, cracked heels, mallender, sallenders, bites, broken heels, &c.

No. 47.

To make a Drawing Ointment.

Take elder-root and the seed of Jamestown-weed and fry it in lard. It will draw any splinters out of the flesh, or any thing else in man.

No. 48.

How to make Blue Water, to cure Wounds in Horses.

Take 1½ pounds unslaked lime; put it into an earthen pot, (glazed;) pour 2 quarts warm water on it; let it stand 3 days; stir it 3 or 4 times a day; after it is settled, pour off the pure water; add 2 ounces sal ammoniac and 3 grains camphor; dissolve the sal ammoniac and camphor in alcohol; let it stand 12 hours; put it in a copper vessel and mix well.

No. 49.

Another excellent Simple Salve for Wounds in Horses.

Take lime-water as much as you will; pour into it linseed-oil, and stir it well all the time until it is the consistency of salve, and anoint the wound with it; in a short time the wound or scald will be healed.

No. 50.

To make Oil-Paste Shoe-Blacking. No. 1.

Take 8 pounds ivory-black.
     1 gallon molasses, (the cheapest you can get.)
     1 pint fish-oil.
     2 pounds oil of vitriol.

Mix the molasses, ivory-black, and the fish-oil thoroughly, and then pour on the oil of vitriol in small quantities at a time, and keep stirring until the boiling is over; then put it in boxes while it is warm.

N.B.—The oil of vitriol will cause the boiling. You will have to use a stone or earthen pot.

No. 51.

A Cure for the Dropsy.

Take a stone jug and put in 1 gallon good cider, 2 handfuls parsley, with the root cut fine, 1 handful grated horseradish, 2 tablespoonfuls bruised mustard-seed, $\frac{1}{2}$ ounce squill, 1 ounce juniper-berries. Mix all together, and let it remain 24 hours near the fire, shaking it often; then strain it. *Dose.*—$\frac{1}{2}$ gill 3 times a day, on an empty stomach. Don't drink much while taking the medicine. Eat dry meals.

No. 52.
A Cure for Rheumatism. No. 1.

Take 1 pint best brandy.
  1 ounce gum guaiacum.

Mix. *Dose.*—Take as much as you can bear, and take it clear. Repeat the dose until a cure is effected.

No. 53.
Another Cure for Rheumatism. No. 2.

Take 2 ounces centaury.
  2 ounces senna.
  4 ounces boletus of oak.
  4 ounces canella alba.
  2 ounces zadora-root, pulverized.
  2 ounces gum myrrh.
  2 ounces caraway-seed.
  1 gallon rum.

Mix all together, and infuse for 8 or 10 days, when it will be ready for use. *Dose.*—1 tablespoonful, always before meals.

No. 54.
Hamilton's Celebrated Vermifuge.

Take ½ gallon castor-oil.
  ½ pound Baltimore wormseed-oil.
  ½ ounce oil of aniseed.
  2 ounces tincture of myrrh.
  2½ ounces pinkroot.
  1 ounce senna.

Boil the pinkroot and senna together in 2 quarts of water, enough to take the strength out; then strain it through flannel; boil the tea again down to half; then mix it with the above, and shake it well, so that it shall be mixed thoroughly while you put it into vials.

Dose.—1 teaspoonful, morning and evening, for a child 3 years old. The vial must always be well shaken before it is given, so that the sediment is well mixed.

N.B.—I myself paid 15 dollars for this recipe. It was also sold to a party in this county (Lebanon) for 100 dollars nearly 30 years ago.

No. 55.

To make Eye - Water.

Take 2 scruples white vitriol.
2 scruples sugar of lead.
1 teaspoonful laudanum.

Mix in ½ pint rain-water.

No. 56.

Collyrium, or Eye - Water.

Collyrium of alum: Take ½ drachm of alum, and agitate it well together with the white of an egg.

It is used in inflammation of the eyes, to allay heat, and restrain the flux of humours. It must be spread upon linen and applied to the eyes, but should not be kept on above 3 or 4 hours at a time.

No. 57.

Vitriolic Collyrium, or Eye-Water.

Take ½ drachm white vitriol.
6 ounces rose-water.

Dissolve the vitriol in the rose-water, and filter the liquor.

It is a useful application in weak, watery, inflamed eyes.

No. 58.

A simple Cure for Liver-Complaint.

Take 1 tablespoonful pulverized charcoal and ½ teacupful sweet fresh milk in the morning and evening. Continue for some time.

No. 59.

A Cure for Consumption.

Take hart's tongue.
     lungwort, (or pulmonary.)
     liverwort.
     sarsaparilla-root.
     speedwell.

One handful of each. Boil on a coal fire, in an earthen pot, well covered; stir it every 5 minutes with a pine stick; let it boil 15 minutes; let it stand until milk-warm, then strain and bottle it close. *Dose.*—For an adult, 1 tablespoonful in the morning, sober; afterward, every 3 hours. Also eat every day spoonwort or water-cresses. Don't eat pork or drink very sour vinegar.

No. 60.

A Remedy for Purifying the Blood.

Take ½ ounce cloves.
    1 ounce cinnamon.
    ½ ounce mace.
    6 cents' worth saffron.
    ½ ounce borax.
    1 handful rosemary.
    1 quart wine.

Distil in the sun or warm stove for 5 or 6 days. *Dose.*—½ gill in the morning and evening. It is good for women when their blood is out of order.

No. 61.

Paregoric Elixir.

Take 1 drachm opium, in powder.
    1 drachm benzoic acid.
    2 scruples camphor.
    1 drachm oil of aniseed.
    1 quart proof spirits of wine, (alcohol.)

Digest for 10 days, and strain. It contributes to allay the tickling which provokes frequent coughing, and at the same time it opens the breast and gives greater liberty to breathing. It is given to children against the chincough, in doses from 5 to 20 drops. Adults, from 20 to 100 drops.

No. 62.

A simple Cure for Scarlet Fever.

For adults, give 1 tablespoonful of good brewers' yeast in 3 tablespoonfuls of sweetened water, 3 times a day; and if the throat is much swollen, gargle with yeast and apply to the throat as a poultice, mixed with Indian meal. Use plenty of catnip-tea, to keep the eruptions out of the skin, for several days.

No. 63.
A Cure for Small-Pox.

Use the above doses of yeast 3 times a day, and milk diet, throughout the entire disease. Nearly every case can be cured without leaving a pockmark.—*Dr. William Fields.*

No. 64.
A Cure for Diarrhœa.

Put into a bottle 3 ounces pimento, (allspice,) upon which pour 1 pint best French brandy; sweeten with sugar.

Dose.—A wineglassful every hour for 3 hours, for adults. For children, dilute, and give a tablespoonful each hour. This remedy has been known to cure violent cases of diarrhœa.

No. 65.
Medical use of Salt.

In many cases of disordered stomach, a teaspoonful of salt is a certain cure. In the violent internal aching termed colic, add a teaspoonful of salt to a pint of cold water. Drink it, and go to bed. It is one of the speediest remedies known. The same will revive a person who seems almost dead from a heavy fall, &c.

In an apoplectic fit, no time should be lost in pouring down salt and water, if sufficient sensibility remain to allow of swallowing; if not, the head must be sponged with cold water until the sense returns, when salt will completely restore the patient from the lethargy. In a fit, the feet should be placed in warm water, with mustard added, and the legs briskly rubbed, all bandages removed from the neck, and a cool apartment procured, if possible.

In many cases of severe bleeding at the lung, and when other remedies failed, Dr. Rush found that two teaspoonfuls of salt completely stayed the blood.

In case of a bite from a mad dog, wash the part with a strong brine for an hour, and then bind on some salt with a rag.

In toothache, warm salt and water held to the part, and removed two or three times, will relieve it in most cases.

If the gums be affected, wash the mouth with brine.

If the teeth be covered with tartar, wash them twice a day with salt and water.

In swelled neck, wash the part with brine, and drink it, also, twice a day, until cured.

Salt will expel worms, if used in food in a moderate degree, and aids digestion; but salt meat is injurious if used much.

No. 66.

A Cure for the Croup.

Take a piece of fresh lard, as large as a butternut, rubbed up with sugar in the same way that butter and sugar are prepared for the dressing of puddings, divided into three parts, and given at intervals of twenty minutes, will relieve any case of croup which is not already allowed to progress to the fatal point.

No. 67.

Said to be a certain Cure for a Felon.

"Take a pint of common soft soap, and stir in it air-slaked lime till it is of the consistency of glaziers' putty. Make a leather thimble, fill it with this composition and insert the finger therein, and change the composition once in twenty minutes, and a cure is certain."—*Buffalo (N. Y.) Com. Advertiser.*

"We happen to know that the above is a certain remedy, and recommend it to any who may be troubled with that disagreeable ailment."—*Public Ledger.*

No. 68.

A sure and simple Cure for Dysentery. No. 1.

Drink a gill (or teacupful) of West India (or Trinidad) molasses. This is a *dose* for adults; children in proportion.

No. 69.

To cure the Cancer. No. 1.

Take bread dough the size of an egg, old hog's lard the same quantity, mix it well, and spread it on white leather, and apply it to the sore.

No. 70.

Another Cure for Cancer. No. 2.

Take alum, vinegar, and honey, equal quantities, and wheat flour, and make a plaster by mixing it all together; renew every twelve hours.

No. 71.

Another for Cancer. No. 3.

Take pulverized alum and fish-worms smashed, and a salve made like a plaster and put on the sore.

No. 72.

To polish Brass.

Take 6 cents' worth sour salts, and pumice-stone pulverized, soft water, and olive-oil, mix all together, and strain the liquor.

No. 73.

To cure Rheumatism. No. 3.

Take 1 quart spirits of wine.
2 ounces camphor.
2 ounces cloves.
3 handfuls salt.
6 heads red pepper.

Infuse for 3 or 4 days in the sun or warm stove, and bathe with it.

No. 74.

To cure White Swelling.

Take 1 handful sarsaparilla-root.
1 handful sassafras-root.
1 handful dittany.
3 quarts water.

Boil down to one-half. *Dose.*—Every morning, sober, 1 gill until it is all used.

While taking the above internally, make the following salve:—

Take 2 quarts cider.
1 pound beeswax.
1 pound sheep tallow, (suet.)
1 pound smoking-tobacco.

Boil this well, and then put it on the sore like plaster is put on, and renew whenever you think proper.

No. 75.

A certain Cure for Colds.

Take 1 teaspoon flaxseed.
1 ounce liquorice.
¼ pound raisins.

Put the above articles into 2 quarts of water, and boil it down with a slow fire to one-half; then add ¼ pound rock-candy pounded fine, and add 1 tablespoonful lemon-juice. *Dose.*—½ pint on going to bed, and take a little when the cough is troublesome.

This receipt generally cures the worst of colds in 2 or 3 days. It is a sovereign balsamic cordial for the lungs.

No. 76.

A Cure for ingrowing Nails on Toes.

Take a little tallow and put it into a spoon, and heat it over a lamp until it becomes very hot; then pour it on the sore or granulation; the effect will be almost magical. The pain and tenderness will at once be relieved. The operation causes very little pain if the tallow is properly heated; perhaps a repetition may in some cases be necessary.

No. 77.

To make a very superior Hair-Oil.

Take half an ounce of alkanet-root, which may be bought for a few cents at the druggist's. Divide this quantity into four portions, and tie up each portion in a separate bit of new bobinet or clean thin muslin. The strings must be white: for instance, coarse white thread or fine cotton cord. Take care to omit any powder or dust that may be found about the alkanet, as if put in it will render the oil cloudy and muddy. Put these little bags into a large tumbler or a straight-sided white-ware jar, and pour on half a pint of the best fresh olive-oil. Cover the vessel, and leave it untouched for three or four days or a week, being careful not to shake or stir it; do not press or squeeze the bags. Have ready some small clear glass vials, or a large one that will hold half a pint. Take out carefully the bags of alkanet and lay them in a saucer. You will find that they have coloured the oil to a beautiful crimson. Put into the bottom of each vial a small portion of any perfume you fancy: for instance, oil of orange-flowers, oil of jessamine, oil of roses, oil of pinks, extract of violets. The pungent oils (cloves, cinnamon, bergamot, lavender, orange-peel, lemon, &c.) are not good for the hair, and must not be used in scenting this oil. Having put a little perfume into the vials, pour into each through a small funnel sufficient of the coloured olive-oil to fill them to the neck. Then cork them tightly, and tie a circular bit of white kid leather over the corks. To use this oil, (observing never to shake the bottle,) pour a little into a saucer or some other small vessel, and with the finger rub it into the root of the hair.

The bags of alkanet may be used a second time.

No. 78.

Another Hair-Oil.

A very excellent hair-oil, which answers all common purposes, is made by mixing 1 ounce of brandy with 3 ounces of sweet oil. Add any scent you prefer; a selection can be got at the drug-store.

No. 79.

Another excellent Hair-Oil.

Take 1 quart olive-oil or fine lard-oil.
2½ ounces spirits of wine.
1 ounce cinnamon powder.
5 drachms bergamot-oil.

Heat them together in a large pipkin, then remove it from the fire, and add four small pieces of alkanet-root; keep it closely covered for 6 or 8 hours, let it then be filtered through a funnel lined with blotting or filtering paper.

No. 80.

To make Imitation of Ox-Marrow Hair-Grease.

Take fresh hog's lard, and melt it on a stove in any tin vessel; when melted, add such fine oil as you wish to perfume it to your fancy, such as extract of violet, oil of orange-flowers, oil of jessamine, oil of roses, oil of pinks, &c. The quantity you must use will depend on the quantity of lard you use. And to make it a bright yellow, take a little turmeric and boil it in a little lard, so that the colouring will be extracted; strain it, and pour it into your scented lard as much as will give the desired colour; this must be done when the scented lard is milk-warm, and must also be well mixed. Then pour it into wide-mouthed vials, such as are used for ox-marrow. Keep the vials well corked. To make it a purple colour, take a little alkanet-root, and proceed the same as with the yellow.

No. 81.

To make Rose Tooth Powder.

Take 3 ounces prepared chalk.
    ¼ ounce cinnamon, ground.
    ½ ounce orris-root, pulverized.
    ½ ounce rose-pink.

Make all very fine by pulverizing it, and mix. (Ready.)

No. 82.

To make very nice Cologne.

Take 2 drachms oil of lemon.
2 drachms oil of rosemary.
1 drachm oil of lavender.
2 drachms oil of bergamot.
10 drops oil of cinnamon.
2 drops oil of rose.
10 drops oil of cloves.
8 drops tincture of musk.
1 quart alcohol, (or spirits of wine.)

Mix all together, and shake well, when it will be ready to use. The older it gets, the better.

No. 83.

A remedy for Black Teeth.

Take equal parts of cream of tartar and salt; pulverize it, and mix it well. Then wash your teeth in the morning, and rub them with the powder.

No. 84.

How to clean the Teeth and Gums.

Take 1 ounce myrrh, in fine powder.
2 tablespoonfuls honey.
A little green sage, in very fine powder.

Mix them well together, and wet the teeth and gums with a little every night and morning.

No. 85.

A Lip-Salve.

Take 2 ounces oil of lemon.
1 ounce white wax.
1 ounce spermaceti.

Melt these ingredients, and while warm add 2 ounces rose-water, and ½ ounce orange-flower water. These make Hudson's cold cream,—a very excellent article.

The lips are liable to excoriation and chaps, which often extend to considerable depth. These chaps are generally occasioned by mere cold. The above salve will be found efficacious in correcting these evils.

No. 86.

To make Cottage Beer.

Take 1 peck good sweet wheat bran, and put it into 10 gallons of water, with 3 handfuls of good hops; boil the whole together in an iron, brass, or copper kettle, until the bran and hops sink to the bottom. Then strain it through a hair sieve, or a thin sheet, into a cooler, and when it is about lukewarm add 2 quarts of molasses. As soon as the molasses is melted, pour the whole into a 9 or 10 gallon cask, with 2 tablespoonfuls of yeast. When the fermentation has subsided, bung up the cask, and in 4 days it will be fit for use.

No. 87.

Brown Spruce Beer.

Pour 8 gallons fresh water into a barrel, and then 8 gallons more boiling hot; add 1 gallon molasses, and ½ pound essence of spruce; when nearly cool, put in ½ pint of good ale yeast. This must be well stirred and well mixed; leave the bung out 2 or 3 days. After which, the liquor may be immediately bottled, well corked and tied, and packed in sawdust or sand, and it will be ripe and fit to drink in two weeks.

No. 88.

To make good Ginger Beer.

Take 1 spoonful ground ginger.
    1 spoonful cream of tartar.
    1 pint yeast.
    1 pint molasses.
    6 quarts cold water.

Mix, and let it stand a few hours, until it begins to ferment; then bottle it, set it in a cool place: in 8 hours it will be good.

No. 89.

To make Imperial Ginger Beer.

Take 1 pound cream of tartar.
    2 ounces ginger, ground.
    7 pounds white sugar.
    1 drachm essence of lemon.
    6 gallons water.
    ½ pint yeast.

Bottle, and tie the corks down.

No. 90.

To make White Spruce Beer.

Take 3 pounds loaf sugar.
    4 gallons water.
    1 ounce ginger.
    ¼ pound essence of spruce.
    A little lemon-peel.
    1 cupful good yeast.

Mix all together, and when fermented bottle it close.

No. 91.

How to make Gas Beer.

Take 4 gallons cold water.
    3 pints molasses.
    1 quart yeast.
    1 handful hops.
    And such spices as you wish.

Then take 1½ pints of the above molasses, and mix it well with the yeast; then take 3 quarts of the above cold water and make it boiling hot; put into this boiling water the other 1½ pints of molasses, and such spices as you wish; then take some more of the above cold water and cool down the boiling water, molasses, and spices until it is milk-warm; then boil the above handful of hops in water, to take the strength out of the hops, and strain the hops out of the liquor. Then put all together into a strong cask, and bung it tight; then put the cask in the sun, or near to a warm stove, about five or six hours; after this put the cask into a tub of fresh or cold water 3 or 4 hours. In 24 hours it will be ripe. Keep the cask all the time closed up tight. You must take a very strong cask, or it will burst.

No. 92.

To make Cream Beer.

Take 2 ounces tartaric acid.
2 pounds white sugar.
3 pints water.
The juice of half a lemon.

Boil all together five minutes; when nearly cold, add the whites of 3 eggs, well beaten, with ½ cup flour, and ½ ounce essence of winter-green. Bottle. Take 2 teaspoonfuls of this syrup for a tumbler of water, and add to it ¼ teaspoonful of baking-soda. Drink it fresh.

No. 93.

How to make Mead.

Take 12 gallons water.
20 pounds honey.
6 eggs, the glair only.

Let it boil 1 hour; then add cinnamon, ginger, cloves, mace, and a little rosemary. When cold, add one spoonful of yeast, from the brewer; stir it well, and in 24 hours it will be good.

No. 94.

Ginger Beer—a pleasant beverage.

Take 10 pounds white sugar.
9 fluidounces lemon-juice.
1 pound honey.
11 ounces ginger, (ground.)

Boil the ginger in 3 gallons water for ½ hour; then add the sugar, the lemon-juice, and the rest of the water, and strain through a cloth. When cold, add the white of an egg, ½ fluidounce essence of lemon. After standing 4 days, it may be bottled off. A glass of this on a hot day, with a lump of ice in it, is very refreshing.

No. 95.

How to make Ginger Beer Powders.

Take 1 ounce and 54 grains (apothecaries') bicarbonate of soda, reduce it to powder, and divide into 16 papers; to each paper add 5 grains ground ginger, and a drachm of white sugar. Then take 1 ounce tartaric acid, which powder divide into 16 parcels, and do it up in separate papers. Two of these papers will make a pint of beer. Dissolve the soda in 2 gills of water in one glass, and the acid in 2 gills in another glass; pour them together, and swallow quickly.

No. 96.

How to make Ginger-Pop.

Take 2 gallons hot water, (boiling;) mix 2 ounces ground ginger and the peel of 2 lemons, 1 teaspoonful cream of tartar, 2 pounds white sugar; let this stand until milk-warm. Then put in the other part of the 2 lemons, 1 teaspoonful saleratus, 4 tablespoonfuls yeast, and the glair of 4 eggs, to clear. Cinnamon and cloves to your taste.

No. 97.

How to make Silver-top, a temperance drink.

Take 1 quart water, 3¼ pounds white sugar, 1 teaspoonful lemon-oil, 1 tablespoonful flour, with the white of 5 eggs, well beat up; mix all the above well together. Then divide the syrup, and add 4 ounces carbonate of soda into one part, and put it into a bottle, and then add 3 ounces tartaric acid to the other part of the syrup, and bottle it also. Take 2 pint tumblers, and put in each tumbler 1 tablespoonful of the syrup, (that is, from each bottle of the syrup,) and fill them half full with fresh cold water; pour it together into one tumbler. Superb.

No. 98.

Sassafras Mead, a cheap beverage.

Stir gradually with 1 quart boiling water, 1½ pounds brown sugar, 3 gills molasses, and 1 drachm tartaric acid. Stir it well, and when cold strain it into a large earthen pan or crock; then mix in 1 drachm essence of sassafras. Transfer it to clean bottles, (it will fill 2 or 3;) cork it tightly, and keep it in a cool place. Have ready a box containing about ¼ pound carbonate of soda, to use with it.

To prepare a glass of it for drinking, pour a little

of the mead or syrup into a tumbler; stir into it a small quantity of soda, and then add sufficient cold fresh water (ice-water, if you have it) to half fill the glass; give it a stir, and it will immediately foam up to the top.

No. 99.

To make Pineapple-ade.

Pare some fresh, ripe pineapples, and cut them into thin slices; then cut each slice into small bits; put them into a large pitcher, and sprinkle powdered white sugar among them; pour on boiling water in proportion of ½ gallon of water to each pineapple; cover the pitcher, stop up the spout with a roll of soft paper, and let the pineapples infuse into the water till it becomes quite cool, stirring and pressing down the pineapple occasionally with a spoon, to get out as much juice as possible. When the liquid has grown quite cold, set the pitcher for a while in ice. Then transfer the infusion to tumblers, add some more sugar, and put into each glass a lump of ice. You may lay a thin slice of fresh pineapple into each tumbler before you pour out the infusion.

No. 100.

How to clarify Sugar.

Take ½ pint water to 1 pound sugar, (loaf sugar;) set it over the fire to dissolve; to 12 pounds sugar thus prepared, beat up an egg very well, put in when cold, and, as it boils up, check it with a little cold water. The second time boiling, set it away to cool.

In a quarter of an hour, skim the top, and turn the syrup off quickly, leaving the sediment which will collect at the bottom.

No. 101.

For frosting Cakes.

Allow for the white of 1 egg, 9 large teaspoonfuls of double-refined sugar, and 1 teaspoonful of nice Poland starch, both powdered and sifted through a very fine sieve. Beat the whites of eggs so stiff they will adhere to the bottom of the plate on turning it upside down; then stir the sugar in gradually with a wooden spoon, stirring constantly about fifteen minutes; add a teaspoonful of lemon-juice, or vinegar, and a little rose-water. Stir in a few grains of cochineal-powder, or rose-pink if you wish to colour pink; or of the powder blue, if you wish to have it of a bluish tinge. Before icing a cake, dredge it all over with flour, and then wipe off the flour; the icing may thus be spread on more evenly. Lay the frosting on the cake with the knife, soon after it is drawn from the oven, (it may be either warm or cold;) smooth it over, and set in a cool place till hard. Allow the whites of 3 eggs for 2 common-sized loaves. The appearance of the cake will be much improved by icing it twice. Put on the first icing soon after the cake is taken out of the oven, and the second the next day, after the first is perfectly dry.

Before cutting an iced cake, cut the icing first, by itself, by pressing the back of the knife nearest the blade-end across the cake, to prevent the cracking and breaking of the icing.

No. 102.

To make Lemon-Cakes. No. 1.

Take 1 teacupful of butter, and 3 of powdered loaf sugar; rub them to a cream; stir into them the yolks of 5 eggs well beaten; dissolve a teaspoonful of saleratus in a teacupful of milk, and add the milk, add the juice and grated peel of 1 lemon, and the whites of the 5 eggs; and sift in, as light as possible, 4 teacupfuls of flour. Bake in 2 long tins about half an hour. Much improved by icing.

No. 103.

Queen-Cake.

Take 1 pound of sifted flour, 1 pound of sugar, and ¾ of a pound of butter; rub the butter and sugar to cream; add the well-beaten yolk of 5 eggs, 1 gill of wine, 1 gill of brandy, and 1 gill of cream, with part of the flour, and 1 pound of stoned raisins, or well-prepared currants, and spices to the taste; and then add the whites of the 5 eggs, beaten to a stiff froth, with the remainder of the flour.

No. 104.

Sponge-Cake.

Beat well together the yolk of 10 eggs with 1 pound white powdered sugar; and then stir in the whites, beaten to a stiff froth. Beat the whole 10 or 15 minutes; then stir in, gradually, half a pound sifted flour. Spice it with a nutmeg or grated rind of lemon. Bake immediately.

No. 105.

White Lemon-Cake.

Rub well together 6 ounces butter, 1¼ pounds flour; add ¼ pint (well beaten) eggs, 1 pound pulverized sugar, 12 drops essence of lemon, and 2 drachms carbonate of ammonia. The ingredients should be mixed into a paste, with as little handling as possible, rolled out about as thick as a silver dollar, cut in cakes, and baked on buttered tins, with a gentle heat.

No. 106.

Strasbourg-Cake.

To 1 pound flour, add 10 ounces pulverized sugar, 10 ounces butter, 2 eggs, half a nutmeg, (grated,) and an equal quantity of ground cinnamon, or mace and cinnamon, mixed. Bake.

No. 107.

How to bake Rusks. No. 1.

Take 1 pint milk, 1 teacupful yeast; mix it thin; when light, add 12 ounces sugar, 10 ounces butter, 4 eggs, flour sufficient to make it as stiff as bread; when risen, again mould and sponge it upon tin.

No. 108.

How to make Mock Mince-Pies.

Mix 1 cup sugar, 1 cup molasses, 1½ cup bread-crumbs, with 1 cup good cider-vinegar, 4 cups water, and 3 eggs; add 1 cup raisins, 1 ounce cloves, 1 ounce soda. This quantity will be sufficient for 3 pies. Bake.

No. 109.
To make Indian Biscuits.

Take 1 quart of cold Indian mush, or hasty pudding; put it into a pan containing about the same quantity of either coarse or fine wheat flour; add milk or sweet cream sufficient to make the mush thin, say ½ pint; then mix the flour, and make up into biscuits as soft as you can well handle them, and bake in a quick oven 20 minutes.

No. 110.
How to bake Lemon Pies.

Grate the peels of 4 lemons, and squeeze the juice into the grated peel. Then take 9 eggs, leaving out half the whites, 1 pound loaf sugar, (white,) ½ pound butter, 1 pint cream or milk, and 4 tablespoonfuls rose-water, and beat them well together, and add the lemon. Divide into 4 pies, with undercrust, and bake.

No. 111.
Cider-Cake.

Take 2 pounds flour, 1 pound sugar, ½ pound butter, 1 pint cider, cloves and cinnamon, with or without fruit, 2 teaspoonfuls soda. Bake.

No. 112.
How to bake Sugar-Cakes.

Take 1 pound flour, ¾ pound sugar, ½ pound butter, 5 eggs. Mix and drop them on tins, and put sugar, sanded on them, just as you put them into the oven, or frost them.

No. 113.

Cup-Cakes.

Take 3 cups sugar, 1 cup butter, 2 teaspoonfuls soda, 3 eggs, 5 cups flour,—all beaten together with as much spice as you please.

No. 114.

Ginger-Cakes.

Take 1 quart molasses, ½ pint thick milk, ¾ pound fresh lard or butter, 1 cent's worth pearlash, 1 cent's worth saleratus, 1 cent's worth anniseed, 1 teacupful ginger. Thicken with flour. Mix and bake.

No. 115.

How to preserve Milk for any length of time.

This process, invented by a Russian chemist named Kirkoff, consists in evaporating new milk by a very gentle fire, and very slowly, until it is reduced to a dry powder. This powder is to be kept in bottles carefully stopped. When it is to be employed, it is only necessary to dissolve the powder in a sufficient quantity of water. According to Mr. Kirkoff, the milk does not lose by this process any of its peculiar flavour.

No. 116.

To make Custards without Eggs.

Take 1 quart new milk, 4 tablespoonfuls flour, 2 tablespoonfuls sugar, season with nutmeg or cinnamon, and add salt to your taste. The milk should be placed over a quick fire, and, when at boiling-point, the flour should be added, being previously stirred up in cold milk. As soon as thoroughly scalded, add the sugar, spice, and salt. It may be baked either in cups or crust. This is an excellent dish, and deservedly prized by every one who has tried it.

No. 117.

How to keep Preserves or Jellies.

It is said that to set newly-made preserves for several days open in the sun, is one of the best methods of making them keep through the summer unfermented. It is worth trying.

No. 118.

To preserve Plums an elegant green.

Take 8 pounds double-refined sugar.
8 pounds of the fruit prepared.

Take the plums whilst a pin will pass through them, set them, covered with water in which a little alum has been dissolved, in a brass kettle on a hot hearth, to coddle. If necessary, change the water; they must be a beautiful grass-green; then, if you prefer, peel them and coddle again; take 8 pounds of this fruit to the above sugar after it has been dissolved in 1 quart of water and nicely skimmed. Then set the whole on the fire, to boil, until clear, slowly skimming them often, and they will be very green; put them up in glasses for use.

No. 119.

To preserve Peaches.

Take 10 pounds nicely-peeled peaches.
10 pounds loaf sugar.

The white clingstone is the nicest. Peel and drop into a pan of water, cut up 2 lemons, break the sugar slightly, put into a well-tinned kettle, (brass will do if nicely cleaned,) with 1 quart of water and the lemons; let it scald, and skim, and, having the required quantity of peaches in a nice stone jar, pour the syrup over; let it stand over night, then put all into the preserving-kettle and boil slowly, until the fruit looks clear; take out the peaches, and boil down the syrup to a proper consistence and pour over the fruit.

No. 120.

To preserve Magnum Bonum Plums.

Take 12 pounds plums.
12 pounds loaf sugar.
2 oranges.

Take 2 pounds of the sugar, and make a weak syrup; then pour it boiling upon the fruit; let it remain over night, closely covered; then, if preferred, skim them, and slice up the 2 oranges nicely, dissolve the rest of the sugar by taking the large cakes, and dip in water quickly, and instantly bring out. If the plums are not peeled, they must be nicely drained from the rest of the syrup, and the skin pricked with a needle. Do them gently until they look clear and the syrup adheres to them. Put them one by one into small pots, and pour the liquor over. These plums will ferment if not boiled in two syrups.

No. 121.
How to preserve Quinces.

Take 1 peck of the finest golden quinces, put them into a bell-metal kettle, cover with cold water, put over the fire, and boil until done soft; then take them out with a fork into an earthen dish; when sufficiently cool to handle, take off the skin, cut open on one side, and take out the core, keeping them as whole as possible. Take their weight in double-refined sugar, put it with a quart of water into the kettle, let it boil, and skim until very clear; then put in your quinces; 2 oranges cut up thin and put with the fruit, is an improvement. Let them boil in the syrup half an hour, then with your fruit-ladle take out the fruit, and boil the juice sufficiently, then pour it over the fruit.

No. 122.
How to make Raspberry Jam.

Take 6 pounds nicely-picked raspberries.
6 pounds loaf sugar.

Put the fruit into a nice kettle over a quick fire, and stir constantly, until the juice is nearly wasted; then add the sugar, and simmer to a fine jam. In this way the jam is greatly superior to that which is made by putting the sugar in first.

No. 123.

How to preserve Barberries.

Take 6 pounds nicely-picked barberries.
6 pounds loaf sugar.

Put the fruit and sugar into a jar, and place the jar in a kettle of boiling water; let it boil until the sugar is dissolved, and the fruit soft; let them remain all night. Next day put them into a preserving-pan, and boil them 15 minutes; then pot, as soon as cool, and set them by the next day, and cover them close.

No. 124.

How to preserve Cherries.

Take 8 pounds cherries.
6 pounds sugar.

Then take 1 quart water, melt some sugar in it, and boil; then the rest boil and skim, then put in the cherries, boil softly but steadily; take them off two or three times and shake them, and put them on again; then let them boil fast. When the fruit looks clear, take it out with a skimmer, and boil the syrup until it will not spread on a china plate; then return the fruit, and let it cool; then put it in pots for use.

No. 125.

How to make Currant Jelly.

Take 4 quarts juice of currants.
8 pounds sugar. (Loaf is the best.)

The currants should be used as soon as they are of a light red; put them, stem and all, into a jar, place that in boiling water, cook, then squeeze the juice, and to every quart put 2 pounds sugar; boil together 15 minutes, then put into glasses.

No. 126.

How to make Bread Cheese-Cakes.

Take 1 nutmeg, grated.
    1 pint cream.
    8 eggs.
    ½ pound butter.
    ½ pound currants.
    1 spoonful rose-water.
    1 penny loaf of bread.

Scald the cream, slice the bread thin as possible, and pour the cream boiling on to it; let it stand 2 hours. Beat together the eggs, butter, and grated nutmegs, and rose-water; add the cream and bread, beat well, and bake in patty-pans on a raised crust.

No. 127.

How to make a Plain Pound-Cake.

Beat 1 pound butter in an earthen pan until it is like a fine thick cream; then beat in 9 whole eggs till quite light. Put in a glass of brandy, a little lemon-peel shred fine; work in ¼ pound flour; put it into the hoop or pan, and bake it for an hour. A pound plum-cake is made the same with putting 1½ pounds clean washed currants, and ½ pound candied lemon-peel.

No. 128.

Rice-Cakes.

Beat the yolks of 15 eggs for nearly half an hour with a whisk; mix well with them 10 ounces of fine sifted loaf sugar, put in ½ pound of ground rice, a little orange-water or brandy, and the rinds of 2 lemons grated; then add the whites of 7 eggs well beaten, and stir the whole together for a quarter of an hour. Put them into a hoop, and set them in a quick oven for half an hour, when they will be properly done.

No. 129.

Lemon-Cakes. No. 2.

Take 1 pound of sugar, ¾ pound of flour, 14 eggs, 2 tablespoonfuls of rose-water, the raspings and juice of four lemons; when the yolks are well beaten up and separated, add the powdered sugar, the lemon-rasping, the juice, and the rose-water; beat them well together in a pan with a round bottom, till it becomes quite light, for half an hour. Put the paste to the whites, previously well whisked about, and mix it very light. When well mixed, sift in the biscuits, and bake them in small oval tins, with six sheets of paper under them, in a moderate heat. Butter the tins well, or it will prove difficult to take out the biscuits, which will be exceedingly nice if well made. Ice them previous to baking, but very lightly and even.

No. 130.

Cream-Cakes.

Beat the whites of 9 eggs to a stiff froth; stir it gently with a spoon, lest the froth should fall; and to every white of an egg grate the rinds of 2 lemons, shake in gently a spoonful of double-refined sugar sifted fine; lay a wet sheet of paper on a tin, and with a spoon drop the froth in little lumps on it near each other; sift a good quantity of sugar over them, set them in an oven after the bread is out, and close up the mouth of it, which will occasion the froth to rise. As soon as they are coloured they will be sufficiently baked; lay them by two bottoms together on a sieve, and dry them in a cool oven.

No. 131.

How to make Muffins.

Mix a gill of fine flour, 1½ pints of warm milk and water, with ¼ pint of good yeast, and a little salt, stir them together for a quarter of an hour, then strain the liquor into a quarter of a peck of fine flour; mix the dough well, and set it to rise for an hour, then roll it up and pull it into small pieces; make them up in the hand like balls, and lay flannel over them while rolling to keep them warm. The dough should be closely covered up the whole time; when the whole is rolled into balls, the first that are made will be ready for baking. When they are spread out in the right form for muffins, lay them on tins and bake them, and as the bottom begins to change colour turn them on the other side.

No. 132.

How to bake Rusks. No. 2.

Beat up 7 eggs, mix them with ½ pint of warm new milk, in which ¼ pound of butter has been melted, add ¼ pint of yeast, and 3 ounces of sugar, put them gradually into as much flour as will make a light paste nearly as thin as batter; let it rise before the fire an hour, add more flour to make it a little stiffer, work it well, and divide it into small loaves or cakes about five or six inches wide, and flatten them. When baked and cold, put them into the oven to brown a little. These cakes when first baked are very good buttered for tea; if they are made with caraway-seeds, they eat very nice cold.

No. 133.

How to make common Buns.

Rub 4 ounces of butter into 2 pounds of flour, a little salt, 4 ounces of sugar, a dessert-spoonful of caraway-seeds, and a spoonful of ginger; put some warm milk or cream to 4 tablespoonfuls of yeast; mix all together into a paste, but not too stiff; cover it over and set it before the fire an hour to rise; then make into buns, put them on a tin, set them before the fire for a quarter of an hour, cover over with flannel, then brush them with very fine warm milk, and bake them of a nice brown in a moderate oven.

No. 134.

How to make Ice-Cream.

Take of new milk and cream each 2 quarts, 2 pounds pulverized sugar, and 12 eggs; dissolve the sugar in the milk, beat the eggs to a froth, and add to the whole; strain, and bring to a scald, but be careful not to burn it; when cool, flavor with extract of vanilla or oil of lemon. Pack the tin freezer in a deep tub, with broken ice and salt, whirl the freezer, and occasionally scrape down from the side what gathers on. The proportions are one quart of salt to every pail of ice.

No. 135.

How to make Japan Black Writing-Ink.

In 6 quarts of water boil 4 ounces of logwood in chips cut very thin across the grain. The boiling may be continued for nearly an hour, adding, from time to time, a little boiling water to compensate for waste by evaporation. Strain the liquor while hot, suffer it to cool, and make up the quantity equal to five quarts by the further addition of cold water. To this decoction put 1 pound of blue galls coarsely bruised, or 1¼ pounds of the best galls, in sorts, 4 ounces of sulphate of iron calcined to whiteness, ½ ounce of acetate of copper, previously mixed with the decoction till it forms a smooth paste, 3 ounces of coarse sugar, and 6 ounces of gum senegal or arabic. These several ingredients may be introduced one after another, contrary to the advice of some, who recommend the gum, &c. to be added when the ink is nearly made. The composition produces the ink usually called Japan ink, from the high gloss which it exhibits when written with, and a small vial of it has been sold for 12 cents. The above ink, though possessing the full proportion of every ingredient known to contribute to the perfection of ink, will not cost more to those who prepare it for themselves than the common ink which can be bought by retail. When gum is very dear, or when no very high gloss is required, 4 ounces will be sufficient, with 1½ ounces of sugar. By using only ¾ pound of galls to 4 ounces sulphate of iron, uncalcined, omitting the logwood, and acetate of copper, and the sugar, and using only 3 ounces gum, a good and cheap common ink will be obtained.

No. 136.

How to make Black Ink.

Take 1 pound logwood, and 1 gallon of water; boil slightly or simmer in an iron vessel one hour; dissolve in a little hot water 24 grains bichromate of potash, 12 grains prussiate of potash, and stir into the liquid while over the fire; take it off and strain it through a fine cloth. No other ink will stand the test of oxalic acid, and it is so indelible that oxalic acid will not remove it from paper.

No. 137.

Another cheap Black Ink.

Take 1 drachm prussiate of potash.
 1 drachm bichromate of potash.
 1 ounce extract of logwood.
 1 gallon water.

Mix all together and shake it well; when dissolved, it is fit for use.

No. 138.

How to make Black Printers' Ink.

Printers' ink is a real black paint, composed of lampblack and linseed-oil, which has undergone a degree of heat superior to that of common drying oils. The manner of preparing it is extremely simple. Boil linseed-oil in a large iron pot for 8 hours, adding to it bits of toasted bread for the purpose of absorbing the water contained in the oil; let it rest till the following morning, and then expose it to the same degree of heat for 8 hours more, or till it has acquired the consistence required; then add lampblack worked up with a mixture of oil of turpentine and turpentine.

The consistence depends on the degree of heat given to the oil, and the quantity of lampblack mixed up with it; and this consistence is regulated by the strength of the paper for which the ink is intended.

The preparation of printers' ink should take place in the open air, to prevent the bad effects arising from the vapour of the burnt oil, and, in particular, to guard against accident by fire.

No. 139.

How to make Indelible Ink.

Take 1½ ounces of nitrate of silver, 5½ ounces liquor ammoniæ fortis; dissolve the nitrate of silver in the liquor ammoniæ fortis; ¾ ounces archil for colouring; and gum mucilage, 12 ounces; when ready for use, put up in drachm vials.

No. 140.

How to make another Indelible Ink.

Take 1 inch of stick nitrate of silver and dissolve it in a little water, and then stir it into a gallon of water, which will make a first-rate ink for cloth.

No. 141.

How to make Red Ink for writing. No. 1.

Boil over a slow fire 4 ounces Brazil-wood, in small raspings or chipped, in 1 quart of water, till a third part of the water is evaporated. Add during the boiling two drachms of alum in powder. When the ink is cold, strain it through a fine clean cloth.

N.B.—Vinegar or stale urine is often used instead of water. In case of using water, I presume a very small quantity of sal-ammoniac would improve this ink.

No. 142.

Another Red Writing-Ink. No. 2.

Take best carmine, 2 grains; rain-water, ¼ ounce; water of ammonia, 20 drops; add a little gum arabic.

No. 143.

How to make Blue Ink for writing. No. 2.

Take soft Prussian blue and oxalic acid, equal parts, powder them finely, and then add soft water to bring it to a thin paste. Let it stand for a few days, then add soft water to make the desired shade of colour, adding a little gum arabic to prevent its spreading.

No. 143½.

How to make Vinegar. No. 1.

Vinegar is used principally as a sauce and to preserve vegetable substances; but it is employed externally when an overdose of strong wine, spirit, opium, or other narcotic poison has been taken. A false strength is given to it by adding oil of vitriol or some acrid vegetable, as pellitory of Spain, capsicum, &c. It is rendered colourless by adding fresh-burned bone-black, 6 ounces to a gallon, and letting it stand for 2 or 3 days to clear. Mix cider and honey, in the proportion of 1 pound of honey to a gallon of cider, and let it stand in a vessel for some months, and vinegar will be produced so powerful that water must be mixed with it for common use.

No. 144.

Another Vinegar. No. 2.

Schele, a celebrated chemist, has recommended the following recipe:—Take 6 spoonfuls of good spirits of ⁓, to this add 3 pints of milk, and put the mixture into a vessel to be corked close. Vent must be given from time to time to the gas of fermentation. In the course of a month this will produce very good vinegar.

No. 145.

Another Vinegar. No. 3.

Put into a barrel of sufficient dimensions a mixture composed of 41 pints of water, and about 4 quarts of whiskey, and 1 quart of yeast, and 2 pounds of charcoal, and place it in a proper situation for fermentation. At the end of 4 months a very good vinegar will be formed, as clear and as white as water.

No. 146.

Common Vinegar.

This is made from weak liquor brewed for the purpose: its various strength is, in England, denoted by numbers, from 18 to 24.

No. 147.

Another Vinegar. No. 4.

To every gallon of water put 1 pound of sugar; let the mixture be boiled and skimmed as long as any scum arises. Then let it be poured into proper vessels; and when it is as cool as beer when worked, let a toast rubbed over with yeast be put to it. Let it work about 24 hours, and then put it into an iron-hooped cask, fixed either near a constant fire or where the summer sun shines the greater part of the day; in this situation it should be closely stopped up; but a tile or brick, or something similar, should be laid on the bunghole, to keep out the dust and insects. At the end of about 3 months (or sometimes less) it will be clear and fit for use, and may be bottled off. The longer it is kept after it is bottled the better it will be. If the vessel containing the liquor is to be exposed to the sun's heat, the best time to begin making it is in the month of April.

No. 148.

Wine Vinegar.

Take any sort of wine that has gone through fermentation and put it into a cask that has had vinegar in it. Then take some of the fruit or stalks of which the wine has been made, and put them, wet, into an open-headed cask, in the sun, with a coarse cloth over it, for 6 days; after which, put them into the vinegar and stir it well about. Then put it in a warm place, if in winter, or, if in summer, put it in a yard, in the sun, with a slate over the bung-hole. When the vinegar is sour enough and fine, rack it off into a clean sour cask and bung it up; then put it in the cellar for use. Those wines that contain the most mucilage are fittest for the purpose. The lees of pricked wine are also a very proper ingredient in vinegar.

No. 149.

Sugar Vinegar.

To each gallon of water add 2 pounds of brown sugar and a little yeast. Leave it exposed to the sun for 6 months, in a vessel slightly stopped.

No. 150.

Gooseberry Vinegar.

Bruise the gooseberries when ripe, and to every quart put 3 quarts of water. Stir them well together, and let the whole stand for 24 hours; then strain it through a cloth bag. To every gallon of liquor add 1 pound brown sugar, and stir them well together before they are put into the cask. Proceed in all other respects as before. This vinegar possesses a pleasant taste and smell; but raspberry vinegar, which may be made on the same plan, is far superior in these respects. The raspberries are not required to be of the best sort: still, they should be ripe and well-flavoured.

No. 151.

Currant Vinegar.

This is made in the same way as that from gooseberry: only pick off the currants from the stalks.

No. 152.

Primrose Vinegar.

To 15 quarts of water put 6 pounds of brown sugar; let it boil 10 minutes, and take off the scum; pour on it half a peck of primroses; before it is quite cold, put in a little fresh yeast, and let it work in a warm place all night; put it in a barrel in the kitchen, and, when done working, close the barrel, still keeping it in a warm place.

No. 153.

Raisin Vinegar.

After making raisin wine, lay the pressed raisins in a heap to heat; then to each 56 pounds put 5 gallons of water and a little yeast.

No. 154.

Cider Vinegar.

The poorest sort of cider will serve for vinegar, in managing which, proceed thus:—

First draw off the cider into a cask that has had vinegar in it before; then put some of the apples that have been pressed into it; set the whole in the sun, and in a week or 9 days draw it off into another cask. This is a good table vinegar.

No. 155.

How to Strengthen Vinegar.

Suffer it to be repeatedly frozen, and separate the upper cake of ice or water from it. All vinegars owe their principal strength to the acetic acid they contain; but the vinegar of wine contains also a tartar, a small proportion of malic acid, alcohol, and colouring-matter; that of cider contains merely the malic acid, little or no alcohol, and a yellowish colouring-matter.

No. 156.

How to make Vinegar from Elder-Flowers, Gilliflowers, Musk-Roses, and Tarragon.

Dry an ounce of either of the above flowers for

two days in the sun; then put them into a bottle, pour on them a pint of vinegar, closely stop the bottle, and infuse for 15 days in moderate heat of the sun.

No. 157.

How to make German Vinegar.

Take 15 gallons soft water, 4 pounds brown sugar, ¼ pound cream of tartar, 2 gallons whiskey. Mix, and keep it lightly covered, in a warm temperature.

No. 158.

How to increase the Sharpness and Strength of Vinegar.

Boil 2 quarts of good vinegar till reduced to 1; then put it in a vessel and set it in the sun for a week. Now mix the vinegar with six times its quantity of bad vinegar in a small cask: it will not only mend it, but make it strong and agreeable.

No. 159.

General Remarks on Dyeing.

Cleanliness in dyeing is very essential. The vessel and the articles to be dyed must be rid of grease and dirt, as grease resists the colouring-particles and dirt leaves a stain. Soft water should always be used for dyeing. Vessels used for dyeing small articles should generally be wash-basins, small copper and tinned pans, and sufficiently large that the dyeing-liquor be not spilled by dipping the articles in and out when dyeing. The quantity of liquor generally necessary for dyeing a dress of muslin, crape, sarcenet, cambric, &c., is about three quarts; for a larger dress, a proportionate quantity.

The dyeing-utensils are simple, being composed of tubs, kettles, horse, or a couple of lathed benches, for the purpose of placing the goods upon when they come from the dye. The horse may be in form of a carpenter's stool. A doll, which is used for beating blankets, counterpanes, &c. in the tub, in order to clean them. For this doll some use an article similar to a pavior's mall, but of smaller dimensions: others have a circular piece of wood, two inches thick, in which four legs are fastened on the under side, and in the centre a pretty long handle, with a cross-piece put through it to work it with. Against the wall or a post fasten a hook or a pin to put on your skeins, and with a small stick wring them out. In fancy-dyeing the various shades of cambric, a winch is put in frequent use.

The liquor should always be stirred with a spoon, rod, or any thing that is clean, previous to the article being dipped in it, to cause the colouring-particles to be equally diffused, so that the article to be dyed receives its colour uniformly; and it is also necessary that the article be moved in and out quickly, and opened to receive the colour more evenly. Colours generally look much darker when wet, therefore allowance should generally be made for drying, which should always be done in a warm room, pinned or stretched to a line.

No. 160.
Aluming.

Is a preparation necessary for some colours in order to receive the colouring-particles, such as crimson scarlet, purple, and some other colours. If any article is directed to be alumed, be careful to rid it well of the soap-suds, as alum turns soap to grease. When the article is put in the alum-liquor, it is to be well dipped in and out and opened, to receive this preparation more equally, for an hour, or all night, if circumstances admit; and, when alumed, it must be well wrung out and rinsed in two waters, and then dyed, the sooner the better, before getting dry.

Note.—The aluming of silks ought to be done cold, or it will be deprived of its lustre.

No. 161.

Preparing of the Dye-Liquors, or Scalding the Wood.

Having something like the end of a tub, about one foot deep, with a copper bottom, bored full of holes about a quarter of an inch in diameter, lay a piece of rather coarse sheeting on this; lay it all together on another tub; fill it with the wood to be scalded. Then, having a copper boiler full of boiling water, fill the tub which contains the wood with boiling water; stir it during the time it is going through; fill it up again, and so repeat the operation till you have got all the strength from the wood.

The criterion by which to know when the strength is gone from the wood is the paleness of the liquor as it runs through. This operation is considered superior to boiling the wood in a copper boiler, especially for the ground wood: but either way will answer. The method of rendering the liquor stronger of course is by evaporation, in a copper vessel, with a constant fire under it. The chips of dyewood are generally superior to the ground wood, as they are not so likely to be adulterated.

No. 162.

Pink on Silk.

After aluming, (see receipt No. 160,) handle the goods to be dyed in peach-wood liquor till of the colour desired; then take out, and put in a little alum-liquor; handle the goods a little longer, take out, rinse in water, and finish.

Note.—In most cases where the shade is not dark enough, the operation must be repeated.

No. 163.

Brown on Silk.

Alum your silk, (see No. 160.) Then take 1 part of fustic-liquor and 3 parts of peach-wood liquor; handle in these till it becomes a good brown; (a little logwood-liquor will darken your shade, if required;) hedge out, and put in a little alum-water; again put in your goods, handle a little longer, then take out, drain, rinse well, and finish.

Note.—By varying the peach-wood and fustic, various shades may be obtained.

No. 164.

Green on Silk.

Take green ebony, boil it in water, and let it settle. Take the clean liquor, as hot as you can bear your hands in it, and handle in it your goods till of a bright yellow. Then take water, and put in a little sulphate of indigo; handle your goods in this till of the shade wanted.

Note.—The ebony may previously be boiled in a bag, to prevent it from sticking to the silk.

No. 165.

Sulphate of Indigo.

Take 3 pounds of vitriol and 1 pound of ground indigo; put in a little at a time, and keep stirring till all dissolved. Let stand for 24 hours, and then it is ready for use.

No. 166.

Blue on Silk.

Indigo, same as for green; you will have a blue.

Note.—The silk ought to be boiled in white soap and water and made quite white, and then rinsed in lukewarm water.

No. 167.

Black on Silk.

Take 1 ounce of bluestone of vitriol, 2 ounces of copperas, and $\frac{1}{2}$ ounce of nitrate of iron. Mix all together with as much water as will do one piece; have the water a little warm. Hedge in this 6 times, backward and forward; take out, and rinse in water. Take another tub, and put in it as much logwood-liquor that has in it 1 pound of logwood and 1 ounce of fustic-liquor; hedge in this liquor with a sufficient quantity of water till black; wash out, and finish.

Note.—In both processes, let them have a chance to air in drying.

No. 168.

Blue Black on Silk.

First run through a mordant of nitrate of iron and water; then run through pearlash-water; then through nitrate of iron again; then put them through logwood-liquor, with a little bluestone of vitriol dissolved in it. If not dark enough, repeat the operation.

No. 169.

Maroon on Silk.

To 3 pounds silk take ½ pound cudbear; put it in water, and let it boil; then put in your silk, and let it boil a few minutes. Keep your silk well handled; take out, and you will have a good handsome colour. To change the shade, put in 2 pounds common salt, and operate as before: this will vary the shade. To vary it still further, take the silk, after boiling it the first time without the salt, and handle it in pearlash-water, or in cream of tartar, and you will have a handsome blue.

No. 170.

Orange on Silk or Cotton.

Take 1 pound silk, 1 ounce annotto, 2 ounces pearlash, and boil them well together. Turn in your goods; when boiled 10 minutes, take out, wash, and finish. If this orange is dark, handle the goods at hand-heat.

Note.—These goods must be well washed out in

soap, and in aluming them you may use a little sugar of lead.

No. 171.

Gray on Silk.

For a silk dress: Take 4 or 6 ounces of fine powdered galls, and pour on them boiling water; handle your silk in this for 20 or 30 minutes. In another form, dissolve a piece of green copperas about the size of a nut. Handle your silk through this, and it will be a gray, more or less dark, according to the quantity of drugs.

No. 172.

Slate on Silk.

To make a slate, take another pan of warm water and about a teacupful of logwood-liquor, pretty strong, and a piece of pearlash of the size of a nut. Take the above gray-coloured goods and handle a little in this liquor, and it is finished.

Note.—If too much logwood is used, the colour will be too dark.

No. 173.

Olive on Silk.

By adding a little fustic-liquor to the above slate, it will form an olive: it may be necessary to run them through a weak pearlash-water to sadden them. Wash in two waters for the above three colours. They will keep their colour very well.

No. 174.

Stone on Silk.

Take the coloured gray, (see Receipt No. 171.) Add a sufficient quantity of purple archil to the gray liquor. To give them a red sandy cast, add a little red archil. Simmer the silk in this a few minutes. Rinse in one or two cold waters. Dry in the air. The red archil is made from purple archil, by adding a small quantity of vitriol and water, which will redden it.

No. 175.

To dye a Silk Dress Brown.

Take 8 ounces sumach, 4 ounces logwood, 8 ounces camwood or madder; boil these drugs in water, then cool down your liquor; wet out your silks; then enter them; handle well; wash out as usual. For a mulberry cast, add as much purple archil as may be necessary.

No. 176.

Drab on Silk.

For a silk dress: Take 4 ounces archil, 1 ounce madder; enter and handle the goods. This may be saddened by taking out your goods and dissolving in the liquor a piece of green copperas, the size of a nut; again handle in this liquor. Or, what is still better, instead of copperas, use a little pearlash to sadden with.

No. 177.

Dove on Silk.

Take Brazil logwood and sumach; vary the quantities as you want your shade; boil them in water, then enter your goods, handle well, and sadden with green copperas.

No. 178.

Yellow on Silk.

Boil quercitron-bark in a copper pan for 20 minutes, any quantity you please. Dip a sufficient quantity to cover your silk in another copper pan, or tinned vessel, to which add a small quantity of muriate of tin; pass your silks first through warm water, and wring them out; then put them into this pan of dye-water, and handle them with a clean stick till cold; when cold, take out, throw out your liquor, take from the first pan as much liquor as before; handle in this 10 minutes, then add muriate of tin according to shade wanted. Rinse out in its own liquor, and dry in a warm room. Annotto affords an orange yellow with equal quantities of pearlash, and gives out its colour to silk in warm water. Turmeric gives out its colour in a similar manner. The roots of barberry afford a yellow of themselves when boiled in water.

No. 179.

Crimson on Silk.

Take cudbear, boil it in water; then just rinse or handle your silks in it for a few minutes, you have the shade wanted. Chamber-lye or any alkaline solution will change the colour.

No. 180.

Flesh-Colour on Silk.

Having first thoroughly cleaned your silk in the usual manner, rinse in warm water; then handle them in a very slight water of alum and tartar,—so slight that you could hardly taste it. Then, if you have been dyeing pinks, (Receipt No. 162,) take some of the old liquor, handle in it till of the shade wanted. The liquor must not be too strong, or the shade will be too heavy.

No. 181.

Brown on Woollen Cloth, or Cloths of any description.

The quantity of woods to be regulated according to the quantity of goods to be dyed. For instance, a pair of men's pantaloons, being first well cleaned from all grease: take 1 pound red-wood, hypernick, or peach-wood, 1 pound fustic, put them in a copper kettle, boil them, then cool down so as to bear in it your hand; then put in a small quantity of cream of tartar; agitate the water; then enter your goods, handle them till they come to a boil, 5 or 10 minutes; take out the goods, put in a strong solution made of 4 ounces copperas, again cool down, re-enter the goods, again bring them to a boil; take out; rinse well in water. (Finished.)

This process makes a good substantial brown, and might be varied in the shade by varying the quantities of woods in their proportion,—also by adding a little alum in the saddening. This is somewhat of an olive.

No. 182.

A Brown on the Red Cast.

Take 2 pounds red-wood, 1 pound fustic; proceed in every respect as in Receipt No. 181: the desired shade will be obtained. The quantity of dye-woods may be regulated according to the quantity of goods to be dyed; in No. 181 also, the copperas and tartar. (On woollen, of course.)

No. 183.

Olive-Brown.

For a pair of pantaloons, providing they weigh 3 pounds, take 2 pounds fustic, 1 ounce logwood, 4 ounces common madder, 2 ounces peach-wood; boil them up; then cool down your liquor; enter your pantaloons; bring the liquor to a boil; let it boil half an hour, occasionally turning over; take out; cool down your liquor; put in 2 ounces dissolved copperas; handle until deep enough. (For wool.) Any quantity of yarn may be dyed on the same principle.

No. 184.

A Brown inclining to Snuff.

Take any quantity of woollen goods; use for every pound 1½ or 2 pounds logwood. First put your logwood into the copper vessel; bring it to a boil; cool down; then enter your goods; bring them to a boil, half an hour, or longer if a large quantity;

take out, wash, and finish. Put, however, a little sumach,—about 2 ounces to the pound of logwood. This will be a good shade of brown. To alter this shade, put into your liquor a proportionally small quantity of alum-liquor, again enter the goods: you will have a good handsome shade on silk as well as woollen.

No. 185.

A Black inclining to Purple, on Wool and Silk.

Take 4 pounds logwood, 1 pound sumach; boil them in a sufficient quantity of water; cool down with water enough to dye 4 or 5 pounds of silk or wool; enter the goods; bring them to a boil, for 10 minutes; take out, partly cool down; put in about 1 pound copperas; again enter your goods, bring them to a boil, take out, wash, and finish. (Chiefly intended for wool.)

N.B.—A pair of pantaloons, or any other article which is old, would not need to be so particular in quantity of dye-stuffs or length of time. It will also answer for cotton, and that without sumach, if the sumach is not at hand. (This is intended chiefly for woollen.)

No. 186.

A Black inclining to Brown, on Silk and Woollen.

Take 1 part sumach, 1 logwood, 1 hypernick or peach-wood; boil the dye-stuffs; cool down; put in the silk or woollen according to the quantity of your dye-woods, bring them to a boil, for 10 minutes, take out the goods, cool down; having put in a sufficient quantity of dissolved copperas, again enter the goods, bring to a boil, take out, wash well, and finish.

To mix the copperas with alum would materially alter the shade, if a variety was wanted. (This is chiefly intended for wool.)

No. 187.

A Jet Black on Wool or Woollen Cloth.

For 7 pounds wool or woollen cloth, take $3\frac{1}{2}$ pounds logwood, $\frac{3}{4}$ pound sumach, $\frac{3}{4}$ pound fustic; boil these drugs in a sufficient quantity of water for 20 minutes; cool down, put in your goods, bring to a boil half an hour, then take out; cool down your liquor; add copperas, dissolved in water, $1\frac{1}{4}$ pounds, bluestone of vitriol, 2 ounces; again enter your goods, bring to a boil, 15 minutes, take out, wash well in cold water, and finish.

No. 188.

Blue Prussian on Woollen.

Take any quantity of calcined copperas, dissolve it in warm water, strong, put in your goods, keep them well handled till the water comes nearly to a boil; still handle 15 minutes; then rinse the goods in cold water; get up another kettle of 1 of urine to 3 of water; bring the water to hand-heat; put in your goods, handle half an hour; again rinse in cold water; get up another kettle of water, hand-heat, and for each pound of goods, 3 ounces prussiate of potash; put some oil of vitriol in the kettle; handle the goods half an hour. If the colour looks green, add a little more vitriol, handle half an hour longer, take out, wash in cold water, and finish.

No. 189.

Green on Wool.

For 6 pounds yarn, worsted, or cloth, take 3 pounds fustic, ¾ pound alum; boil them in a kettle 10 minutes, partly cool down; then put in a small teacupful sulphate of indigo, rake it well up, enter your goods well handled, let boil 20 minutes, (if a larger quantity, boil longer in proportion;) take out, and, if not blue enough, add a little more sulphate of indigo; handle until deep enough. Rinse in cold water, and finish. This shade may be altered in a variety of ways, by adding a little camwood, or logwood, in the first boiling.

No. 190.

Lilac on Wool.

Boil up any quantity of archil, according to the quantity of goods you want to dye; cool the liquor a little, enter the goods, handle carefully, until the shade is deep enough, without boiling the liquor, take out, wash, and finish. One pound of archil will dye 4¼ pounds of goods. Silk may be dyed in the same way. The shades may be altered by soda, pearlash, wine, or common salt, adding a little, and re-entering the goods before washing, and handling a little while longer.

No. 191.

Drab on Woollen.

For about fifteen pounds of woollen goods, take ¾ pounds weld, 9 ounces madder, 4 ounces logwood, 3 ounces archil; put them in water, bring them to a boil for 10 or 15 minutes, cool down; enter the goods, boil 15 minutes, wind up; put in 1 ounce alum, 1½ ounce copperas, ground; boil a few minutes longer, during which time handle well; take out, wash, and finish. The above receipt may serve as a standard of procedure for all the drab shades (which may be altered at pleasure) that can be produced, only varying the quantities of drugs, in some cases adding archil, and in others a little sulphate of indigo. Red tartar and camwood may also be used. The copperas and alum may be varied in quantity, or increased, or the alum left out, thus varying the whole round.

No. 192.

Red on Woollen.

For 10 pounds of woollen goods, take 2 pounds alum, ½ pound red tartar; boil the goods in this 1 hour, (if a larger quantity of goods, boil longer;) then boil up 4½ pounds peachwood in clean water, cool down to a scald, put in 2 ounces No. 1 tin-liquor, enter the goods, handle until dark enough, and finish. The goods must not be washed between the first and second operations.

No. 193.

How to make No. 1 Tin-Liquor.

Take 2 quarts muriatic acid, killed with 24 ounces granulated tin. This will answer for woollen or cotton.

No. 194.

How to make No. 2 Tin-Liquor, for Yellow on Woollen.

About 4 parts muriatic acid to 1 part sulphuric acid, killed with granulated tin. This will answer for yellow on cotton, also.

No. 195.

Slate on Woollen.

For 10 pounds of woollen goods, take 10 pounds sumach, boil it up 10 minutes, cool down, put in your goods, bring them to a boil a few minutes, take out; put in 4 pounds copperas, dissolve, cool down; re-enter the goods, bring them to a boil, take out, wash, and finish. A quantity of iron-liquor, such as the calico-printers use, would be preferable to copperas. This slate may be varied by varying the proportion of copperas and sumach; also, by adding a little peachwood, or any other red wood; in this case, less copperas might be used.

No. 196.

Yellow on Wool.

For 10 pounds of wool, bring a kettle of water to a scald, or to 180 degrees of heat; put in 4 pounds quercitron-bark, (do not allow it to boil, as that would bring out the tannin and dull the yellow,) 1 pound alum, 6 ounces cream of tartar, nearly ½ pint No. 1 tin-liquor; stir up the liquor well, allow it to settle 15 minutes, enter the goods, keep in until dark enough.

No. 197.

Orange on Wool.

First dye the pattern to a full yellow. Then take a clean kettle of water; when a little warm, put in for the above goods 2 pounds madder, peachwood, munjeet, or hypernick; munjeet does very well; put in your goods, keep them well handled, bring the goods to a boil, let boil till dark enough, wash, and finish.

VARIOUS SHADES OF FANCY DYEING ON COTTON.

No. 198.

For any quantity of Thread in Black.

First take thread and boil it in sumach and water; then let it be immersed in lime-water, cold; then in weak copperas-water, cold; then in lime-water again, cold; then in logwood-liquor, warm; take out, put some copperas-liquor into your logwood-liquor, again put in your goods, handle, and finish. This makes a first-rate black.

No. 199.

Turmeric Yellow.

Take about 3 pounds of turmeric, put in a small tub for the purpose; pour on it a tumbler of oil of vitriol, stir it well up; then pour on it hot water, about 2 gallons, stir this well up; then, having half a tubful of water boiling hot from the boiler, pour on it the contents of the small tub; enter 3 pieces, 30 yards each, give them 6 or 8 ends, as the workmen term it, fold up. The next process is to have another tub of water, put in it half a pailful of alum-liquor, give the pieces 3 or 4 ends in this, take out, and finish. Renew with the same quantity for the next 3 pieces, and proceed. *Note.*—By ends is meant rinsing the pieces backward and forward over the wince in the tub. Half a hogshead will answer the purpose.

It will be understood that these cotton colours are intended for linings or cambrics. It will also be understood that the liquors must be prepared as in Receipt No. 161, or by boiling in a copper cistern; the former is most generally adopted for this kind of dyeing. It will be necessary to have a number of tubs for the different liquors, and in dyeing various shades to have the liquors prepared in readiness.

No. 200.

Green on Cotton.

Take as much hot fustic-liquor as will cover 3 pieces, in which is put a very little lime-liquor, put it in a tub, enter your goods, give them 5 ends, hedge them out; take another tub, half full of water, (cold,) put into it a sufficient quantity of blue-stone of vitriol liquor to set the tub, about 2 quarts; enter your goods in this, give them 5 ends, hedge out; then take a couple of pailfuls of the fustic-liquor, renew the first tub, enter 3 pieces more, and so proceed as at first; then renew your blue vitriol tub with half the quantity of liquor, not taking any out, and proceed as at first. In this way do as many the first and second time as you can finish that day; then commence to finish them. Take half a tubful of old fustic-liquor, that has been used once, and put to it 1½ pailfuls of logwood-liquor; enter your pieces 3 at the time, give them 5 ends, and finish. Renew with a little more logwood-liquor, enough to make them dark enough, having first thrown away a couple of pailfuls from the tub, and renew with the same from the old tub, and so proceed in finishing.

No. 201.

Buff on Cotton.

Take as much hot fustic-liquor and water as will half fill a tub, enter 3 pieces, give them 5 ends, hedge out; take another tub of lime-water cold, enter the same pieces, and give them 5 ends in this; take out, and in a short time they will be buff. Renew your first and second tub, and proceed as at first. This is all required for buff.

No. 202.

Annotto-Orange on Cotton.

Having prepared your annotto-liquor by boiling it in a copper vessel for 20 minutes, take out your liquor, put it in a tub, partly fill your boiler with water, bring it to a boil; having kept in the boiler the sediment of the annotto, make it strong enough with annotto-liquor to the shade you want to dye; enter 3 pieces when boiling, give them 3 ends, take out; enter them into cold alum-water, give them 4 ends, take out, and finish. Renew your annotto-boiler with a sufficient quantity of annotto-liquor, and proceed as before; then renew your alum-tub, proceed as before in the second process. This finishes them.

The liquor that is left in the boiler at night will do to boil the annotto in the next day, so that nothing is lost.

No. 203.

Red on Cotton.

Take 3 pieces, enter them into a tub with hot redwood or peachwood liquor, give them 5 ends, then run them into your wince; have another tub, called the spirit-tub, close by, half full of cold water, put into it about 3 tumblerfuls of spirits; then run the pieces from the other wince over the wince of the spirit-tub, give them 5 ends in the spirit-tub, then wind them on the wince of the spirit-tub, then back again to the red-tub; give them 5 ends without having renewed the tub, they are finished.

Throw away the red-tub liquor, put in fresh liquor, and proceed as before; but the spirit-tub must be renewed always; even at night it may be left in a tub, and renewed the next day.

No. 204.

Brown on Cotton.

The first process is to give them 5 ends in hot sumach-liquor, or let them lie all night in the large tub, same as for blacks; then give them 5 ends in copperas, hedge out, give them 5 ends in lime-tub; then hedge out, lay them one side till you get enough to finish that day. You next renew your tubs, and repeat the operation as before. Then comes the finishing part. Make up a tub of hot redwood-liquor, enter 3 pieces, give them 5 ends, put the pieces one side the tub, put in some alum-liquor, stir up, give them 5 ends more, hedge out, and finish.

No. 205.

Drab on Cotton.

Take half a tub of hot sumach and fustic liquor; more fustic than sumach, according to shade wanted; enter 3 pieces, give them 5 ends, hedge out; give them 5 ends in the copperas-tub, and finish. Renew your tubs, and proceed as before. The copperas-tub is a half tub of water, with a couple of pailfuls of copperas-liquor to set in the first place; renewed each time.

No. 206.

Slate on Cotton.

Make up a tub of about 2 of logwood to 1 of fustic liquor,—both hot; enter 3 pieces; give them 5 ends; hedge out; give them 5 ends in copperas-liquor; have it stronger or weaker, according to shade wanted. This finishes them. Renew your tubs, and proceed as before.

No. 207.

Purple on Cotton.

Get up a tub of hot logwood-liquor, enter 3 pieces, give them 5 ends, hedge out; enter them into a clean alum-tub, give them 5 ends, hedge out; get up another tub of logwood-liquor, enter, give them 5 ends, hedge out; renew your alum-tub, give them 5 ends in that, and finish.

No. 208.

Black on Cotton.

First take your pieces and boil them in sumach-liquor, in a large copper vessel, if you have it, that will hold 60 or 70 pieces, in which you put about a bushel and a half of sumach; let them stay all night, if it is convenient; take out, and enter them into the lime-tub, 3 at a time; give them 4 ends, hedge out; enter them into the copperas-tub, give them 5 ends, hedge out; enter them into the lime again, give them 4 ends, hedge out; enter them into another tub with tolerably strong logwood-liquor, give them 5 ends; put them to one side of the tub; put in enough copperas-liquor to blacken them, (about a couple of quarts,) then give them a few more ends, and they are finished. With this process it is the same as with the greens. After sumaching, liming, copperasing, and second liming is repeated, till you get as many as will answer you to finish that day, the tubs being renewed after each 3 pieces, then comes the finishing; after each 3 pieces, the logwood and copperas liquor is thrown away, because the copperas kills the logwood, and so renders it unfit for the next pieces. It is frequently the case that, instead of the first process of sumach-boiling, they collect the old sumach, and fustic, and logwood-liquor, that has no copperas or lime in it, into a large tub, and all the pieces that are spoiled in the other colours they throw into this tub, and let them lie a few days till they are ready to dye blacks, and this answers instead of the sumaching.

For the foregoing cotton shades, the pieces are first taken and boiled in a wood or copper cistern, as circumstances may be, in order to take out the sizing, and prepare them to receive the dye.

No. 209.

How to put a fine Gloss on Silk.

Take a fair white potato, cut it in very thin slices, pour on it boiling water, let stand till rather cool, take out the slices of potato, run your silk through this water, squeeze out, smooth while damp, and you will have a very superior gloss. It was tried on black silk, and it was found to answer well. If it should not answer on lighter colours, try the following one. If a quantity of silk, of course proportion your potatoes.

No. 210.

Another way to put a Gloss on Silk.

Instead of a potato, use a small quantity of isinglass; dissolve in water. Use it the same as the above in every particular. 1 ounce of isinglass will answer for 1 pound of silk.

No. 211.

Tin-Liquor for Pinks, Scarlets, Crimson, &c.

Take 1 part muriatic acid, and 1 part nitric acid, and kill with tin.

No. 212.

Tin-Liquor for Scarlets, Crimson, &c. on Silks.

Take 1 pound nitric and 1 pound muriatic acid, and about 1½ ounces sal-ammoniac; kill with granulated tin.

No. 213.

How to set an Indigo-Vat for Cotton.

Having a sufficiently large vat, nearly fill it with water; put in 30 pounds ground indigo, 50 pounds copperas, 50 pounds slaked lime; occasionally stir it up, for 2 days. When perfectly settled, it is ready for use. When the vat is exhausted, renew with 4 pounds pearlash, 4 pounds lime, and 12 pounds copperas.

No. 214.

A Blue-Vat for Silk and Woollen.

Take 8 pounds indigo, and about 2 gallons vinegar, work it well in the mill till fine; if this is not convenient, put them on a slow fire for 24 hours till dissolved; put in 1 pound madder; mix these well, and put them into a vat containing 100 gallons urine; stir well twice a day for one week. It may be then worked, always previously stirring it. This vat continues to be good till exhausted. Mazarine blues, and deep purples, may be managed with this vat and archil-dye; take care to rinse it well from one to the other. Archil forms a dye of itself without mordant, on silk and woollen, when boiled in water.

No. 215.
How to dye Straws Red.

Boil ground Brazil-wood in a lye of potash, and boil your straw in it.

No. 216.
Blue on Straw.

Take a sufficient quantity of potash-lye, 1 pound of litmus, or lacmus, ground; make a decoction, and then put in the straw and boil it.

No. 217.
Turkey-Red on Leather.

After the skin has been properly prepared with sheep or pigs' dung, &c., take strong alum-water, and sponge over your skin; when dry, boil a strong gall-liquor, (it cannot be too strong;) then boil a strong Brazil-wood liquor, the stronger the better; take a sponge, dip it in your liquor, and sponge over your skin: repeat this, till it comes to a full red. To finish your skin, take the white of eggs and a little gum-dragon, mix the two together in $\frac{1}{2}$ gill of water, sponge over your skin, and, when dry, polish it with a bottle, or piece of glass prepared for the purpose.

No. 218.

Red on Leather.

Red is given by washing the skins, and laying them two hours in galls, then wringing them out, dipping them in a liquor made with ligustrum, alum, and verdigris, in water, and lastly in a dye made of Brazil-wood boiled with lye.

No. 219.

Yellow on Leather.

Infuse quercitron-bark in vinegar, in which boil a little alum, and brush over your skins with the infusion. Finish same as No. 217.

No. 220.

Another Yellow on Leather.

Take 1 pint whiskey, 4 ounces turmeric; mix them well together; when settled, sponge your skin over, and finish the same as No. 217.

No. 221.

Blue on Leather.

For each skin, take 1 ounce indigo; put it into boiling water, and let it stand one night; then warm it a little, and with a brush smear the skin twice over. Finish same as No. 217.

No. 222.

Black on Leather.

Put your skin on a clean board, sponge it over with gall and sumach liquors strong, then take a strong logwood-liquor, sponge it over 3 or 4 times; then take a little copperas, mix it in the logwood-liquor, sponge over your skin, and finish the same as No. 217.

No. 223.
How to make different Shades on Leather.

The pleasing hues of yellow, brown, or tan-colour are readily imparted to leather by the following simple process: steep saffron in boiling water for a number of hours, wet a sponge or soft brush in the liquor, smear the leather. The quantity of saffron, as well as of water, will of course depend on how much dye may be wanted, and their relative proportions on the depth of colour required.

No. 224.
To dye Leather Purple.

First sponge the leather with alum-liquor strong, then with logwood-liquor strong, or mix them both and boil them, and sponge with the liquor. Finish the same as No. 217.

No. 225.
Painters, how to mix Colours to form different Shades.

The various colours that may be obtained by mixture of other colours are numberless. It is only proposed to give some of the simplest and best modes of preparing those most frequently required.

Compound colours formed by the union of only two colours are called by painters virgin tints.

The smaller the number of colours of which any

compound colour is composed, the purer and the richer it will be.

Light gray is made by mixing white lead with lampblack, using more or less of each material as you wish to obtain a lighter or a darker colour.

Buff is made from yellow ochre and white lead. *Silver or Pearl gray.*—Mix white lead, indigo, and a very slight portion of black, regulating the quantities by the shade you wish to obtain. *Flaxen gray* is obtained by a mixture of white lead and Prussian blue, with a small quantity of lake. *Brick colour.*—Yellow ochre and red lead, with a little white. *Oakwood colour.*—¾ white lead, and ¼ part umber and yellow ochre: the proportions of the last two ingredients being determined by the required tints. *Walnut-tree colour.*—⅔ white lead, and ⅓ red ochre, yellow ochre, and umber, mixed according to the shade sought. If veining is required, use different shades of the same mixture, and for the deepest places, black. *Jonquil.*—Yellow, pink, and white lead. This colour is only proper for distemper. *Lemon yellow.*—Realgar and orpiment. Some object to this mixture on account of the poisonous nature of the ingredients. The same colour can be obtained by mixing yellow pink with Naples yellow; but it is then only fit for distemper. *Orange colour.*—Red lead and yellow ochre. *Violet colour.*—Vermilion, or red lead, mixed with black or blue, and a small portion of white. Vermilion is far preferable to red lead, in mixing this colour. *Purple.*—Dark red mixed with violet-colour. *Carnation.*—Lake and white. *Gold colour.*—Massicot or Naples yellow, with a small quantity of realgar, and a very little Spanish white. *Olive colour.*—This may be obtained by various mixtures: black, and a little blue, mixed with yellow; yellow pink, with a little verdigris and lampblack; or ochre and a small quantity of white, will also produce a kind of olive colour. For distemper, indigo and yellow pink, mixed with white lead or Spanish white, must be used. If veined, it should be done with umber. *Lead colour.*—Indigo and white. *Chestnut colour.*—Red ochre and black for a dark chestnut. To make it lighter, employ a mixture of yellow ochre. *Light timber colour.*—Spruce ochre, white, and a little umber. *Flesh colour.*—Lake, white lead, and a little vermilion. *Light Willow-green.*—White, mixed with verdigris. *Grass-green.*—Yellow pink mixed with verdigris. An endless variety of greens can be obtained by the mixture of blue and yellow in different proportions, with the occasional addition of white lead. *Stone colour.*—White, with a little spruce ochre. *Dark Lead colour.*—Black and white, with a little indigo. *Fawn colour.*—White lead, stone ochre, and a little vermilion. *Chocolate colour.*—Lampblack and Spanish brown. On account of the fatness of the lampblack, mix some litharge and red lead. *Portland Stone colour.*—Umber, yellow ochre, and white lead. The varieties of shades of brown that may be obtained are nearly as numerous as those of green. *To imitate Mahogany.*—Let the first coat of painting be white lead, the second orange, and the last burned umber or sienna; imitating the veins according to your taste and practice. *To imitate Wainscot.*—Let the first coat be white, the second half white and half yellow ochre, and the third yellow ochre only. Shadow with umber of sienna. *To imitate Satin-wood.*—Take white for your first coating, light blue for the second, and dark blue or dark green for the third.

No. 226.

Names of the different Colours used in Painting.

Whites.—*White Lead, Ceruse, and Flake.*—The more common sorts are called white lead; the purer, ceruse; the very best, flake-white. The white colours are generally used in house-painting.

Spanish or Bougival White is generally sold in cakes of an oblong form. It is much better for house-painting than any whites that contain a mixture of chalky substances, and it is not unfrequently used instead of white lead for priming, being far cheaper, though much less durable.

Gypsum, or Plaster of Paris.—When employed in house-painting, it requires to be mixed with a great quantity of water, and it then forms a very valuable article for white-washing apartments, and for painting in distemper.

White of Troyes, or White Chalk.—It is generally used for common white-washing, though gypsum is much preferable for this purpose.

Blacks.—*Ivory-Black* is extremely rich and intense in colour; but, being costly, it is seldom employed in common work.

Lamp-Black is used more than any other black in common painting.

Charcoal-Black.—The woods that furnish the best charcoal for painters are the beech and vine; the former yielding a black of a bluish cast, and the latter one of a grayish cast. When charcoal obtained from any of these sources is employed in painting, it should be mixed with a very small portion of white lead, and made up for use with drying-oil.

Reds. — *Vermilion* is the most brilliant of all the light reds. The body of vermilion is very delicate, and will grind as fine as oil itself. No colour looks better, works smoother, bears a better body, or goes farther.

Minium, or Red Lead.—When it is well ground and made fine, it is lighter than any other red in general use, bears a good body in oil, and binds very fast and firm. It has likewise the advantage of drying readily.

Carmine is a more dazzling red than vermilion, and is almost too brilliant for the eye to endure. There are various sorts of carmine, numbered in the order of their relative value. Thus, No. 1 is the best; No. 2 the second best; and so on.

Lake.—There are two sorts of colours known under this name: lakes derived from cochineal,—the richest and finest of all dark reds; and lakes prepared from madder,—not quite so good.

Spanish Brown.—The deeper the colour, and the freer from gritty particles, the better it is for use. It is much employed by painters for priming or first colour.

Other Reds.—Besides the above reds may be mentioned, as among those in use by painters, English red and Prussian red; red ochre, which is very extensively used, especially in distemper; rose-colour, composed of a portion of white lead mixed with pure lake; and realgar.

Yellow Ochre.—Of this colour there are two kinds, the bright yellow and dark yellow. The former is sometimes called plain ochre, and the latter spruce ochre. It will grind very fine, resists the weather well, and bears a good body.

Massicot is a good light yellow for general use, and very serviceable, mixed with blue, for making greens.

Chrome Yellow is a very rich and brilliant yellow, and employed to advantage in house and coach painting.

Turner's, or Patent, Yellow.—It is a very beautiful colour, much in use among coach-painters.

Orpiment.—It is good for some purposes, particularly for the production of straw-colour in painting doors, windows, &c. It likewise, in common with all bodies that contain arsenic, produces a bad effect on any metallic substance exposed to its action.

Naples Yellow.—The best of all yellows. It is milder and more unctuous than either orpiment, massicot, or any of the ochres. It is necessary to use it with great care. It must be ground well on a slab of porphyry or marble, and scraped together with an ivory knife, as both stone and steel have a tendency to turn it to green.

Yellow of Antimony.—It holds an intermediate place between chrome yellow and Naples yellow. It is chiefly used for giving a yellow colour to glass and earthenware.

Yellow Pink.—It grinds and dissolves in water easily; but care must be taken not to bring it in contact with iron, as the astringent principle which it contains in abundance instantly dissolves that metal, which in its turn destroys the clearness of the colour.

Prussian Blue.—There are blue colours superior to this, both in clearness and durability, but none which, volume for volume, contains so large a quantity of colouring-matter. A practical colourman says that it contains even ten to one more than any other colouring-matter. It is, on this account, much used in house-painting, and also in colouring paper-hangings.

Indigo.—Another blue colour, much used in common painting. None but the best and purest kind of this colour is proper for oil-painting: that of an inferior quality is only fit for distemper, as the oil renders it black or green. Indigo grinds fine, and bears a very good body. Its natural colour, however, being very dark, almost indeed approaching to black, it is seldom or never used without a small mixture of white.

Ultramarine is the richest, mellowest, most beautiful, and lasting of all blues; but its extravagant price —nearly equal, when pure, to its weight in gold— prevents its being introduced, unless very rarely indeed, into house-painting.

Smalt, Zaffre, Azure, Saxon Blue, or Enamel Blue.— It is of a lovely azure hue, but, if not bought in the form of powder, is very difficult to grind, and it can be used only in a peculiar manner.

Blue Verditer.—This is a beautiful blue, obtained from the waste nitrate of copper of the refiners by adding to it a quantity of chalk; but it is only proper for distemper: it does not admit of being used with oil, unless a considerable mixture of white is introduced.

Greens. — Verdigris.—This is the best simple green, and the one most in use. It has a bluish tint, but, when lightened by the addition of a little yellow pink, it makes a beautiful grass-green. It grinds very fine, and works easily, and in a good body. When delicate painting is required, the dross mixed with the common verdigris makes it improper, and it becomes necessary to use distilled verdigris, which can be had at the shops, and is free from all impurities; but it is too expensive for ordinary purposes.

Italian, or Verona, Green.—It is of the same colour as chlorine, which derives its name from the Greek word *chloros,* signifying a yellowish green. It is very durable, and not acted on by acids, but, being obtained from an earth, does not incorporate well with oil.

Saxon, or Hungary, Green.—The colour which bears this name is a carbonate of copper, found in a natural state, in the mountains of Saxony and Hungary, mixed with earthy matters, which give it a polish hue.

Scheele's Green.—This colour, called after the celebrated chemist by whom its composition was first made known, is of a light sea-green colour. It grinds well with oil, and is much in request for the painting of cabins of ships.

Schweinfurt Green.—A green which has recently obtained great reputation on the continent, and which is said to surpass Scheele's both in beauty and splendour.

Brunswick Green.—A colour thus named is much used for paper-hangings and coarse kind of painting water-colours.

Green Verditer.—This is obtained from the same substance as blue verditer, by a process nearly similar. Without the addition of white lead or Spanish white it is unfit for oil-painting; and, in any way, it is better adapted for distemper. Its colour may be obtained in oil by mixing two or three parts of verdigris with one of white lead.

Green Lake, or Venetian Emerald.—A very simple mode has recently been discovered, at Venice, of producing a fine unchangeable emerald colour. A quantity of coffee is boiled in river-water,—if spoiled coffee, so much the better. The green lake obtained by this process is said to have resisted the action of acids, and even the influence of light and moisture.

Browns.—*Umber*, or, as it is sometimes called, brown ochre, is an impure native oxide of iron and manganese. It is much employed by painters, and is the only simple brown in common use.

New Brown, discovered by Mr. Hatchet. This celebrated chemist has suggested to painters that a simple brown colour, far superior in beauty and intensity to all the browns, whether simple or compound, hitherto known, may be obtained from the prussiate of copper, (a combination of prussic acid with copper.) The following is the process which he recommends:—

Dissolve the green muriate of copper in about ten times its weight of distilled or rain water, and add a solution of prussiate of lime, until a complete precipitation is effected. The precipitate is then to be washed with cold water, filtered, and set to dry in the shade.

No. 227.

Of different Oils used in Painting and Varnishing.

Oil of Spike is, if pure, a volatile oil, and has the advantage of drying more quickly than any other fat-oil.

Oil of Lavender.—Its property of drying more equally and gradually than perhaps any other oil renders it also of service to the varnisher. It is also used by enamellers, to whom it is very valuable.

Oil of Poppies is, that of being perfectly colourless. The only objection is of being insufferably tedious in drying.

Nut and Linseed Oils.—Both in very general use, and rank among the fat-oils. Their fatness, indeed, is so great, that it is mostly found necessary, before employing them in colouring, to give them a drying quality, which may be done in the following manner:—

Take 1 pound white vitriol and 4 pounds litharge, and let them be reduced to as fine a powder as possible; then mix them with 1 gallon nut or linseed oil, and place the mixture over a fire just brisk enough to keep the oil slightly boiling. Let it continue to boil till the oil entirely ceases to throw up any scum. Then take the vessel off the fire, and let it stand in a cool place for about three hours, and a sediment, which contains the fattening part of the oil, will be formed at the bottom. Pour off the oil which is above (being careful not to let any of the sediment mix with it) into wide-mouthed bottles.

Let it remain a sufficient time to clear itself perfectly before it is used, and you will find it possessed of the proper drying quality.

Oil of Turpentine is more used than any of the preceding oils: the varnisher, indeed, scarcely employs any other. Fat-oils are oftentimes mixed with oil of turpentine, as well as other volatile oils. Drying oils, which are composed of particular substances mixed with some of the oils before mentioned, are useful for several purposes. They are most valuable when so manufactured as to be colourless. They are much used in preparing varnishes, and, in oil-painting, are not unfrequently employed as a varnish, either alone or diluted with a little oil of turpentine.

No. 228.

How to prepare Linseed-Oil to Boil Varnishes.

Take 5 gallons green linseed-oil, 1½ pounds litharge, and 1½ pounds amber. Put all together into a proper vessel, and let it boil 1½ or 2 hours; then it will be ready for use when cold. You must also strain it.

No. 229.

How to boil Linseed-Oil to mix with Paint.

Take 2½ gallons green linseed-oil, 14 ounces litharge, and 4 ounces amber. Boil all together until it is clear from scum,—say 6 or 8 hours; be careful in stirring it well. If you want to have the oil to dry very quick, add double the quantity of litharge and amber.

No. 230.

How to make Copal Varnish. No. 1.

The foundation of all varnishes are gummy and resinous substances, and the only liquids that can be combined with them, so as to form varnishes, are oils, spirits of turpentine, and spirits of wine.

To make copal varnish: Take 22 ounces gum copal, (good and clear,) and dissolve it in a proper copper vessel. As soon as it is properly dissolved, add 1 pint of the prepared linseed-oil. (See No. 228.) When well incorporated, take it off the fire, let it cool off a little, add nearly 1 quart spirits of turpentine, mix it thoroughly, and strain through flannel. Let it stand 5 or 6 days, when it will be fit for use.

No. 231.

Another Copal Varnish. No. 2.

Take 1 ounce copal, and ½ ounce shellac; powder them well, and put them into a bottle or jar containing a quart of spirits of wine. Place the mixture in a warm place, and shake it occasionally, till you perceive that the gums are completely dissolved; and when strained the varnish will be fit for use.

No. 232.

Gold-Coloured Copal Varnish.

Take 1 ounce powdered copal, 2 ounces essential oil of lavender, and 6 ounces essence of turpentine. Put the oil of lavender into a matrass of a proper size, placed on a sand-bath subject to a moderate heat. When the oil is very warm, add the copal from time to time, in very small quantities, and stir the mixture with a stick of white wood rounded at the end. When the copal has entirely disappeared, put in the turpentine in almost a boiling state, at three different times, and keep continually stirring the mixture till the solution is quite complete.

No. 233.

Seed-Lac Varnish.

Take 3 ounces seed-lac, and put it, with a pint of spirits of wine, into a bottle of which it will not fill more than two-thirds. Shake the mixture well together, and place it in a gentle heat till the seed-lac appears to be dissolved: the solution will be hastened by shaking the bottle occasionally. After it has stood some time, pour off the clear part, and keep it for use in a well-stopped bottle. The seed-lac should be purified before it is used, by washing it in cold water; and it should be in coarse powder when added to the spirit.

This varnish is next to that of copal in hardness, and has a reddish-yellow colour: it is, therefore, only to be used where a tinge of that kind is not injurious.

No. 234.

Shell-Lac Varnish.

Take 5 ounces of the best shell-lac, reduce it to a gross powder, and put it into a bottle in a gentle heat, or a warm, close apartment, where it must continue 2 or 3 days, but should be frequently well shaken. The lac will then be dissolved, and the solution should then be filtered through a flannel bag; and, when the portion that will pass through freely is come off, it should be kept for use in well-stopped bottles.

The portion which can only be made to pass through the bag by pressure may be reserved for coarse purposes. Shell-lac varnish is rather softer than seed-lac varnish, but is the best of varnishes for mixing with colours to paint with, instead of oil, from its working and spreading better in the pencil.

No. 235.
To dissolve Copal in fixed Oil.

Melt, in a perfectly clean vessel, by a very slow heat, 1 pound clear copal; to this add from 1 to 2 quarts prepared linseed-oil. When these ingredients are thoroughly mixed, remove the vessel from the fire, and keep constantly stirring it till nearly cold; then add a pound of spirits of turpentine, strain the varnish through a piece of cloth, and keep it for use. The older it is, the more drying it becomes. This varnish is very proper for woodwork, house and carriage painting.

No. 236.
Amber Varnish.

Amber varnish forms a very excellent one: its solution may be effected by boiling it in drying linseed-oil.

Oil varnishes which have become thick by keeping are made thinner with spirits of turpentine.

No. 237.
Linseed-Oil Varnish.

Boil any quantity of linseed-oil for an hour, and to every pint of oil add ¼ pound good clear rosin, well powdered; keep stirring it till the rosin is perfectly dissolved and, when this is done, add 1 ounce spirits of turpentine for every pint of oil, and when strained and cool it will be fit for use.

This varnish is much used for common purposes. It is cheap, is a good preservative of wood, and not liable to sustain injury from the application of hot water.

No. 238.

Turpentine Varnish.

Take 5 pounds clear good rosin, pound it well, and put it into a gallon of oil of turpentine; boil the mixture over a stove till the rosin is perfectly dissolved, and when cool it will be fit for use.

No. 239.

White Hard Varnish.

Take 1 pound mastic, 4 ounces gum anima, and 5 pounds gum sandarac; put them all together, to dissolve, into a vessel containing 2 ounces rectified spirits of wine, which should be kept in a warm place and frequently shaken till all the gums are quite dissolved; then strain the mixture through a lawn sieve, and it will be fit for use.

No. 240.

Varnish for Harness.

Take ½ pound India-rubber, 1 gallon spirits of turpentine; dissolve enough to make it into a jelly by keeping almost new-milk-warm; then take equal quantities of good linseed-oil (in a hot state) and the above mixture, incorporate them well on a slow fire, and it is fit for use.

No. 241.
Leather Varnish for Shoemakers and Saddlers.

Take 1 gallon spirits of wine, 2½ pounds gum shellac, 1 pound white clear rosin, ¼ pound Venice turpentine, 1½ ounces lampblack. Dissolve all with a gentle heat: when cool it will be fit for use; if too thick, thin it with spirits of wine.

No. 242.
How to make Venice Turpentine.

Take 1 quart spirits of turpentine, ½ pound rosin. Dissolve over a gentle heat: when cool it will be fit for use.

No. 243.
How to boil a Leather Varnish.

Take 1 gallon spirits of wine, 1 pound gum shellac, 1¾ pounds black sealing-wax, ¼ pound asphaltum, ½ ounce Venice turpentine. Boil over a slow fire, in a water-bath.

No. 244.
How to make Shoes and Boots Water-Proof.

Take neats'-foot oil, and dissolve in it caoutchouc, (India-rubber,) a sufficient quantity to form a kind of varnish; rub this on your boots. This is sufficient. The oil must be placed where it is warm, the caoutchouc put into it in parings. It will take several days to dissolve.

No. 245.

Another Water-Proof for Leather.

Take linseed-oil 1 quart, yellow wax and white turpentine each ¼ pound, Burgundy pitch 2 ounces: melt, and colour with lampblack.

No. 246.

A Water-Proof and Leather-Preservative.

Take ½ pound fine lampblack, (Eddies' New York best,) 2 pounds rosin, 3 quarts linseed-oil, 2½ ounces oil of lavender, 6 pounds sheep's tallow, (suet:) melt and mix over a gentle fire, when it will be ready for use, and be put up in tin boxes.

Directions.—Let your leather be clean and damp when the blacking is applied, and allow time to dry moderately before wearing. Apply it plentifully at first, with a brush or otherwise, until the leather is filled with it: after that, a little occasionally will answer. One box, used with economy, will be sufficient to last one person a year.

Directions.—For carriage-tops and harness. Mix about a pint of oil (fish or tanners') to a box, by warming it well. Have your leather clean and damp before you apply it.

N.B.—Leather that this is applied to will not mould,—which, every one knows, is very injurious to leather.

This blacking will not produce a polish, but will make the leather soft, water-proof, and much more durable. Polish-blacking can be used immediately and produce a fine polish.

No. 247.

Excellent Liquid Blacking. No. 1.

Take 7 pounds ivory-black powdered, 2 pints molasses, 1 pint sweet oil, good malt vinegar, 1 quart, stale beer, but good, 2 quarts, oil of vitriol, ½ ounce, soft distilled water, 3 quarts. Mix the molasses and water together, and to the powder add the oil, well mixed; then add the beer and vinegar in a pan; stir well together 1 hour with a stick, then fit for use.

N.B.—Put the oil of vitriol in water and mix, and then add the whole together.

No. 248.

Liquid Blacking. No. 2.

Put 1 gallon vinegar into a stone jug; add 1 pound ivory-black, well pulverized, ½ pound loaf sugar, ½ ounce oil of vitriol, and 1 ounce sweet oil; incorporate the whole by stirring. This is a blacking of very good repute, and on which great praise has been very deservedly bestowed. It has decidedly been ascertained, from experience, to be less injurious to the leather than most public blackings; and it certainly produces a fine jet polish, which is rarely equalled, and never yet surpassed.

No. 249.

Black Varnish for Straw or Chip Hats.

Take ½ ounce best black sealing-wax, pound it well, and put it into a 4-ounce vial containing 2 ounces rectified spirits of wine. Place it in a sand-bath, or near a moderate fire, till the wax is dissolved; then lay it on warm, with a fine soft hair-brush, before a fire, or in the sun. It gives a good stiffness to old straw hats, and a beautiful gloss equal to new. It likewise resists wet.

No. 250.

Coating Sheet-Iron with Varnish to protect it from the action of the atmosphere.

First take clean sheet-iron plates, and dip them in a solution of the chloride of iron, by which they become covered with a thin tin scale; they are then washed well with warm water, and dipped into a melted composition of rosin and tallow; after this they are allowed to dry, and then dipped into a hot solution composed of ¾ pound shellac and ¼ pound rosin dissolved in 2 gallons alcohol. Finally, they are taken out and dried in an oven. Common tin plates for roofing, exposed to sea-winds, where tin is liable to rust, will, if coated in this manner, stand exposure to the weather well.

No. 251.

Another Oil-Paste Blacking. No. 2.

Take ¼ pound oil of vitriol, 10 ounces tanners' oil, 4 pounds ivory-black, 10 ounces molasses; mix the oil of vitriol and the tanners' oil together, and let it stand one day, then add the ivory-black and molasses, and the white of 2 eggs, and stir it well together to a thick paste. This is an excellent blacking, and will not injure the leather.

No. 252.

How Compound Spirits of Cordials for beverage is manufactured.

The perfection of this grand branch of manufacturing depends upon the observation of the following general rules, which are easy to be observed and practised. First, The manufacturer must always be careful to use a well-cleansed spirit, or one freed from its own essential oils. For, as a compound cordial is nothing more than a spirit impregnated with the essential oil of the ingredients, it is necessary that the spirit should have deposited its own. Second, Let the time of previous digestion be proportioned to the tenacity of the ingredients, or the ponderosity of the oil. Third, Have a due proportion of spirits, the grosser and less fragrant parts of the oil not giving the spirit so agreeable a flavour, and at the same time rendering it thick and unsightly. This may, in a great measure, be effected by leaving out the feints, and making up to proof with fine soft water in their stead.

It is sometimes necessary to filter cordials. This may be done by letting it run through some proper cloth. If fining should be necessary, it may be done by adding from 5 to 7 eggs to the barrel. A syrup is made by taking the best white sugar. Take 8 pounds loaf sugar, 2 quarts water. Dissolve the sugar in the water on a gentle fire, and remove the scum as it rises; as soon as it commences boiling, take it from the fire, and strain it immediately. This is called by the art simple syrup, and is used in the manufacture of many kinds of liquors.

No. 253.

How to manufacture Anniseed-Cordial.

Take 30 gallons pure rectified whiskey, 5 drachms oil of anniseed cut in alcohol, 20 gallons good clear soft water, 8 gallons of the above syrup; mix all together, and let it lie from 10 to 12 days, when it will be good to use.

No. 254.

How to make Citron-Cordial.

Take 30 gallons pure rectified whiskey, and add 10 pounds rind of lemons, 5 pounds orange-peel, 5 ounces broken nutmeg, and let it lie for 12 or 14 days; then add again 15 gallons water, and 8 gallons of the mentioned syrup; and in a few days you may draw it off. (Ready for use.)

No. 255.

How to make Peppermint-Cordial. No. 1.

Take 30 gallons pure rectified whiskey; cut up in alcohol 5 drachms oil of peppermint in 1 quart alcohol, and let it stand 1 or 2 days, then add it to the whiskey; after this, add 30 gallons water, and 10 gallons simple syrup. Mix all well together, and, if not clear, fine it by dissolving 1¼ pounds alum in 2½ quarts water, and add to the cordial; stir it for 5 or 10 minutes, then let it stand for 10 days.

No. 256.

How to make Cinnamon-Cordial.

Take 6 gallons rectified whiskey, 2 drachms oil of cinnamon cut in alcohol, 3 gallons water, 1¾ gallons syrup; mix, and proceed as before.

No. 257.

How to make Orange-Cordial.

Take 5 gallons pure proof rectified whiskey, add ½ pound fresh lemon-peel, 2 pounds dried orange-peel, and 3 pounds fresh orange-peel; let it stand for 10 or 14 days, then draw it off, and add 3 gallons soft water, 1½ gallons syrup, and proceed as before.

No. 258.

How to make Clove-Cordial.

Take 6 gallons pure rectified whiskey, 1 drachm oil of cloves cut in alcohol, 3 gallons water, 2 gallons syrup; mix, and let stand as before.

No. 259.

How to make Strawberry-Cordial.

Take 5 gallons pure rectified whiskey, to which add 8 quarts strawberries, and let it stand 10 or 12 days; then draw it off, and add 3 gallons water and 2 gallons syrup, and manage as before.

No. 260.

How to make Rose-Cordial.

Take 6 gallons pure proof rectified whiskey, from 40 to 60 drops oil of roses cut in 1 pint alcohol, 4 gallons soft water, and 7 quarts syrup, and mix all together; manage as before.

No. 261.

Another Peppermint-Cordial. No. 2.

Boil 4 gallons or 24 pounds common brown sugar in 4 gallons water and 3 ounces alum, and scum it as long as any scum will rise. Then add 1 ounce oil of peppermint, 10 gallons pure spirits, 14 gallons clear rain-water, and stir all well; and in 24 hours it will be clear and fit for use.

N.B.—Any other flavour can be given by adding other essential oils: such as oil of cinnamon, oil of roses, oil of cloves, oil of lemon, oil of anniseed, oil of wintergreen, &c. If it should not be clear, add the white of eggs, or a little alum, alone, or a little carbonate of soda or potassa dissolved in water; in from 10 days to 2 weeks it will be clear.

If the quantity is too much or too little in the foregoing receipts, you can make any quantity by taking the ingredients proportionate to the quantity you wish to make.

No. 262.

How to make Cider.

After the apples are gathered from the trees, they are ground into what is called pomace, or pulp, either by means of a common pressing-stone, with a circular trough, or by a cider-mill, which is either driven by hand or by horse power. When the pulp is thus reduced to a great degree of fineness, it is conveyed to the cider-press, where it is formed by pressure into a kind of cake, which is called the cheese.

This is effected by placing clean sweet straw or hair-cloth between the layers of pomace or pulp, till there is a pile of 8 or 10 to 12 layers. This pile is then subjected to different degrees of pressure in succession, till all the must or juice is squeezed from the pomace. This juice, after being strained in a coarse hair sieve, is then put either into open vats or close casks, and the pressed pulp is either thrown away or made to yield a weak liquor, called washings, or, as we call it, water-cider.

After the liquor has undergone the proper fermentation in these close vessels, which may be best effected in a temperature of from 40 to 60 degrees of Fahrenheit, and which may be known by its appearing tolerably clear, and having a vinous sharpness upon the tongue, any further fermentation must be stopped by racking off the pure part into open vessels exposed for a day or two in a cool situation. After this, the liquor must again be put into casks, and kept in a cool place during winter. The proper time for racking may always be best known by the brightness of the liquor, the discharge of the fixed air, and the appearance of a thick crust formed of fragments of the reduced pulp. The liquor should always be racked off anew as often as a hissing noise is heard, or as it extinguishes a candle held to the bung-hole.

When a favourable vinous fermentation has been obtained, nothing more is required than to fill up the vessels every 2 or 3 weeks, to supply the waste by fermentation. In the beginning of March the liquor will be bright and pure, and fit for final racking, which should be done in fair weather. When the bottles are filled they should be set by uncorked till morning, when the corks must be driven in tightly, secured by wire or twine and melted rosin, or any similar substance.

No. 263.

How to manage Cider.

To fine and improve the flavour of 1 hogshead, take a gallon good French brandy, with $\frac{1}{2}$ ounce cochineal, 1 pound alum, and 3 pounds rock-candy; bruise them all well in a mortar, and infuse them in the brandy for a day or two; then mix the whole with the cider, and stop it close for 5 or 6 months. After which, if fine, bottle it off.

Cider, when bottled in hot weather, should be left a day or two uncorked, that it may get flat; but if too flat in the cask, and soon wanted for use, put into each bottle a small lump or two of rock-candy, 4 or 5 raisins of the sun, or a small piece of raw beef; any of which will much improve the liquor, and make it brisker.

Cider should be well corked and waxed, and packed upright in a cool place. A few bottles may be kept in a warmer place, to ripen and be ready for use.

No. 264.

To make cheap Cider from Raisins.

Take 14 pounds raisins, with the stalks; wash them out in four or five waters, till the water remains clear; then put them into a clean cask with the head out, and put 6 gallons of good water upon them; after which cover it well up, and let it stand 10 days. Then rack it off into another clean cask, which has a brass cock in it, and in 4 or 5 days' time it will be fit for bottling. When it has been in the bottles 7 or 8 days, it will be fit for use. A little colouring should be added when putting into the cask the second time. The raisins may afterwards be used for vinegar.

No. 265.

Observations on Cider.

From the great diversity of soil and climate in the United States of America, and the almost endless variety of its apples, it follows that much diversity of taste and flavour will necessarily be found in the cider that is made from them.

To make good cider, the following general, but important, rules should be attended to. They demand a little more trouble than the ordinary mode of collecting and mashing apples of all sorts, rotten and sound, sweet and sour, dirty and clean, from the tree and the soil, and the rest of the slovenly process usually employed; but in return they produce you a wholesome, high-flavoured, sound, and palatable liquor, that always commands an adequate price, instead of a solution of "villanous compounds," in a poisonous and acid wash, that no man in his senses will drink. The finest cider was made of an equal portion of ripe, sound pippin and crab apples, pared, cored, and pressed, etc., with the utmost nicety. It was equal in flavour to any champagne that ever was made.

No. 266.

General Rules for making Cider.

1. Always choose perfectly ripe and sound apples. 2. Pick the apples by hand. An active boy, with a bag slung over his shoulders, will soon clear a tree. Apples that have lain any time on the soil contract an earthy taste, which will always be found in the cider. 3. After sweating, and before being ground, wipe them dry, and if any of them are found bruised or rotten, put them in a heap by themselves, for an inferior cider to make vinegar. 4. Always use hair cloth, instead of straw, to place between the layers of pomace. The straw when heated gives a disagreeable taste to the cider. 5. As the cider runs from the press, let it pass through a hair sieve into a large open vessel, that will hold as much juice as can be expressed in one day. In a day, and sometimes less, the pomace will rise to the top, and in a short time grow very thick; when little white bubbles break through it, draw off the liquor by a spigot, placed about three inches from the bottom, so that the lees may be left quietly behind. 6. The cider must be drawn off into very clean casks, and closely watched. The moment the white bubbles before mentioned are perceived rising at the bung-hole,

rack it again. When the fermentation is completely at an end, fill up the cask with cider in all respects like that already contained in it, and bung it up tight; previous to which a tumblerful of sweet oil may be poured into the bung-hole. Sound, well-made cider, that has been produced as described, and without any foreign mixtures, excepting always that of good cognac brandy, (which, added to it in the proportion of 1 gallon to every 30, greatly improves it,) is a pleasant, cooling drink, and useful beverage.

Cider prepared as above is generally used to imitate the different kinds of wine.

No. 267.

Another Rule for making good Cider.

In grinding the apples, reduce the whole fruit to a uniform pomace. Allow the pulp to remain from 2 to 6 or 8 days; if warm weather, for a shorter time, and if cold, a longer time, according to the state of the weather, stirring it every day, until put to the press. If there should be any wanting of the saccharine matter, add sugar before fermentation takes place, and after fermentation add spirits of wine. After the liquor has remained a few days, (after its having been strained through a sieve,) taking off the scum as it rises, then draw it off into casks, and place in a cool cellar; or let it be, a short time after the pressing, placed in a cool place, put into strong, light casks, and after the pomace has all overflown, drive the bung close, and bore with a gimlet a hole through the bung, and put in a spile to draw, when the cask appears to be in danger of bursting.

No. 268.

How to keep common Cider good for years.

Take the cider when you think it will suit your taste, put it into a kettle, and boil it very little. Make a bag and put into it ¼ pound of hops, then put the bag with hops into the kettle with the cider, and tie it fast to the handle so that the bag with hops will not touch the bottom of the kettle; scum off the cider while you have it on the fire, and after it has boiled a short time take it off the fire, and let it cool down lukewarm; put it into a good sweet barrel, and add 1 pint good fresh brandy, bung it up, and it will keep the same as you put it into your barrel for years.

No. 269.

Another way to keep Cider.

Take cider after it is taken from the press, or when it suits your taste, and put it into a good, strong, tight, sweet barrel, and add 3 gallons apple whiskey, and 6 cents' worth mustard-seed, and bung it up tight, and let it ferment in the barrel; bore a gimlet-hole through the bung, and put a spile into it, so that you can let some of the gas out, to prevent the cask from bursting. When the fermentation is subsided, draw it off clear, and clean out your barrel, and put the cider in again, and bung it up close.

N.B.—This cider will also be good to imitate all kinds of wines; that is, if the cider is clear.

No. 270.

How to put up a simple Stand for Rectifying Raw Whiskey.

Purifying spirituous liquors consists in passing the liquor through prepared charcoal, sand, or gravel, or fine-broken brick, (washed very clean,) flannel, blanket, and charcoal, particularly prepared for this purpose.

Take a good, common, tight barrel for a stand, and bore one of the heads full of $\frac{1}{2}$ inch holes, $\frac{1}{2}$ inch apart, so that it appears like a sieve, or riddle; when this is done, take the perforated bottom out, and sink down into the barrel within 2 inches of the lower bottom; first nail 3 or 4 strips of wood, 2 inches thick, to answer for legs, (so that there will be an empty space of 2 inches between the two bottoms,) to rest the second bottom on, between which you will have to bore a hole through the side, to put in a brass or wooden spigot, between the empty space of the two bottoms, to draw out the rectified liquor, which, if the rectifier is good, should not run out faster than the thickness of a middle-sized knitting-needle, or still less; and after you have the perforated bottom at its proper place, put a layer of flannel or blanket over this bottom, so that it will come all round up the sides a little; now take some fine, clean sand, and put from 4 to 6 inches on the flannel or blanket; now put another layer of flannel on the sand, and on the top of this put from 12 to 15 inches of the prepared charcoal, and on the top of this put another layer of blanket or flannel; on the top of this flannel lay 4 or 6 bricks, to keep the flannel down, or else if you pour in your liquor it would rise on the top of the liquor; now your stand is ready to receive the liquor you wish to purify. This stand is capable to rectify 10 barrels of strong whiskey, when the coal will be worn out; and when the coals are worn out, renew them, the same as before. Observe, there will be left a great deal of strength in the coal after it stops running; to get that strength out, pour water on and let water through, until no strength of the liquor remains in it. To ascertain this, a hydrometer is indispensably necessary to try the liquor; by this mode you can find how many degrees of spirits you have in the water. These spirits can be used for liquor that is over proof, to bring it down to proof.

You may put up as many stands as you wish, of the same size, or make them as large as you please. Some rectifiers put up two, one above the other, and let the whiskey through them both; and if you want your spirits very fine, you can let it run through 3 or 4 times; the oftener, the finer your spirits gets. Keep your rectifier always in use, or the coal will become mouldy and unfit for use.

The charcoal ought to be prepared from sugar maple wood. Some rectifiers use raw cotton, or straw, instead of flannel, and put between the sand and charcoal, malt, or lime, according to fancy.

Recapitulation of Directions in putting up a Rectifying Stand.

1. Take a good, tight barrel, or any other good cask.

2. Bore holes through one of the heads, as described.

3. Take out the head and sink it down within 2 inches of the bottom.

4. Cover with a layer of flannel this perforated bottom.

5. Put 4 to 6 inches washed sand on the top of the flannel.

6. Put another layer of flannel on the top of the sand.

7. Put 12 or 15 inches of charcoal on the top of the flannel.

8. Put another layer of flannel on the coal.

9. Put 4 or 6 bricks on the flannel, to keep it from rising up to the top.

10. Keep the stand, after you have poured liquor on, well covered.

The spirituous liquor which is rectified thus is called pure spirits or sweet liquors, and is flavoured for wines, brandies, spirits, rum, Monongahela whiskey, cordials, etc., and should be clear of all foreign matter.

No. 271.

How to make Monongahela Whiskey. No. 1.

Take 36 gallons pure spirits, and add ¼ pound young hyson tea, 6 pounds dried peaches, baked brown, not burned, 4 pounds loaf sugar, 4 ounces cloves, 4 ounces cinnamon. Mix them all together, and stir them well for 3 or 4 days, and in a few weeks it will be good.

N.B.—You can put double or triple the quantity

of flavouring in, and then take 3, 4, 5, or 6 gallons of it and pour it into a barrel of pure rectified whiskey, and add 2 pounds loaf sugar to each barrel. The longer your flavouring will lie, the better.

No. 271½.

Another way to make Monongahela Whiskey.   No. 2.

Take 30 gallons pure rectified whiskey; add 12 ounces burned barley, ground or bruised, 6 drachms sweet spirits of nitre, 4 pounds dried peaches, 4 pounds New Orleans sugar, 3 ounces allspice, 2 ounces cinnamon; mix them all together, and let stand from 6 to 12 days, and stir them every day. Draw off.

No. 272.

How to make Wheat Whiskey.

Take 30 gallons pure rectified whiskey, proof; add 1 ounce spirits nitre dulc., ½ ounce tincture of rhatany, 1 pint simple syrup, 4½ gallons pure wheat whiskey, 2 ounces tincture of cinnamon; mix them all together, and colour it with sugar-colouring if you wish.

No. 273.

How to make good Apple Whiskey.

Take 30 gallons pure rectified whiskey, from 5 to 10 degrees above proof; add 4½ gallons pure apple whiskey, 1½ pints simple syrup, 2 good pineapples, (the juice of them only.) Mix thoroughly, and let stand for 2 weeks. Then ready for use.

No. 274.

How to imitate Old Bourbon Whiskey.

Take 30 gallons pure rectified whiskey, 6 gallons pure Bourbon whiskey, 3 half-pints simple syrup, 1½ ounces sweet spirits of nitre; mix them all together, and colour with sugar-colouring.

No. 275.

How to imitate Irish Whiskey.

Take 30 gallons pure rectified whiskey, proof, 6 gallons pure Irish whiskey, 6 drachms acetic acid, 1 drachm acetic ether, 75 drops kreosote cut in 3 half-pints alcohol, 3 half-pints simple syrup, and manage as before.

No. 276.

How to imitate Scotch Whiskey.

Take 30 gallons pure proof rectified whiskey, 6 gallons pure Scotch whiskey, 1½ ounces acetic acid, 3 pints simple syrup; mix, and add 45 drops kreosote cut in 1 pint alcohol; let stand a few days, when it will be ready for use; stir it well.

No. 277.

How to imitate Holland Gin. No. 1.

Take 30 gallons pure spirits, add 2 gallons pure imported Holland gin highly flavoured, 4 ounces sweet spirits of nitre, 1 ounce pure oil of juniper, 2 drachms oil of caraway. Cut the oil of juniper and oil of caraway in 1 pint alcohol, and mix all together, when it will be ready for use. The older, the better.

No. 278.

Another imitation of Holland Gin. No. 2.

Take 30 gallons pure rectified whiskey, 1 gallon pure imported Holland gin, 1 ounce pure oil of juniper, 2 drachms oil of caraway, (cut the oil of juniper and caraway in 1 pint alcohol,) 1 ounce sal-ammoniac. Mix them all together, and in a short time it will be good for use.

No. 279.

Holland Gin. No. 3.

Take 30 gallons pure rectified whiskey, 4 gallons pure Holland gin, 1 ounce oil of juniper cut in alcohol, 1 pound coriander-seed. Mix them all together, let it stand, and stir it well for 3 or 4 days; then draw off and strain.

No. 280.

Holland Gin. No. 4.

Take 10 gallons pure rectified whiskey, 1½ gallons pure Holland gin, 1 drachm oil of juniper cut in alcohol, ½ drachm fennel-seed, ½ drachm caraway-seed. Infuse the fennel and caraway seed in 2 quarts rectified whiskey for 8 or 10 days, then mix.

No. 281.

Holland Gin. No. 5.

Take 5 gallons pure spirits, and add 1 gallon pure imported Holland gin. Good.

No. 282.

How to make Country Gin.

Take 32 gallons pure rectified whiskey. Infuse 4 pounds juniper-berries in 4 gallons of the pure rectified whiskey for 8 or 10 days; separate the juice from the berries, and add it to the rest of your liquor.

N.B.—The pure rectified whiskey, or pure spirits, ought to be from 3 to 5 degrees above proof, for good gin.

No. 283.

How to imitate Jamaica Rum. No. 1.

Take 28 gallons pure spirits, 3 gallons pure Jamaica rum, 3 ounces sweet spirits of nitre, 1 ounce tincture of kino. Mix them all together.

No. 284.

Jamaica Rum. No. 2.

Take 32 gallons pure spirits. Then boil in 2 gallons of pure spirits 4 pounds foreign locks, 4 pounds bitter orange-peel, 4 ounces anise-seed, until the flavour is drawn out, and strain it while hot; add it to the rest of your liquor.

No. 285.

How to make Tincture of Kino.

Take 1¾ ounces powdered kino, and macerate it in 1 pint alcohol for 2 weeks; then filter it through paper.

No. 286.

How to make Jamaica Spirits.

Take 30 gallons pure rectified whiskey, 6 gallons pure Jamaica rum, 1 ounce tincture of kino, 1½ pints syrup, 1¾ ounces butyric acid cut in 2 quarts alcohol. Mix well, and colour.

No. 287.

New England Rum. No. 1.

Take 28 gallons pure spirits, 2 gallons St. Croix rum, 4 ounces sweet spirits of nitre, 1 ounce sal-ammoniac, 50 drops nitric acid. Mix all together.

No. 288.

Another Rum. No. 2.

Take 29 gallons pure spirits, 1 gallon rum, 2 ounces sweet spirits of nitre, 3 ounces tincture of argol, 2 ounces spirits of hartshorn; mix well.

No. 289.

St. Croix Rum. No. 1.

Take 32 gallons pure spirits, and boil 6 pounds liquorice-sticks, 2 pounds winter-bark, ½ pound aniseseed, until the flavour is drawn out; strain it while hot, and add it to your pure spirits; bung it tight, and in 3 days it will be good.

No. 290.

Another St. Croix Rum. No. 2.

Take 5 gallons pure spirits, 1¼ gallons St. Croix

rum, ½ pint syrup, ½ ounce tincture of catechu, ⅜ ounce butyric acid; cut, mix, and let stand 5 days. Colour with sugar-colouring.

No. 291.
How to make Tincture of Catechu.

Take 3 ounces catechu, and macerate it in 1 quart diluted alcohol for 2 weeks, and filter through paper or strain through cloth.

No. 292.
Another Jamaica Rum. No. 3.

Take 32 gallons pure spirits; add 5 gallons pure imported Jamaica rum from the custom-house.

No. 293.
Cognac Brandy. No. 1.

Take 31 gallons pure spirits, 4 pounds peach-pits, 1 pound winter-bark, 4 pounds bitter orange-peel; steep the peach-pits, winter-bark, and the orange-peel in a few gallons of pure spirits, until the flavour is drawn out; then pour it off, and put it into your pure spirits, and add as much pure imported cognac brandy as you wish.

No. 294.
Another Cognac Brandy. No. 2.

Take 31 gallons rectified whiskey; set the barrel on the head. Then take of this whiskey 2 gallons, and boil 4 pounds peach-pits, 1 pound winter-bark, and 4 pounds bitter orange-peel, the whole broken together until the flavour is drawn out, and while hot strain it into other liquor, and stop tight 2 hours. Then add ½ pound sweet oil cut up clear in alcohol, and pour it into your barrel, and draw and pour back until well mixed, and in 3 days it will be fit for use. Colour.

No. 295.
Another Cognac Brandy. No. 3.

Take 35 gallons pure rectified whiskey, from 10 to 15 degrees above proof, and add 7½ gallons pure cognac brandy, 1⅞ drachms cognac-oil cut in alcohol, 1¼ ounce œnanthic acid, 1⅓ ounce acetic acid, 2¼ ounces tincture of kino, 3 half-pints syrup, and mix it thoroughly, and colour it to your fancy.

No. 296.
Another Cognac Brandy. No. 4.

Take 5 gallons pure sweet liquor, ¼ gallon pure cognac brandy imported, 2½ pounds bruised raisins, ¼ ounce acetic acid, 2 pounds loaf sugar, 1 ounce tincture of catechu, and mix. Manage as before.

No. 297.
Imitation of French Brandy. No. 1.

Take 32 gallons pure spirits. Then take ½ gallon dried peaches baked brown, (not burned,) beat them to powder, and put them to your pure spirits in the barrel. Then take ¾ pound crude or red tartar, boil it in 4 gallons water until it is reduced to 2 gallons, then strain the liquor through a fine cloth, and when cold put them into the cask and stir them well together; then add to it 8 gallons pure French brandy, fourth proof, allowing the pure spirits to be first proof; or cider brandy is the best. The above will make 42 gallons of first-rate French brandy in 6 months, and scarcely distinguishable from French brandy by the best of judges.

No. 298.

Another imitation of French Brandy. No. 2.

Take 30 gallons pure spirits, 10 to 15 degrees above proof; then take some of the pure spirits and mix with it 3 ounces tincture of japonica and 9 ounces sweet spirits of nitre, and, when this is well incorporated, pour it into the barrel with your spirits. Mix it thoroughly. (Ready.) The older, the better.

No. 299.

How to prepare Tincture Japonica.

Take of the best saffron, and dissolve, 1 ounce; mace, bruised, 1 ounce; infuse them into a pint of brandy till the whole tincture of the saffron is extracted, which will be in 7 or 8 days: then strain it through a linen cloth, and to the strained liquor add 2 ounces tartar japonica powdered fine; let it infuse till the tincture is wholly impregnated.

No. 300.

Rochelle Brandy. No. 1.

Take 30 gallons pure rectified whiskey, 5 degrees above proof, 3 gallons pure Rochelle brandy, 6 pounds raisins, 6 ounces tincture of kino, 1 pound loaf sugar, 1 ounce acetic ether; mix, and colour.

No. 301.
Cognac Brandy. No. 5.

Take 30 gallons pure sweet liquor, 3 ounces acetic ether, 3 ounces acetic acid, 5 ounces tincture of kino, 7½ pounds raisins, 3 pints simple syrup; mix, and let it stand 2 weeks, then draw it off clear.

No. 302.
Rochelle Brandy. No. 2.

. Take 30 gallons pure rectified whiskey, 7½ gallons pure imported Rochelle brandy, 2¼ drachms oil of cognac, 2 ounces œnanthic acid, 1½ ounces acetic ether, ¾ ounce acetic acid, 6 ounces tincture of kino; mix, and colour with sugar-colouring.

No. 303.
Bordeaux Brandy.

Take 30 gallons sweet liquor, 15 degrees above proof, 7½ gallons pure Bordeaux brandy, ¾ ounce oil of cognac, 2 ounces œnanthic acid, 4¾ ounces acetic ether, 3 ounces tincture of kino, 1½ quarts simple syrup. Mix and colour.

No. 304.
Cherry Brandy. No. 1.

Take 10 gallons pure rectified whiskey, proof, 2 gallons water, 9 pounds sugar, ½ pound bruised bitter almonds, ½ ounce tincture of cardamom-seed, ½ ounce tartaric acid, 1 drachm orange-flower-water. Let it stand 20 days, draw off, and colour dark.

No. 305.
Common Brandy.

Take 28 gallons rectified whiskey, add 3 gallons brandy, 1 ounce spirits of nitre dulc., 1 ounce tincture of kino: mix, and let stand 24 hours. Good.

No. 306.
Domestic Brandy.

Take 28 gallons rectified whiskey, pure, 2 gallons fourth-proof brandy, high-flavoured, 4 ounces tincture of kino, 2 ounces sweet spirits of nitre, 100 drops nitric acid, and a few pounds burnt raisins; mix all together, and let it stand a few weeks, and draw off. (Ready for use.)

No. 307.
French Brandy. No. 3.

Take 35 gallons pure spirits, 15 degrees above proof, 1 pound stone-lime, ½ pound pulverized alum, 3 ounces sweet spirits of nitre, 2 pounds liquorice-sticks, 1 pound winter-bark. Put them all into your cask together, stir, and mix them well; let them stand 24 hours, then draw it off; take good care that you draw it off very clear. Put into a clean barrel. Then add 6 gallons fourth-proof French brandy, 2 pounds burnt raisins, 1½ ounces mace, 1 ounce nutmeg, 1 quart peach-pits, 2 quarts red-oak sawdust: it will be good in a few days, but the older the better.

No. 308.

Another French Brandy. No. 4.

Take 10 gallons pure spirits, ½ pint tincture of bitter almonds, 2½ gallons good brandy; mix, and colour with sugar-colouring.

No. 309.

Another Brandy. No. 5.

Take 29 gallons pure spirits, 1 gallon pure brandy, 2 ounces sweet spirits of nitre, 4 ounces tincture of kino, 100 drops nitric acid. Mix.

No. 310.

Peach Brandy.

Take 20 gallons pure rectified whiskey, 6 gallons good peach brandy, 4 pounds loaf sugar, ½ drachm oil of bitter almonds cut in alcohol, ½ pint orange-flower-water; mix, colour, and let stand 6 or 8 days, and it is ready.

No. 311.

Blackberry Brandy. No. 1

Take 10 gallons pure proof rectified whiskey, 2¼ gallons raspberry brandy, 2 gallons water, 5 pounds sugar, ½ ounce tincture of cinnamon, ½ ounce tincture of cardamom; colour, and let stand 10 days; draw off, and it is fit for use.

No. 312.

Another Cherry Brandy. No. 2.

Take sweet black cherries ½ bushel, put them in a clean barrel, pour on them good rectified whiskey to cover them well, then let it lie until you get good cider, which you have to boil and skim off clean; then fill up the barrel which contains the cherries and whiskey with the cider, and let it lie, and in a few months it will be good.

No. 313.

Raspberry Brandy.

Take 10 gallons pure spirits, proof, 13 quarts raspberries, 2 gallons water, 6 pounds loaf sugar, $\frac{1}{2}$ ounce, unground cloves, $\frac{1}{2}$ ounce cinnamon; mix, and let stand 25 days; draw off, and fine if necessary.

No. 314.

Another Cherry Brandy. No. 3.

Take 10 gallons pure rectified whiskey, 13 quarts wild cherries, bruised; let stand 8 days; strain it, and add 6 pounds loaf sugar, and 2 gallons water.

No. 315.

Rose Brandy.

Take 10 gallons pure sweet liquor, $2\frac{1}{2}$ gallons water, 10 pounds sugar, 15 drops oil of roses cut in alcohol, 2 drachms tartaric acid; colour, and let stand a few days, when it will be good.

No. 316.

Blackberry Brandy. No. 2.

Take 10 gallons rectified whiskey, 12 quarts blackberries, 4 gallons soft water, 6 pounds loaf sugar, 2 drachms unground cloves, ½ ounce cinnamon, bruised; mix, and let stand 2 or 3 weeks; draw off, strain, and fine if necessary.

No. 317.
Rochelle Brandy.   No. 3.

Take 15 gallons pure spirits, 9 pounds bruised raisins, 3 ounces acetic ether, 1½ ounces acetic acid, 3 ounces ground cinnamon, 3 pounds loaf sugar, 8 ounces tincture of kino, 3 ounces tincture of catechu; mix, and manage as the last.   Colour.

No. 318.
Lavender Brandy.

Take 5 gallons pure spirits, proof, ¼ drachm oil of lavender dissolved in alcohol for 10 or 12 hours, then add it to your pure spirits; also add 1½ gallons soft water, 2 drachms tincture of cinnamon, 1 quart simple syrup. Colour with sugar-colouring.

No. 319.
Ginger Brandy.

Take 10 gallons pure sweet liquor, add ½ ounce tincture of cardamom-seed; then take ¼ pound ground ginger-root, infuse in 1 quart alcohol for 6 or 8 days; filter, and add to your liquor; mix thoroughly. Then add 2½ gallons soft water, and 2 quarts simple syrup.

No. 320.
How to make Tincture of Cinnamon.

Take 4½ ounces ground cinnamon, alcohol, diluted, 3 pints: infuse for 2 weeks.   (Ready.)

No. 321.

How to make Tincture of Cardamom-Seed.

Take 2 ounces cardamom-seed, bruised, and 1 pint alcohol, diluted; macerate it for 2 weeks, and filter.

No. 322.

How to make Tincture of Rhatany.

Take 6 ounces rhatany, 1 quart diluted alcohol: macerate for 2 weeks, and filter.

No. 323.

How to make Tincture of Allspice.

Take 4 ounces allspice, 2 quarts alcohol, and infuse for 2 weeks; filter.

No. 324.

How to make Tincture of Saffron.

Take 1 ounce saffron, 1 pint rectified whiskey, pure first-proof, and infuse for 2 weeks; filter.

No. 325.

How to make Tincture of Red Sanders.

Take ½ pound ground red sanders, 1 quart alcohol; macerate for 2 weeks; express and filter.

No. 326.

How to make Tincture of Cloves.

Take 2 ounces ground cloves, infuse it in alcohol for 2 weeks, and filter.

No. 327.

How to imitate Port Wine. No. 1.

Take 6 gallons good prepared cider, 1½ gallons good imported Port wine, 1½ gallons juice of elderberries, 3 quarts good brandy, 1½ ounces cochineal. This will produce 9½ gallons. Now pulverize the cochineal very fine, put it with the brandy into a stone jug, let it remain at least 2 weeks, shake it every day, and at the end of 2 weeks have your cider ready; put 5 gallons of the cider into a 10-gallon cask, add to this the elder-juice and Port wine and the brandy and cochineal; take the remaining 5 gallons of cider, with part of which clean out your jug that contained the brandy, and pour the whole into your cask, bung it tight, and in 6 weeks it will be ready for use.

No. 328.

Another Imitation of Port Wine. No. 2.

Take 10 gallons prepared cider, 2 gallons good pure imported Port wine, 3 quarts good sweet liquor, 2 quarts good brandy, 1 pound bruised raisins, 1 ounce tincture of kino, ½ ounce extract of rhatany, 1 pint simple syrup. Colour, if necessary, with tincture of red sanders; let it stand 2 weeks; rack and fine until perfectly clear and transparent; keep cool.

No. 329.

How to imitate Madeira Wine. No. 1.

Take of white Havana sugar 30 pounds, water 10 gallons, white tartar 6 ounces; boil the whole half an hour, and skim it well; let it stand until cool; then add 8 gallons strong beer-wort from the vat while working; stir it well together, and let it stand until next day; then put it into a sweet cask; then add to it 6 pounds bruised raisins, 1 quart French brandy, ½ pound brown rock-candy, 2 ounces isinglass. After the wine is put into the cask, put a piece of muslin over the bung-hole; and when it has done working, which will be in about 6 weeks, then add 2 green citrons; let them remain until the wine is bottled; it will be ready for bottling in about 6 months.

No. 330.

Another Imitation of Madeira Wine. No. 2.

Take 10 gallons prepared cider, 1½ gallons pure imported Madeira wine, 3 quarts sweet liquor, 1 ounce tartaric acid, ¼ drachm oil of bitter almonds cut in alcohol, 2 pounds bruised raisins, 2 quarts brandy; let stand 10 days; then rack and fine until clear.

No. 331.

How to imitate Lisbon Wine.

Take 10 gallons prepared cider, 2½ gallons pure imported Lisbon wine, 2½ pounds grapes in cluster, ½ ounce tincture of rhatany, ½ ounce tincture of kino, 1 gallon sweet liquor, 1½ pounds loaf sugar; let stand 10 days, and manage as before.

No. 332.

How to imitate Malaga Wine.

Take 10 gallons good cider, 2 gallons imported

Malaga wine, 1 ounce cream of tartar, 2 pounds raisins, 1 pint good brandy, ¼ ounce tincture of kino, 1 pint syrup. Colour with sugar-colouring, and manage as before.

No. 333.
How to imitate Claret Wine.

Take 5 gallons cider prepared, 3 quarts good imported claret wine, 24 drachms cream of tartar, ½ drachm citric acid, ½ pound raisins, 1 gill honey, ½ ounce tincture of red sanders, 1 quart water. Manage as before.

No. 334.
How to imitate Sherry Wine.

Take 12 gallons prepared cider, 9 quarts imported pure sherry wine, 6 quarts native wine, ⅜ drachm oil of bitter almonds dissolved in alcohol, 9 pints rectified whiskey, 1½ pounds loaf sugar, 1½ ounces tincture of saffron. Mix, and manage as before.

No. 335.
How to imitate Teneriffe Wine.

Take 10 gallons cider, 2½ gallons pure imported Teneriffe wine, 3 quarts sweet liquor, 2 drachms citric acid, ½ pint simple syrup. Mix, and let stand for 6 or 8 days, then draw off.

No. 336.
How Racking Wine is performed.

This is an operation highly requisite to the keeping of wine good,—to its purification, strength, colour, brilliancy, richness, and flavour,—and is performed by drawing off the wine and leaving the sediment in the cask. A siphon should be used; but, if not, the cask should be tapped 2 or 3 days previously. It may be racked off into another cask again, after it has been well cleaned; and, if requisite, the cask may be slightly fumigated, immediately before the wine is returned into it. If the wine, on being tasted, is found weak, a little spirits to be given to it, the cask filled up, and bunged tight. The racking off ought to be performed in temperate weather; and, as soon as the wines appear clear, a second racking will make them perfectly brilliant; and, if so, they will want no fining.

No. 337.

How to fine or clear Wine.

One of the best finings is as follows: Take 1 pound fresh marshmallow-roots, washed clean, and cut into small pieces; macerate them in 2 quarts of soft water for 24 hours, then gently boil the liquor down to 3 half-pints, strain it, and, when cold, mix with ½ ounce pipe-clay or chalk in powder; then pour the mucilage into the cask, and stir up the wine, so as not to disturb the sediment or lees, and leave the vent-peg out for some days after.

Or, take boiled rice, 2 tablespoonfuls, the white of 1 new egg, and ½ ounce burnt alum in powder. Mix with a pint or more of the wine, then pour the mucilage into the cask, and stir the wine with a stout stick, but not to agitate the sediment or lees.

Or, dissolve, in a gentle heat, ½ ounce isinglass in

a pint or more of the wine; then mix with it ½ ounce chalk in powder. When the two are well incorporated, pour it into the cask, and stir the wine, so as not to disturb the sediment or lees. As soon as the wines are clear and bright, after being fined down, they ought to be racked into a sweet and clean cask,—the cask to be filled up and bunged tight.

No. 338.

How the Bottling of Wine is performed.

Fine clear weather is best for bottling all sorts of wines; and much cleanliness is required. The first consideration in bottling wines is to examine and see if the wines are in a proper state. The wines should be fine and brilliant, or they will never brighten after. White wines, before being bottled, must go through the process of fining. For 1 hogshead, (or any quantity in proportion, more or less,) take 2 ounces isinglass, and dissolve it in 1 quart water, and mix with 2 quarts of the wine. Red wines are fined by beating to a froth the white of 7 eggs, and mixing them with 3 times the bulk of water; then, adding 2 quarts of the wine, mix well, and pour it into 1 barrel of your wine.

The bottles must be all sound, clean, and dry, with plenty of good, sound corks.

The cork is to be put in with the hand, and driven well in with a flat wooden mallet, the weight of which ought to be 1¼ pounds, but, however, not to exceed 1½ pounds; for, if the mallet be too light or too heavy, it will not drive the cork in properly, and may break the bottle. The corks must so completely fill up the neck of each bottle as to render them air-tight, but leave a space of an inch between the wine and the cork.

When all the wine is bottled, it is to be stored in a cool cellar, and on no account on the bottles' bottoms, but on their sides, and in sawdust.

No. 339.

How to make Currant Wine.

To every quart of currant-juice, add 3 pounds sugar and 3 quarts water. Put all together into your cask, (be careful to take such a cask that you can fill up to the bung-hole. Should it not quite fill up your cask, add a little water until it is full.) When your cask is full, leave the bung out, and lay thin gauze or bobinet over the bung-hole, to keep the flies out; let it ferment until it stops. After fermentation, draw it off, and clean out your cask very clean; return the liquor, bung your cask up tight, and it will be fit for use in 3 or 4 months. If you wish, you can add 1 quart brandy to every 10 gallons before you bung it up tight.

N.B.—The following wines can all be made on the above principle: Morelle jerries, sour jerries, blackberries, elderberries, raspberries, strawberries, and grape of every kind.

No. 340.

How to make Cider Wine.

Take 25 gallons good cider, add 1 gallon good French brandy, 4 gallons good wine, ¼ pound crude tartar, 1 pint new milk.

No. 341.

How to make Cypress Wine.

To 10 gallons soft water, add 5 quarts juice of elderberries. The berries are to be slightly pressed: each quart of the liquid will contain 6 ounces juice; and to the whole quantity add 2 ounces ginger and 1 ounce cloves. Boil the whole for an hour. Skim the liquid, and pour it into a vessel which should contain the whole, throwing in 1½ pounds bruised grapes, which leave in the liquor until the wine is of a fine colour.

No. 342.

How to make Apple Wine.

To every gallon of cider, immediately as it comes from the press, add 2 pounds loaf sugar. Boil it as long as any scum arises, then strain it through a sieve, and let it cool; add some good yeast, mix it well; let it work in the tub 2 or 3 weeks, then skim off the head; draw it off close and tun it; let stand 1 year, then rack it off, and add 2 ounces isinglass to the barrel; then add ½ pint spirits of wine to every 8 gallons.

No. 343.

How to boil Sugar-Colouring.

Take 3 or 4 pounds brown sugar, boil it well, and burn it so that it tastes very bitter; thin it with water while on the fire; pour in very little at a time, and keep stirring all the time you are pouring water on it. If you pour too much in at a time, it will explode, and may burn you badly. As soon as the sugar commences to boil, you must commence stirring, and continue all the time, else it will boil over for you. Very much care is required to make good sugar-colouring. After you have thinned it down to its proper consistency, strain it while warm.

No. 344.
How to make Simple Syrup.

Take 1 pint water to every 2 pounds loaf sugar; dissolve it over the fire; remove the scum that will arise; as soon as it commences to boil, remove it from the fire; and, while hot, strain it.

No. 345.
How to make Pure Spirits.

Take 38 gallons rectified whiskey, as pure as you can rectify it, 5 degrees above proof, add 1 pound stone-lime, ½ pound sweet spirits of nitre, 1 pound alum. Put the lime, nitre, and alum into the whiskey; stir them well together, let stand 24 hours; then add 1 pound liquorice-stick, and ¼ pound winter-bark; let them stand 36 hours, then draw it off as pure as possible.

No. 346.
How to make Pure Spirits by Distillation.

Prepare a work as a copper-still. Take good rectified whiskey, for every barrel add 1 bushel fine-pulverized charcoal, 1 pound rock-salt, and 1 pound orris-root; put the whole together in the still with your liquor, and run it off by a slow fire.

No. 347.

How to make Yeast for Distillers, Brewers, with Hops.

Take 6 quarts soft water, and 2 handfuls wheat or barley meal; stir the latter in the water before the mixture is placed over the fire, where it must boil till two-thirds are evaporated. When this decoction becomes cool, incorporate with it, by means of a whisk, 2 drachms salt of tartar, and 1 drachm cream of tartar, previously mixed. The whole should be kept in a warm place. For bread, it ought to be diluted with pure water, and passed through a sieve, before it is kneaded with the dough, in order to deprive it of its alkaline taste.

No. 348.

Another Yeast.

Boil 1 pound good flour, ¼ pound brown sugar, and a little salt, in 2 gallons water for 1 hour; when milk-warm, bottle it and cork it close: it will be fit for use in 24 hours. One pint of this yeast will make 18 pounds of bread.

No. 349.

How to make a Beer to make Yeast.

Take 9 gallons boiling water, and let it stand until it is 170 degrees; then add 1 peck malt, put it in by degrees; then let it stand 3 hours until it is settled, then pour it off and add ½ pound hops; then boil down to half, which must be strained through a tin strainer, and squeeze the hops out well. This will make about 4 gallons juice, well squeezed out; then let it stand until 90 degrees; then put into this juice 1 quart good yeast; let it stand and work for a few days until the foam will fall back; put the beer into a stone jug, and it will be good for months.

N.B.—This is very valuable for distillers and brewers.

No. 350.

How to make French Raspberry Vinegar.

Take a sufficiency of the ripe raspberries, put them into a deep earthen pan, and mash them with a wooden beetle in a large linen bag, and squeeze and press out the liquor into a vessel beneath. Measure it, and to each quart of the raspberry-juice allow a pound of powdered white sugar and a pint of the best cider vinegar. First mix together the juice and the vinegar, and give them a boil in a preserving-kettle. When it has boiled well, add gradually the sugar, and boil and skim it till the scum ceases to rise. When done, put it into clean bottles, and cork them tightly. It is a very pleasant and cooling beverage in warm weather, and for invalids who are feverish. To use it, pour out half a tumbler of raspberry vinegar, and fill it up with ice or fresh cool spring-water.

No. 351.

How to make British Champagne.

Take gooseberries before they are ripe, crush them with a mallet in a wooden bowl, and to every gallon of fruit put a gallon of water; let it stand 2 days, stirring it well; squeeze the mixture well with the hands through a hop-sieve; then measure the liquor, and to every gallon put 3½ pounds loaf sugar; mix it well in the tub, and let it stand 1 day; put a quart good brandy into the cask, and leave it open 5 or 6 weeks, taking off the scum as it rises; then make it up, and let it stand 1 year in the barrel before it is bottled. The proportion of brandy to be used for this liquor is 1 pint to 7 gallons.

FARRIERY.

No. 352.

To cure Wounds in Cattle.

When horses, cattle, or any of our domestic animals are wounded, the treatment may be very simple, and much the same as with the human race. It is extremely improper to follow a practice that is common in many parts of the country among farriers, cow-doctors, and even shepherds,—that of applying to the wound, or putting into the sore part, common salt, powder of blue vitriol, or tar, or cloths dipped in spirits, as brandy, rum, &c., or turpentine, or any other stimulant articles; for all such very much increase the pain, and by irritating the sore may increase the inflammation even to the length of inducing mortification. Though the treatment may be varied according to circumstances, yet, in most cases, it may be sufficient to take notice of the following particulars:—It will be proper to wash away any foulness or dirt about the part, and to examine particularly its condition.

No. 353.

To stop the Bleeding.

Should any large blood-vessel be cut, and discharging copiously, it will be right to stop it, by some lint or sponge, with moderate compression, or bandaging, at the same time, and not taking it off for 2 or 3 days. Should the pressure fail of effect, caustic applications, such as lunar-caustic, or even the actual cautery, the point of a thick wire sufficiently heated, may be tried; or, if a surgeon be at hand, the vessel may be taken up by a crooked needle, with waxed thread, and then tied.

No. 354.

Adhesive Plaster and Sewing.

When there is no danger of excessive bleeding, and a mere division of the parts, or a deep gash or cut, it will be right to adjust the parts, and keep them together by a strip of any common adhesive plaster; or, when this will not do by itself, the lips of the wound, especially if it be a clean cut, may be closed by one or more stitches with a moderately coarse needle and thread, which, in each stitch, may be tied, and the ends left of a moderate length, so that they can be afterwards removed when the parts adhere. It is advisable to tie the threads, because sometimes the wounded part swells so much that it is difficult to get them cut and drawn out without giving pain and doing some mischief.

No. 355.

Bandages.

If the part will allow a roller or bandage to be used to keep the lips of it together, this may likewise be employed; for, by supporting the sides of the wound, it would lessen any pain which the stitches occasion. With this treatment the wound heals often in a short time, or in a few days, rarely exceeding 5 or 6, and sooner in the young and healthy than in the old and relaxed, and sooner in the quiet and motionless than in the restless and active.

Should the wound be large, and inflammation, with the discharge of matter, likely to take place, it may still be proper, by gentle means, to bring the divided parts near to each other, and to retain them in their natural situation by means of a bandage. This should not be made too tight, but merely to support the part. In this way, and by avoiding stimulant applications, the wound will heal more readily than otherwise, and the chance of any blemish following will be diminished. Washes of spirits, brandy, and the like, "Friar's balsam," spirits of wine and camphor, turpentine, or any other irritating applications, are highly improper, and sometimes make a fresh clean wound (that would readily heal almost of itself) inflame and perhaps mortify, or become a bad sore.

No. 356.

Sores and Bruises.

Over the whole sore, or where the part is bruised, or where there is a tendency to suppuration, a poultice should be applied and kept on by suitable bandages. The poultice may be made of any kind of meal, fine bran, bruised linseed, or of mashed turnips, carrots, &c. The following has been found useful as a common poultice. "Fine bran, 1 quart; pour on it a sufficient quantity of boiling water to make a thin paste; to this add linseed-powder enough to give it a proper consistence." The poultice may be kept on for a week or 10 days, or even longer, if necessary, changing it once or twice a day; and clean the wound when the poultice is removed, by washing it by means of a soft rag or linen cloth with water not more than blood-warm, (some sponges are too rough for this purpose;) or, where the wound is deep, the water may be injected into it by a syringe, in order to clean it from the bottom.

No. 357.

Ointment.

In the course of a few days, when the wound, by care and proper management with the poultices, begins to put on a healthy appearance, and seems to be clean and of a reddish colour, not black or bloody, then there may be applied an ointment made of tallow, linseed-oil, beeswax, and hog's lard, in such proportion as to make it of a consistence somewhat firmer than butter. The ointment should be spread on some soft clean tow; and when applied to the sore, it ought never to be tied hard upon it, (which is done too frequently, and very improperly,) but only fixed by a bandage of a proper length, (for a mere cord is often improper,) so close and securely as to keep it from slipping off. This application may be changed once a day; or, when nearly well, and discharging but little, once in 2 days.

No. 358.

Green Ointment for Wounds.

Put into a well-glazed earthen vessel 2 ounces beeswax; melt it over a clear fire, and add 2 ounces rosin; when that is melted, put in ½ pound hog's lard; to this put 4 ounces turpentine; keep stirring it all the time with a clean stick or wooden spatula. When all is well mixed, stir in 1 ounce finely-powdered verdigris. Be careful that it does not boil over; strain it through a coarse cloth, and preserve it in a gallipot. This ointment is very good for old and recent wounds, whether in flesh or hoof,—also galled backs, cracked heels, mallender, sallenders, bites, broken knees, &c.

No. 359.

Treatment, according to appearance of the part.

When the wounded part begins to discharge a whitish, thick matter, and is observed to fill up, the general treatment and dressings to the sore, now mentioned, should be continued; and, in the course of the cure, the animal, when free of fever, may be allowed better provision, and may take gentle exercise. If the animal be feeble from the loss of blood originally, or from the long continuance of a feverish state produced by the inflammation attending the wound, or from weakness arising from confinement, or connected with its constitution naturally, and if the wound appear to be in a stationary state, very pale and flabby on its edges, with a thin discharge, then better food may be given to it; and, if still no change should be observed along with the better food, the wound may be treated somewhat differently from what has been already advised. The ointment may be made more stimulant, by adding to it some rosin and less beeswax,—or, what would be more stimulant still, some common turpentine; but it is only in very rare cases that oil of turpentine can be requisite. The effects of an alteration in the mode of treatment should be particularly remarked, and stimulants should be laid aside, continued, or increased according as may be judged proper. Before changing the dressings applied to the wound, or before rendering them more stimulant and active by using heating applications, the effect of closer bandaging may be tried; for, sometimes, by keeping the parts a little more firmly together the cure is promoted.

No. 360.

Food and Regimen.

In case of severe wounds, attention should be paid to the condition of the animal in other respects. There being always in such cases a tendency to violent inflammation and fever that may end fatally, means should be employed to moderate both. The apartment should be cool and airy, and so quiet that the animal should not be disturbed; the drink should not be warm, but rather cold, and given freely, though not in too large quantities at a time; the food should be sparingly given, and of a poorer quality than usual, and should be rather succulent and laxative than dry or apt to produce costiveness. Bleeding may be employed, either generally from a vein, or in some cases, when it can be done, by cupping from the hurt part, as in the case of a bruise, (though this last will seldom be requisite,) if found convenient; and it may be done more than once or twice, as may seem proper. Laxative medicines also ought to be given and repeated as there may be occasion.

No. 361.

Abscess.

These are swellings containing matter, that make their appearance in different parts of the body. The remedies are, first, to bleed, then to wash the swollen part with a quart of vinegar, in which are dissolved 2 ounces sal-ammoniac, and ½ ounce sugar of lead. If the swelling does not abate in 2 or 3 days, apply the suppurating poultice. When the tumour becomes soft and points, open it with a lancet, and let out the matter. Then dress it with basilicon ointment.

No. 362.

Anbury or Wart.

Tie a strong silk, or 2 or 3 horse-hairs, round the

neck of the wart, tightening it gradually till it falls away. Then dip a piece of tow in alum-water and bind it on the spot for a whole day. Heal the sore with the green ointment.

No. 363.

The Staggers.

Bleed the animal copiously, (the disease is a true apoplexy,) 2½ quarts at once; then give him ½ pint linseed-oil, the same of castor-oil, 40 grains calomel, 60 grains jalap, and 2 ounces tincture of aloes. Give him twice a day warm bran mashes.

No. 364.

For Loss of Appetite.

Take 1 quart blood from the neck, and give him a purging ball, made as follows: aloes, 1 ounce; jalap, 1 drachm; rhubarb, 1 drachm; make into a ball with castor-oil and ½ drachm ginger.

No. 365.

Inflamed Bladder.

Make the animal drink largely of flaxseed tea, barley or rice water, or any mucilaginous liquid, and inject a portion of the same frequently. Bleeding, and a dose of castor-oil, are never to be omitted. After the oil has operated, give the following ball every six hours: powdered nitre, ½ ounce; camphor, 1 drachm; liquorice-powder, 3 drachms; honey sufficient to form the ball. Should these means not relieve the animal, omit the ball, and give 1 drachm opium twice a day.

No. 366.
Blood Spavin.

Clip off the hair from the swelling, and rub all round outside of the swelling with a piece of hard brown soap; then apply to the swelling a blister made of the following

No. 367.
Blistering Ointment.

Take hog's lard, ½ ounce; beeswax, 3 drachms; sublimate, in fine powder, ½ drachm; Spanish flies, 2 drachms. Mix them all well, and spread it on white leather, and apply it to the spavin.

No. 368.
Bone Spavin.

This may be treated like the former: it is, however, generally incurable. The operation of firing, (which should be done by a professed farrier,) and turning to grass, afford the only reasonable chances of relief.

No. 369.
Bots.

Three kinds of worms infest the bowels of horses, called by the English farriers bots, truncheons, and maw-worms. The bot infests the great gut near the anus: it is a small worm with a large head, and may be frequently observed in the dung.

The truncheon is short and thick, with a blackish head, and is found in the maw, where, if suffered to remain, it sometimes pierces through, and thus is many a fine horse destroyed.

The maw-worm is of a pale-red colour, resembling an earth-worm, from 2 to 3 inches long, occupying also the maw.

No. 370.

Symptoms of Worms in Horses.

Stamping forcibly on the ground with either of his forefeet, and frequently striking at his belly with his hind ones; belly projecting; and hard looking frequently behind him, and groaning as if in great pain.

No. 371.

Remedies for Worms.

Keep the horse from all kinds of food for one day; at night give him a small quantity of warm bran mash, made as usual, and, directly after, a ball made of 1 scruple calomel, 1 scruple turpeth mineral, and as much crumb of bread and honey as will form the mass. Next evening give him a pint of castor and ½ pint of linseed oil. The animal is then to be fed as usual for 2 or 3 days, and the same plan again to be employed.

No. 372.

Inflammation of the Bowels.

This not very common—but, when it does occur,

dangerous—disorder is of two kinds. The first, or peritoneal, inflammation, begins with an appearance of dulness and uneasiness in the animal; appetite diminished or totally gone; constant pawing with the forefeet, frequently trying to kick the belly; he lies down, rises suddenly, looks round to his flanks, —countenance strongly expressive of pain; urine small, high-coloured, and voided with great pain; pulse quick and small; legs and ears cold; profuse sweats; mortification and death.

The second species of the disorder is when the inflammation attacks the internal coat of the intestines, and is generally accompanied by a violent purging and some fever. The symptoms of the latter, however, are much less violent; nor does the animal appear to be in so much pain.

No. 373.

Treatment.

In the first, or peritoneal, inflammation, the only dependence is on early and large bleedings. In addition to this, rub the whole belly well with the mustard embrocation, clothe the animal warmly, (with fresh sheepskins if possible,) insert several rowels about the chest and belly,—putting into them the blistering ointment. As the horse is generally costive, give him a pint of castor-oil, and inject clysters of warm flaxseed tea; give him warm water, or thin gruel, or flaxseed tea, to drink; rub his legs with the hands well, and see that he has plenty of clean fresh litter. If in six hours the disease is not relieved, bleed him again; and should the costiveness continue, repeat the oil and clysters. If, after giving all these remedies a faithful and continued trial, the pain should continue, recourse may be had to the anodyne clyster.

In the second species of this disorder, bleeding need not be resorted to unless the febrile symptoms run high. Clothe the horse warmly, use the mustard embrocation freely, and omit the oil. Give him frequently, by means of a bottle, (if he will not drink it,) quantities of very thin gruel or flaxseed tea. If in spite of this the disease continues, use the anodyne clyster; if that fail, the astringent draught.

The pain occasioned by physicking is to be relieved by large clysters of thin gruel of flaxseed, which produce copious evacuations and relief.

No. 374.

Broken Wind.

This is an incurable disease; all that can be done is to relieve the animal for a time, so as to enable him to perform a day's work. To do this, make the following

No. 375.

Paste-Ball for Broken-Winded Horses.

Assafœtida 2 ounces, elecampane 2 ounces, flowers of colt's-foot 2 ounces, powdered squills 2 drachms, linseed powder 1 ounce, honey as much as will make the mass. Divide it into 4 balls, and give 1 morning and evening. Much benefit may result from bleeding in this disorder, at an early period of the complaint. His food should be carrots or turnips. The hay, oats, or whatever is given, should be in small quantities at a time, and always sprinkled with clean, soft water.

No. 376.

Broken Knees.

Apply a poultice of bread and milk, or bread and warm water, to reduce the inflammation; then dress the wound with basilicon.

No. 377.

Burns and Scalds.

If slight, apply cold lead-water; if extensive, a liniment made of equal parts of linseed-oil and lime-water. If there is much fever, bleed.

No. 378.

Canker.

Cut away freely all the diseased parts, and if necessary draw the frog; then apply the following liniment.

No. 379.

Liniment for Canker.

Warm 6 ounces tar, mix with it, drop by drop, 1 ounce, by measure, oil of vitriol; then add 1 ounce oil of turpentine. Bind this firmly on the part, destroying all the diseased protuberances with lunar-caustic. When the wound looks healthy, dress it with the green ointment.

No. 380.

Capped Hocks.

If the swelling proceed from a bruise or a blow, bathe it three or four times a day with salt and vinegar, made warm. If it proceed from natural cause, apply the suppurating poultice, and when matter is formed, let it out; then use the green ointment.

No. 381.

Cold.

Take a quart of blood from the neck, then give warm mashes, with a scruple of nitre in them. Purge with castor and linseed oil, and keep the stable warm.

No. 382.

Convulsions.

Symptoms.—The horse raises his head higher than usual, and pricks up his ears; neck stiff and immovable, skin tight. He stands in a straddling posture, pants, and breathes with difficulty.

Cure.—Bleed him, if his strength will permit it, and his pulse is high, eyes red, etc.; otherwise not. If you observe bots, or any other kind of worms, pursue the treatment recommended for them.

No. 383.

Cough.

Take 1 quart of blood from the neck, and give the following ball for cough:—Take ½ ounce Venice soap, ½ ounce nitre, 10 grains tartar-emetic, and 10 grains opium. Make these into a ball with honey, and give one every other night. Keep the horse warm, and remedy costiveness by castor-oil.

No. 384.

Corns.

Let the farrier cut them out with a sharp knife. Should they show a disposition to grow again, touch them with oil of vitriol, or caustic, and dress them with green ointment. Be careful, in shoeing, not to let the shoe press on the corn.

No. 385.

Curb.

Cauterize the curb in a line down its middle, and then apply the blistering ointment.

No. 386.

Cracked Heels.

Poultice the parts with carrots, or turnips, boiled soft, three or four times; then anoint them with yellow basilicon, mixed with a little green ointment.

No. 387.

The Gripes.

As soon as the disease is observed, give the draught below, and a clyster composed of warm water. If there is great pain, with quick pulse, take away 3 quarts of blood. The belly should be well rubbed with the mustard or other stimulating embrocation. If no relief is obtained in 2 hours, repeat the draught and embrocation, and should even this fail, give him a pint of castor-oil, with 1½ ounces laudanum. If castor-oil cannot be had, 1¼ pints linseed oil may be used.

No. 388.

Draught for Gripes. No. 1.

Take balsam copaiva 1 ounce, oil of juniper 1 drachm, spirits of nitrous ether ½ ounce, mint-water 1 pint. Mix for 1 dose.

No. 389.

Diabetes.

This disorder, which consists in an involuntary discharge of the urine, which is pale and thin, frequently proves fatal. To cure it, take a quart of blood from the neck, and give the following ball:—

No. 390.

Ball for Diabetes.

Take 4 ounces Peruvian bark, 1 drachm ginger; if costive after it, give a pint of castor-oil. Repeat, if necessary.

No. 391.

Eyes.

Inflammation of the eyes is often cured by scarifying with a lancet the inside of the upper and lower brow, and the distended vessels of the eye itself. It is to be remembered that in treating an inflammation of this important organ we should proceed precisely as if treating a human being labouring under the same complaint, and keep the animal on short allowance, prevent costiveness, keep the stable cool and dark.

Soreness or weakness of the eyes is cured by bleeding from the neck and using the following eye-water:—

No. 392.

Eye-Water, No. 1.

To 1 quart water put 3 drachms sugar of lead, and 2 drachms white vitriol. When dissolved, let it settle, and pour off the clear liquor for use. A drop may be put into each eye, 3 times a day, with a feather.

No. 393.

Film, or Cataract.

There is no remedy for this but an experienced farrier. There are a variety of washes, etc., recommended by various authors, but they are useless.

No. 394.

Farcy.

This disease commences in small, hard knots, which soon become soft and ulcerous, generally situated on the veins and extending upwards. It is a contagious disorder, and not unfrequently ends in the glanders.

No. 395.

Cure for Farcy.

Open the ulcers, and touch the inside of the edges slightly with powdered verdigris, by means of a camel's-hair pencil. At the same time give the following ball: White arsenic 8 grains, and corrosive sublimate 6 grains, powdered and mixed with flour or bread, or any other vehicle that will form a ball with molasses. Keep the animal warm, mix chopped carrots with his mashes. Intermit one day, and give a similar ball; if it purge, add 10 grains opium to it. Attend constantly to the ulcers; wash them with warm soap-suds, and keep the animal by himself; if the disease gains the nostrils and head, and becomes glanders, shoot him at once. There is no remedy.

No. 396.

Grease.

Wash the part well with warm soap-suds twice a day, and if the swelling is great apply a poultice to it; when the sores are cleansed, touch them with a rag or feather dipped in the vulnerary-water.

No. 397.

Foundered Feet.

This is known by the contraction of the hoof, which will appear considerably smaller than the sound one. The horse just touches the ground with the toe of the foundered foot, on account of pain, and stands in such a tottering way that you may shove him over with your hand.

Cure.—Take off the shoe, bleed freely from the thigh-vein, and purge 2 or 3 times. Keep the hair close-trimmed and the parts clean.

No. 398.
Hoof-Bound.

Cut several lines from the coronet down to the toe, all round the hoof, and fill the cuts with tallow and soap mixed. Take off the shoes and (if you can spare him) turn the animal into a wet meadow, where his feet will be kept moist. Never remove the sole nor burn the lines down, as this increases the evil.

No. 399.
Lampass.

This consists in a swelling of the first bar of the upper palate. It is cured by rubbing the swelling two or three times a day with half an ounce of alum and the same quantity of double-refined sugar mixed with a little honey.

No. 400.
Laxity.

Never attempt to stop the discharge too suddenly or too soon; this common but erroneous practice has killed many fine horses. To begin the cure, give the following

Mild purgative-ball: Rhubarb, in powder, 1 ounce; magnesia, ½ ounce; calomel, 1 scruple; oil of anise-seed, 1 drachm. Make up a ball with honey and liquorice-powder. Next day give the horse 1 fluid-ounce liquid laudanum, with 20 grains tartar-emetic, in a pint of water. On the third day, repeat the purge, then the drench, until the animal is well.

No. 401.
Inflammation of the Lungs.

Bleed the animal copiously as soon as the complaint is perceived, and repeat in six hours if the fever, quickness of breathing, &c. do not abate. Blister his sides, rowel the chest, and give the following ball, which is to be taken, morning and evening, until the stalling is considerably increased: one day will then be sufficient. Grass or bran mashes should be the food.

The ball: Powdered nitre, 6 drachms; camphor, 1 drachm; as much syrup and linseed-meal as will form the ball.

No. 402.
Mallenders.

Wash the cracks well with warm soap-suds and a sponge, and then with the vulnerary-water, twice every day. Wipe the parts dry, and apply the green ointment.

No. 403.
Mange.

Wash with soap-suds and vulnerary-water, and purge with castor-oil. Feed the horse well, and work him moderately.

No. 404.
Molten Grease.

Bleed and purge moderately, and feed regularly on a diminished allowance.

No. 405.
Poll-Evil.

Bring the swelling to a head, as any other tumour, by the suppurating poultice, which is made as follows:—

No. 406.
Suppurating Poultice.

Take four handfuls of bran and three middling-sized turnips; boil them till soft, and beat them well together; then boil them again in milk to a thick poultice, adding to it 2 ounces linseed and ½ pound hog's lard.

No. 407.
Quitter.

Make an opening for the matter to descend from all the neighbouring sinuses. Keep the parts well cleaned with warm soap-suds; then inject the vulnerary-water into the sinuses. If there is a core, touch it with caustic; when this is discharged, dress with the green ointment.

No. 408.
Ringbone.

If recent, blister the part; if an old affection, recourse must be had to firing.

No. 409.

Sand-Crack.

Remove the shoe, and ascertain carefully the extent of the injury. If the crack is superficial, fill it with the composition below, and keep the foot cool and moist. If the crack has extended to the sensitive parts, and you can see any fungus flesh, with a small drawing-knife remove the edges of the cracked horn that press upon it. Touch the fungus with caustic, dip a roll of tow or linen in tar, and bind it firmly over it. The whole foot is to be kept in a bran poultice for a few days, or until the lameness is removed. A shoe may then be put on so as not to press on the diseased part. The pledget of tow may now be removed, the crack filled with the composition, and the animal turned into some soft meadow.

No. 410.

Composition for Sand-Crack.

Take 4 ounces beeswax, 2 ounces yellow rosin, 1 ounce turpentine, and ½ ounce tallow or suet: to be melted together.

No. 411.

Sitfasts

Are horny substances on the back, under the saddle. Take hold of them with a pair of pincers and cut them out radically. Leave no part behind, or they will grow again. Dress the wound with green ointment.

No. 412.

Sallenders

Require the same treatment as mallenders, which see.

No. 413.

Strains.

In whatever part of the body this accident occurs, the treatment should be perfect rest, moderate bleeding, and purging till the inflammation is reduced, when any stimulating embrocation may be used.

No. 414.

Strangury.

Take away 1 quart of blood, and throw up a laxative clyster; then give 1 ounce saltpetre and 1 fluid-ounce sweet spirits of nitre in a pint of water.

No. 415.

Strangles.

This is known by a swelling between the jaw-bone and the root of the tongue. If a large tumour appear under the jaw, apply the suppurating poultice. When it is ripe, open it, squeeze out the matter, and re-apply a warm poultice. In a few days it will run off. Give warm bran mashes and gentle exercise.

No. 416.

Thrush.

Remove the shoe, and pare off all the ragged parts

so as to expose the diseased parts. After cleaning the frog nicely, apply a solution of blue vitriol, and shortly after pour some melted tar-ointment into the cleft of the frog and cover its whole surface with tow soaked in the same; and place on the tow a flat piece of wood, about the width of the frog, one of its ends passing under the toe of the shoe, the other extending to the back part of the frog, and bound down by cross-pieces of wood, the ends of which are placed under the shoe. Repeat the dressing every day.

No. 417.
Vives.

This is a disease most common to young horses, and consists in a long swelling of the parotid gland, beginning at the roots of the ears and descending downward. If it is painful and inflamed, apply the poultice; if it suppurates, open the lump, let out the matter, and dress with the green ointment. If it is hard and indolent, apply strong mercurial ointment, to disperse it, and bleed moderately.

No. 418.
Wind-Galls.

These swellings appear on each side of the back sinew, above the fetlock. It is dangerous to puncture them, as is sometimes done, as it may produce an incurable lameness. Tight bandages and moistening the parts frequently with a strong solution of sal-ammoniac in vinegar may do some good.

No. 419.

Wounds.

All the rules laid down in this book for the treatment of wounds in the human subject apply strictly to horses. As in simple cuts, however, sticking-plaster cannot be used, the edges of the wound should be neatly stitched together. Much can be done also by the judicious application of bandages. Farriers generally are in the habit of pursuing such absurd, cruel, and fatal practices in these cases, either by cutting off a part that appears to be partly torn from its connection, or by using stimulating applications, that it becomes necessary to repeat again that all the rules laid down for the treatment of wounds in this work as applicable to man are equally so to the noble animal of which we are speaking. Read over these rules, substitute the word "horse" for "patient," and you will be at no loss how to proceed.

No. 420.

Bleeding in General.

Bleeding is often the most useful and efficacious means of curing diseases in horses. In inflammatory affections, it is generally the first remedy resorted to; and its immediate salutary effects are often surprising.

When it is necessary to lessen the whole quantity of blood in the system, open the jugular or neck vein. If the inflammation is local, bleed, where it can be conveniently done, either from the part affected or in its vicinity, as by opening the plate vein, superficial vein of the thigh, or temporal arteries.

In fevers of all kinds, and when inflammation attacks any important organ, as the brain, eyes, lungs, stomach, intestines, liver, kidneys, bladder, &c., bleeding is of the greatest use. It diminishes the quantity of blood in the body, and by this means prevents the bad consequences of inflammation. The quantity of blood to be taken varies according to the age, size, condition, and constitution of the horse, and the urgency of the symptoms.

From a large, strong horse, 4 or 6 quarts will generally be requisite; and this may be repeated in smaller quantities if the symptoms demand it. The blood, in these diseases, must flow from a large orifice made in the vein. A horse should never be suffered to bleed upon the ground, but into a measure, in order that the proper quantity may be taken. Horses have sometimes much constitutional irritation, which bleeding relieves. But in these affections it is very rarely necessary to bleed to the same extent as in fevers, &c.; 2 or 3 quarts generally suffice to be taken away.

No. 421.

Fulness of Blood.

Moderate bleeding, as from 2 to 4 quarts, is also used to remove fulness of habit, or plethora, attended with slight inflammatory symptoms. In this case the eyes appear heavy, dull, red, or inflamed, frequently closed as if asleep; the pulse small and oppressed; the heat of the body somewhat increased; the legs swell, the hair also rubs off. Horses that are removed from grass to a warm stable, full fed on hay and corn, and not sufficiently exercised, are very subject to one or more of these symptoms. Regulating the quantity of food given to him, proper exercise, and occasional laxatives, as the following powder, will be commonly found sufficient after the first bleeding, and operation of an aloetic purge. In slight affections of this kind, a brisk purge will often alone be sufficient.

No. 422.
Laxative and Diaphoretic Powder.

Take of crocus of antimony, finely levigated, nitre, cream of tartar, and flour of sulphur, each 4 ounces. Powder and mix them well together for use. One tablespoonful of this mixture may be given every night and morning, in as much scalded bran, or a feed of corn moistened with water, that the powder may adhere thereto.

This powder will be found excellent for such horses as are kept on dry food, whether they be in the stable or travel on the road; also for stallions in the spring of the year, as they not only keep the body cool and open, but cause him to cast his coat, and make his skin appear as bright as silk.

No. 423.
Purging.

In obstinate grease and swellings of the legs, accompanied with lameness of the joints, dry coughs, worms, diseases of the skin, farcy, apoplexy or staggers, affections of the liver, and several other diseases treated of in this book, mercurial purges are of the greatest service. The purges destroy worms, generally increase the flow of urine, operate upon the skin, liver, and other viscera in a peculiar manner, cause a healthful action in these parts, and remove many chronic complaints incident to the horse. Great caution is necessary during their operation, lest the horse take cold. The water given him must be warm, and when exercised he should be properly clothed.

Horses that are kept on dry food, and are full fed, with little or no exercise, require regular purging every six months, with 2 or 3 doses each time, allowing proper intervals between each; and those horses which run in stage-coaches, (whose labour is often more than their natural strength is able to bear,) and those whose legs are inclined to swell, all require purgative medicines, the use of which would be a means of preventing many of the diseases that attack this useful animal.

No. 424.

To prepare Horses for Physic.

After violent exercise, horses are liable to lose their appetite, and to have their stomach loaded with crudities and undigested matter, the non-removal of which by the use of proper physic is the chief cause why so many die daily. Previous to administering a purge, the body should be prepared.

The proper method of preparing a horse for

physic is to give him 2 or 3 mashes of scalded bran and oats, and warm water, for 3 or 4 days together. This will soften the fæces and promote the operation of the medicine. But if a strong purge be given to a horse of costive habit without preparation, it will probably occasion a violent inflammation.

No. 425.
Purgative Balls for Horses.

Take of Barbadoes aloes 7½ ounces, Castile soap 1½ ounces, powdered ginger 1½ ounces, oil of aniseseed 2 drachms, syrup a sufficient quantity to make 6 balls, each of which is a dose.

No. 426.
Drink to check Over-Purging.

Take of prepared chalk, ginger, and anise-seed, in powder, each 1 ounce, essential oil of peppermint 15 drops, rectified spirits of wine ½ ounce. Mix the whole in a pint and a half of warm linseed gruel, and give it.

Another.—Take of prepared chalk 2 ounces, aniseseed and caraway-seed, prepared, each 1 ounce, opium ½ drachm. Mix, and give it in a pint of linseed gruel.

No. 427.
Astringent Drink after Looseness.

If the looseness continues after the above drink has been administered for 2 or 3 days, the following may be given:—

Take of pomegranate-shell, in powder, and prepared testaceous powder, each 1 ounce, Dover's powders, and ginger powdered, each 2 drachms. Mix, and give in a pint of warm gruel, and repeat twice a day.

No. 428.

Cough Drink.

Take of Barbadoes tar, anisated balsam of sulphur, each 1 ounce. Incorporate them with the yolk of an egg; then add nitre 1 ounce, ginger ¼ ounce, tincture of opium 1 ounce. Mix them together.

Let this drink be gradually mixed in a pint of warm ale or linseed tea, and give it in the morning, fasting; let the horse stand without food for 2 hours after, then give him a mash of scalded bran and oats and warm water. Repeat every other morning, three or four times.

No. 429.

Fever-Balls for Horses.

Take of antimonial powder, tartarized antimony, and camphor, each 1 drachm, nitre, and Castile soap, each 2 drachms, Barbadoes aloes 2 drachms. Mix, and beat them into a ball with syrup of buckthorn. Let this ball be given to the horse about 2 hours after bleeding, and in 6 hours after giving him the ball, let him have the following

Purgative drink.—Take of Epsom salts 4 ounces, nitre ½ ounce, coarse sugar 2 tablespoonfuls. Dissolve them in a quart of gruel, then add 10

ounces castor-oil. Mix it while new-milk-warm. After the first ball given, the aloes may be left out, and then the ball and drink may be given once a day (one in the morning and the other in the evening,) until a proper passage be obtained.

No. 430.

Powerful Mixture for Fevers.

If the fever still continues to increase, it will be proper to take a little more blood from him, and then to have recourse to the following fever-powder.

Take of emetic tartar 1 ounce, calcined antimony 2 ounces, calcined hartshorn 1 ounce. Mix, and grind them in a mortar to a fine powder; then put them in a bottle for use. 2 drachms of these powders are a proper dose for a horse.

A dose of this powder, with an ounce of nitre, may be given twice or three times a day, in a pint of warm gruel, or to be made into a ball with conserve of roses. If the fever be violent, and the horse in a raging state, $\frac{1}{2}$ ounce tincture of opium may be added to each dose of powders.

No. 431.

Drink for an Inflammatory Fever.

Take of tartar-emetic 1 drachm, prepared kali $\frac{1}{2}$ ounce, camphor 1 drachm, rubbed into powder, with a few drops spirits of wine.

This drink is excellent for all kinds of inflammatory fevers, especially such as are attended with imminent danger. It may be given every 4 hours, or 3 times a day, in a pint of water-gruel.

No. 432.

Purging-Ball for Jaundice.

Take of Barbadoes aloes from 4 to 5 drachms, white antimonial powder, and Castile soap, each 2 drachms, calomel 1 drachm. Mix, and beat them into a ball with a sufficient quantity of syrup of buckthorn.

The horse should have a couple of mashes the day before this ball is given, by way of preparation, and the ball should be given fasting the morning following; let him fast for 2 hours after, then give him a mash of scalded bran and oats, with warm water, and treat him in the same manner as for other physic.

No. 432½.

Hove or Hoven in Cattle.—Mr. Gowen's simple Remedy.

He says, Let a straw or hay rope, made of two strands of thumb rope laid or twisted together, be introduced between the jaws of the animal bridle-wise, drawing it back by both ends, and tying it tightly around the roots of the horns at the back of the head, till the jaws are fully opened and gagged. If this is done in the stall and the animal is able to stand or walk, it should be turned out at once and kept moving about, when in a few minutes the distension will subside and all will be well again.

No. 433.
Restorative Balls after Jaundice.

Take of gentian and caraway-seeds, in powder, each 8 ounces, powdered ginger, and precipitated sulphur of antimony, each 6 drachms, Castile soap, 1½ ounces, and honey sufficient to form into 6 balls.

One of these balls should be given every other day for some time.

No. 434.
Pectoral Balls for Broken Wind.

Take of Barbadoes tar, Venice turpentine, and Castile soap, each 2 ounces, squills in powder, 1 ounce; then add nitre 2 ounces, anise-seed and caraway-seeds, fresh powdered, each 1 ounce; beat them into a mass with honey and liquorice-powder, and divide into 10 balls.

No. 435.
Alterative Balls for Surfeit, Mange, &c.

Take of precipitated sulphur of antimony and gentian-root, and Socotrine aloes, each 1 ounce, in fine powder, nitre 2 ounces, calomel and cantharides, in powder, each 2 drachms. Mix, and make them into a mass of balls with honey or molasses. Each ball to weigh 1½ ounces.

This ball will be found very useful in many diseases, such as surfeit, hide-bound, mange, grease or swelled legs, lameness of the joints, molten grease, inflammation of the eyes, and, indeed, in all lingering and obstinate diseases. One ball may be given every other morning for 2 or 3 weeks.

No. 436.

Astringent Ball for Profuse Staling.

Take of galls and alum, in fine powder, each 2 drachms; Peruvian bark, ½ ounce. Make into a ball with honey or molasses.

It will be proper to repeat this ball every morning, and, if the disease is obstinate, every night and morning, and continue until the urine is diminished to about its natural quantity.

No. 437.

Restorative Balls for Profuse Staling.

Take of gentian-root, in powder, ½ ounce, ginger, powdered, 2 drachms, alum 1 drachm, molasses sufficient to make into a ball.

No. 438.

Mercurial Balls for Worms.

Take of calomel and Castile soap, each, 1 drachm, wormseed, in powder, ½ ounce. Beat them into a ball with syrup of buckthorn.

This ball should be given at night, and the following drink or purging-ball the next morning:—

No. 439.

Drink for Worms.

Take of Barbadoes aloes from 3 to 6 drachms, (according to their size and strength,) wormseed and gentian in powder, each, ½ ounce, caraway-seed, in powder, 1 ounce; mix, and give in a pint of strong decoction of wormwood, and repeat in about 4 or 5 days; but omit giving the mercurial ball after the first time.

No. 440.

Purging-Ball for Worms.

Take of Barbadoes aloes 8 drachms, ginger, Castile soap, and oil of savin, each, 2 drachms, syrup of buckthorn sufficient to make them into a ball.

This purge is calculated for a strong horse; but it may be made weaker by lessening the quantity of aloes to 6 or 7 drachms, which is in general sufficient after a mercurial ball. The horse should have mashes, warm water, and proper exercise.

No. 441.

Stomach-Drink after the Expulsion of the Worms.

Take of compound spirit of ammonia, and sweet spirits of nitre, each 1 ounce, gentian-root, in powder, 1½ ounces, Peruvian bark and hiera-picra, in powder, each, ½ ounce, horse-spice 2 ounces.

Mix the whole in 3 pints of ale, and divide into 3 parts, and give one part every morning, fasting.

Two hours after, give him a mash and warm water. The virtues of this drink deserve the highest recommendation in restoring horses which have been much reduced by some long-continued disease, as in lowness of spirits, debility, and relaxation of the solids, a loss of appetite, and for such also as are over-ridden either in the field or on the road.

No. 442.

Balls for the Staggers.

Take of James's powder 2 drachms, turmeric and cream of tartar, each, ½ ounce. Make them into a ball, with conserve of roses or honey a sufficient quantity.

No. 443.

Clyster for Convulsions.

Take of linseed and valerian-root, each, 4 ounces; boil them in 3 quarts of water to 4 pints; add Epsom salts 4 ounces, assafœtida ½ ounce, opium 2 drachms. Dissolve the whole in the above while hot, and apply it new-milk-warm.

This is a most powerful clyster in all disorders of the intestines that are attended with pain and convulsions or spasms in those parts, such as a violent attack of the colic proceeding from an obstruction of the urinary passage.

No. 444.

To cure Gripes in Horses.

This disorder goes by different names in different districts of the country; as fret,—from the uneasiness attending it; bots,—from its being thought to arise from these animals or worms, &c. The animal looks dull and rejects his food; becomes restless and uneasy, frequently pawing; voids his excrements in small quantities, and often tries to stale; looks round, as if toward his own flank or the seat of complaint; soon appears to get worse, often lying down, and sometimes suddenly rising up, or at times trying to roll, even in the stable, &c. As the disorder goes on, the pain becomes more violent; he appears more restless still, kicks at his belly, groans, rolls often, or tumbles about, with other marks of great agitation; becomes feverish, and has a cold moisture at the roots of his ears and about his flanks, and, when he lies at rest a little while, begins to perspire strongly, and to get covered with sweat more or less profuse.

In most cases of ordinary gripes, signs of flatulence, or of the presence of air confined in the bowels, occur, and constitute a part of the disease, or increase it. The removal of it is, therefore, an object to which the attention of most grooms has been in a chief degree directed; and as it can frequently be got rid of, and the disease cured, by exciting the powerful action of the intestines, cordial and stimulating medicines are had recourse to, and no doubt in many have afforded relief. Some farriers, indeed, without much care in distinguishing cases, almost exclusively rely upon such, and employ them too freely. This, however, should not be done; for it sometimes happens that disorders not unlike flatulent colic or gripes occur when there is neither pent-up air present, nor any relaxation or want of energy and action in the intestines themselves; and stimulating medicines might then do no good, but often much mischief.

When the disorder is early discovered, or has newly come on, it will be proper to lose no time to get ready a clyster, and likewise a medicinal draught for removing the wind and abating the pain. After removing with the hand any excrement in the great gut that can be reached by it, a clyster, made of 5 or 6 quarts of water or water-gruel, blood-warm, and 6 or 8 ounces of common salt, may be injected; and one or the other of the following draughts may be given before, or about the same time:—

No. 445.

Draught for the same. No. 2.

Take of Venice turpentine 1 ounce, beat it up with the yolk of an egg, and then add of peppermint-water, or even of common water, if the other is not at hand, 1½ pints and 2 ounces of whiskey or gin. This will serve for one dose.

Another.—Take of table-beer, a little warmed, 1½ pints, common pepper, or powdered ginger, 1 teaspoonful; gin, whiskey or rum, from 2 to 4 ounces or from 1 to 2 glassfuls: these mix together for one dose.

Another.—Oil of turpentine 1 ounce, and water-gruel 1½ pints, mixed, for a dose.

These and the like preparations may be given, either out of a bottle or drench-horn, one or two persons raising and keeping properly up the horse's head, while another, who administers the medicine, pulls out, and a little aside, the tongue, with his left hand, and with the other pours in the draught.

No. 446.

Further Treatment.

Cordial drenches of the kinds recommended, with the clyster, will have the effect, in ordinary cases, to relieve the disorder. But should this not be the case, after waiting an hour or two, (longer or shorter according to the severity of the ailment, or the period since its commencement,) then the medicine should be repeated, but in a less dose than at first,—perhaps one-half or two-thirds of the former quantity. The horse should be occasionally walked out, properly covered with cloths, lest the chill air bring on shivering and give rise to feverishness; and his belly should be now and then rubbed a considerable time at once, 5 or 10 minutes, but with intervals of rest, so that it may have time to stale or dung. If the disorder does not yield to these remedies, then others must be employed of a more active nature. Some persons recommend castor-oil, in the proportion of half a pint to a pint, with an ounce or two of laudanum or tincture of opium, mixed with water-gruel in the quantity of a pint or rather less. In case the horse has lain down, and continued so for some time, and is covered with sweat, when he rises, two or more persons should be employed to rub him dry; and he should also be kept well clothed. The stable should be airy, moderately cool, and his place in it roomy and well littered, to keep him from hurting himself should he roll about.

No. 447.

White's Ball for Gripes.

Draughts of liquid medicine operate more speedily than any other form; but, as the disorder may attack a horse during a journey, where such cannot readily be procured, Mr. White has given a receipt for a ball for the convenience of those who travel; and if it be wrapped up closely in a piece of bladder, it may be kept a considerable time without losing its power. The ball is composed of the following ingredients, viz.: Castile soap, 3 drachms; camphor, 2 drachms; ginger, 1½ drachms; and Venice turpentine, 6 drachms: to be made into a ball for one dose.

No. 448.

Laudanum Draught.

Laudanum may be used in cases of urgency, especially in the wet or lax gripes. Take a quart of beer, and make it a very little warmer than blood-heat; then put a tablespoonful of powdered ginger into it, and a small wineglassful of laudanum, just before it is given to the horse. This, in most cases, will give ease in a short time; but, if the complaint is exceedingly violent, give about half the above quantity again in 15 or 20 minutes. As soon as the pain seems to be abated, if the belly is costive, give the horse a purgative. In case of looseness, no purgative must be given: the laudanum, which is of a binding nature, will correct it.

When pain is occasioned by inflammation, it is seldom proper to employ opium, or any medicine of that kind; but when it depends upon spasm or irritation, no medicines are so beneficial. In inflammation of the bowels, for example, opium would certainly do much injury; but in flatulent or spasmodic colic, or gripes, it seldom fails of success.

No. 449.

Another Anodyne Medicine.

When horses are affected with colic, or where the use of anodynes is requisite, the following preparation may be given, namely: opium, 1 drachm, or 60 grains; Castile soap, 2 drachms; and powdered aniseseed, ½ ounce, or 4 drachms: to be made into a ball with syrup for one dose.

In speaking of the medicines for gripes, or the flatulent colic, sometimes termed fret, Mr. White mentions, "Domestic remedies may be employed when proper medicines cannot be procured in time. For this purpose a draught may be readily made up of a pint of strong peppermint-water, with about 4 ounces of gin, and any kind of spice."

Another.—A pint of Port wine, with spice or ginger.

Another.—Half a pint of gin diluted with 4 ounces water, and a little ginger.

Another.—Take of Epsom salts, 6 ounces; Castile soap, sliced, 2 ounces. Dissolve them in $1\frac{1}{2}$ pints warm gruel; then add tincture of opium, $\frac{1}{2}$ ounce; oil of juniper, 2 drachms. Mix, and give them new-milk-warm.

This drink may be repeated every 4 or 5 hours, till the symptoms begin to abate.

No. 450.

The same when on a Journey.

Take tincture of opium, and oil of juniper, each, 2 drachms; sweet spirits of nitre, tincture of benzoin, and aromatic spirit of ammonia, each $\frac{1}{2}$ ounce. Mix them together in a bottle for one drink, and give it in a pint of warm gruel.

For the colic, flatulency, and colicky pains of the intestines, this drink will be found a valuable cordial.

Another.—The complaint may be removed by warm beer and ginger, or a cordial ball mixed with warm beer.

It is necessary to repeat the caution given respecting the necessity of distinguishing the flatulent, or windy, or spasmodic colic, from the inflammatory one, and from that which depends on costiveness. It is always necessary to empty the bowels by means of clysters; and, should the horse have appeared dull and heavy previous to the attack, it will be advisable to bleed. If costiveness attends it, give a laxative drench after the paroxysm, which will prevent its return.

No. 451.

To cure Surfeit or bad Coat in Horses.

Take crocus metallorum, or liver of antimony, 1 ounce; sprinkle it with water, or mix it with moist bran. This may be given to horses subject to this disorder once a day, among their oats: it relieves the appetite, destroys worms, sweetens the blood, against all obstructions opens the passage, and improves tired and lean horses in a great degree; it is also of great service in coughs and shortness of breath. It may be given daily from 2 to 4 weeks, and will soon produce a fine coat. The horse may be worked while he is taking the medicine, care being taken not to expose him to wet or cold.

No. 452.

Urine-Balls for Horses.

Mix together 1 ounce oil of juniper, 1 ounce balsam of sulphur, 2 ounces Venice turpentine, 4 ounces sal-prunella, and 1 pound black rosin.

Melt all together gently, over a slow fire, in an

iron pot, and make up into balls of the size of a nutmeg.

Another.—Take nitre, 3 pounds; rosin, 3 pounds; soap, 1½ pounds; juniper-berries, 1 pound; oil of juniper, 1½ ounces.

To be made up into balls, of the common size, with spirits of turpentine.

No. 453.

Remedy for Lameness in Horses.

Mr. Sewell, of the Veterinary College, stated his having discovered a method of curing horses which are lame in the forefeet. It occurred to him that this lameness might originate in the nerves of the foot, near the hoof; and in consequence he immediately amputated about an inch of the diseased nerve,—taking the usual precaution of guarding the arteries and passing ligatures, &c. By this means the animal was instantly relieved from pain, and the lameness perfectly cured.

No. 454.

To Cure the Thrush in Horses' Feet.

Simmer over the fire, till it turns brown, equal parts of honey, vinegar, and verdigris, and apply it with a feather or brush occasionally to the feet. The horse at the same time should stand hard, and all soft dung and straw be removed.

No. 455.

Ointment for Mange.

Take common turpentine, 1 pound; quicksilver,

4 ounces; hog's lard, ½ pound; flour of sulphur, 4 ounces; train-oil, ½ pint.

Grind the quicksilver with the turpentine, in a marble mortar, for 5 or 6 hours, until it completely disappears; and add a little oil of turpentine to make it rub easier; then add the remainder, and work them all well together till united.

This ointment must be well rubbed on every part affected, in the open air, if the sun shine and the weather be warm; but, if it be winter, take the horse to a blacksmith's shop, where a large bar of iron must be heated, and held at a proper distance over him, to warm the ointment.

No. 456.

Liniment for the Mange.

Take white precipitate, 2 ounces; strong mercurial ointment, 2 ounces; sulphur of vivum, 1 pound; flour of sulphur, ½ pound; rape-oil, 2 quarts.

First grind the white precipitate in a little oil; afterwards add the remainder, taking care that they are well mixed.

This liniment must be well rubbed in with a hard brush, in the open air, provided the day be fine and the weather warm. If the horse draws in a team, the inside of the collar must be washed, or the inside of the saddle, if a saddle-horse; for the disease is highly contagious.

No. 457.

Eye-Water. No. 2.

Take camphor, 2 drachms, dissolved in 2 ounces

rectified spirits of wine; Gould's extract, 1 ounce; rose-water, 1 quart. Shake all together in a bottle for use.

Let the eye and the eyelids be well bathed 3 or 4 times a day with a clean linen rag dipped in the eye-water.

No. 458.

For Inflammation of the Lungs.

Take white antimonial powder, 2 drachms; prepared kali, ½ ounce; Castile soap, 2 drachms; aromatic confection, ½ ounce. Beat them into a ball.

This ball must be given to the horse as soon as it can be prepared, after he has been bled; and continue it 2 or 3 times a day as long as the inflammation continues. About six hours after, give him a purging drink, and repeat it every night and morning until a passage is obtained, or the bowels are sufficiently opened.

No. 459.

Embrocation for Sprains.

Take of soap-liniment and camphorated spirits of wine, of each 8 ounces, and oil of turpentine, ½ ounce. Mix, and shake when used.

This evaporating and discutient embrocation is well calculated to remove pain and inflammation, which is generally effected in the course of a fortnight or three weeks. During that time the horse should not be allowed to go out of the stable or farm-yard.

No. 460.

Bracing Mixture for Sprains.

After the above embrocation the following bracing mixture must be rubbed on the part once a day.

Take of Egyptiacum, 2 ounces; oil of turpentine, 1 ounce. Shake well together; then add camphorated spirits of wine and compound tincture of benzoin, each 1 ounce, and vinegar, 11 ounces. Mix, and shake well together every time it is used.

No. 461.

Paste to stop Bleeding.

Take of fresh nettles, 1 handful, and bruise them in a mortar. Add blue vitriol, in powder, 4 ounces; wheat flour, 2 ounces; wine vinegar, $\frac{1}{2}$ ounce; oil of vitriol, $\frac{1}{2}$ ounce. Beat them all together into a paste.

Let the wound be filled up with this paste, and a proper pledget of tow laid over the mouth, in order to prevent it from falling out, and then bandage it on with a strong roller. This dressing must remain on the wound 10 or 12 hours.

No. 462.

Ointment for Scratched Heels.

Take of hog's lard, 1 pound; white lead, 4 ounces; alum, in fine powder, 2 ounces; white vitriol, 1 ounce; sugar of lead, $\frac{1}{2}$ ounce; olive-oil, 3 ounces.

Grind all the powders in a marble mortar with the oil, or on a marble slab; then add the lard, and work the whole together till united.

This is a neat composition, and very proper to

keep in the stable during the winter. It will not only be found useful for greasy and scratched heels, but also for stubs and treads of every description. A small quantity must be rubbed on the part affected every night and morning, in slight cases; but in treads, or wounds upon the heels, it will be best to spread the ointment on pledgets of tow and secure them with bandages.

No. 463.

Astringent Embrocation for Strains in different parts.

Take of camphor, 2 drachms, dissolved in $\frac{1}{2}$ ounce strong rectified spirits of wine; nitre, 1 ounce, dissolved in $\frac{1}{2}$ pint wine vinegar; spirits of turpentine, 4 ounces; white lead, or Armenian bole, in powder, $\frac{1}{2}$ ounce; aqua-fortis, 1 ounce. Mix, and shake them all together in a bottle for use.

No. 464.

Mixture for Canker in the Mouth.

Take of wine vinegar, $\frac{1}{2}$ pint; burnt alum and common salt, each 1 ounce; Armenian bole, $\frac{1}{2}$ ounce. Mix, and shake them together in a bottle for use.

It will be proper to dress the horse's mouth with this mixture, every morning and evening, in the following manner:—

Take a small cane, or a piece of whalebone, half a yard long, and tie a linen rag, or a little tow, round one end; then dip it into the mixture, pass it up his mouth, and gently remove it to all the affected parts. Let him champ it well about in his mouth; after which let him fast an hour, then give food as usual.

No. 465.

Distemper among Cattle.

Examine your cow's mouth, though she appears very well; and if you find any pimple in it, or on the tongue, or if you perceive any within the skin ready to come out, immediately house her, keep her warm, and give her warm tar-water. To a large beast give 1 gallon; to a small one, 3 quarts. Give it four times every day, but not every time the quantity you first gave. Lessen the dose by degrees, but never give less than 2 quarts to a large beast, nor less than 3 pints to a small one; and house her every night for some time, and give her warm gruel and malt mash.

No. 466.

To make Tar-Water for Cows.

Take 1 quart tar, put to it 4 quarts water, and stir it very well 10 or 12 minutes; let it stand a little while, and then pour it off for use. You must not put water to the same tar more than twice. Let the first dose be made of fresh tar. Continue to give it till the beast is well. Don't let her go too soon abroad.

No. 467.

For the Garget in Cows.

This disorder is very frequent in cows after ceasing to be milked; it affects the glands of the udder with hard swellings, and often arises from the animal not being clean milked. It may be removed by anointing the part three times a day with a little ointment composed of camphor and blue ointment. Half a drachm or more of calomel may be given in warm beer, from a horn or bottle, for three or four mornings, if the disorder is violent.

No. 468.

To cure the Red Water in Cattle.

Take 1 ounce Armenian bole, ½ ounce dragon's blood, 2 ounces Castile soap, and 1 drachm rock-alum. Dissolve these in a quart of hot ale or beer, and let it stand until it is blood-warm. Give this as one dose, and, if it should have the desired effect, give the same quantity in about 12 hours after. This is an excellent medicine for changing the water, and acts as a purgative. Every farmer that keeps any number of cattle should always have doses of it by him.

No. 469.

To cure the Scouring in Cattle.

The following composition has been found to succeed in many cases which were apparently drawing to a fatal termination :—

Take of powdered rhubarb, 2 drachms; castor-oil, 1 ounce; kali, prepared, 1 teaspoonful.

Mix well together in a pint of warm milk. If the first dose does not answer, repeat it in 36 hours. If the calf will suck, it will be proper to allow him to do it.

No. 470.

Cure for Cattle Swelled with Green Food.

When any of your cattle happen to get swelled with an overfeed of clover, frosty turnips, or such like, instead of the usual method of stabbing in the side, apply a dose of train-oil, which, after repeated trials, has been found to prove successful. The quantity of oil must vary according to the age or size of the animal. For a grown-up beast, of an ordinary size, the quantity recommended is about an English pint, which must be administered to the animal with a bottle, taking care at the same time to rub the stomach well, in order to make it go down. After receiving this medicine, it must be made to walk about until such time as the swelling begins to subside.

No. 471.

To cure Measles in Swine.

It sometimes happens, though seldom, that swine have the measles. While they are in this state their flesh is very unwholesome food. This disorder is not easily discovered while the animal is alive, and can only be known by its not thriving or fattening as others. After the animal is killed and cut up, its fat is full of little kernels, about the size of the roe or eggs of a salmon. When this is the case, put into the food of each hog, once or twice a week, as much crude pounded antimony as will lie on a shilling. This is very proper for any feeding swine, even though they have no disorder. A small quantity of the flour of brimstone, also, may be given among their food when they are not thriving, which will be found of great service to them. But the best method of preventing disorders in swine is to keep their sties perfectly clean and dry, and allow them air, exercise, and plenty of clean straw.

No. 472.

Rupture in Swine.

Where a number of swine are bred, it will frequently happen that some of the pigs will have what is called a "rupture,"—*i.e.* a hole broken in the rim of the belly, where part of the guts comes out and lodges betwixt the rim of the belly and the skin, having an appearance similar to swelling in the testicles. The male pigs are more liable to this disorder than the females. It is cured by the following means:—

Geld the pig affected, and cause it to be held up with its head downward. Flay back the skin from the swollen place, and, from the situation in which the pig is held, the guts will naturally return to their proper place. Sew up the hole with a needle, which must have a square point, and also a bend in it, as the disease often happens between the hind-legs, where a straight needle cannot be used. After this is done, replace the skin that was flayed back, and sew it up, when the operation is finished. The pig should not have much food for a few days after the operation, until the wound begins to heal.

No. 473.

Cure for the Foot-Rot in Sheep. No. 1.

Take a piece of alum, a piece of green vitriol, and some white mercury,—the alum must be in the largest proportion; dissolve them in water, and after the hoof is pared anoint it with a feather, and bind on a rag over all the foot.

No. 474.

Another Cure for Foot-Rot in Sheep. No. 2.

Pound some green vitriol fine, and apply a little of it to the part of the foot affected, binding a rag over the foot, as above. Let the sheep be kept in the house a few hours after this is done, and then turn them out to a dry pasture. This is the most common way of curing the foot-rot.

No. 475.

Another Cure for Foot-Rot in Sheep. No. 3.

Some anoint the part with a feather dipped in aquafortis or weak nitrous acid, which dries it at once. Many drovers that take sheep to market carry a little bottle of this with them, which, by applying to the foot with a feather, helps a lame sheep by hardening its hoof, and enabling it to travel better. Some may think aqua-fortis of too hot a nature; but such a desperate disorder requires an active cure, which, no doubt, is always to be used cautiously.

Another.—Spread some slaked quick-lime over a house-floor pretty thick, pare the sheep's feet well, and then turn them into this house, where they may remain for a few hours; after which, turn them into a dry pasture. This treatment may be repeated 2 or 3 times, always observing to keep the house clean, and adding a little more quick-lime before putting them in.

The feet must be often dressed, and the sheep kept as much as possible on dry land. Those animals that are diseased should be kept separate from the flock, as the disorder is very infectious.

No. 476.

Prevention and Cure of the Foot-Rot in Sheep.

On suspected ground, constant and careful examination ought to take place; and when any fissures or cracks, attended with heat, make their appearance, apply oil of turpentine and common brandy. This in general produces a very beneficial effect; but where the disease has been long seated, and becomes in a manner confirmed, after cleaning the foot and paring away the infected parts, recourse is had to caustics, of which the best seems to be sulphuric acid and the nitrate of mercury. After this, pledgets are applied, the foot bound up, and the animal kept in a clean dry situation until its recovery is effected.

But it often happens, where the malady is inveterate, that the disease refuses to yield to any or all of the above prescriptions.

The following mode of treatment, however, if carefully attended to, may be depended upon as a certain cure. Whenever the disease makes its appearance, let the foot be carefully examined, and the diseased part well washed, and pared as nigh as possible not to make it bleed; and let the floor of the house where the sheep are confined be strewn 3 or 4 inches thick with quick-lime hot from the kiln; and the sheep, after having their feet dressed in the manner above described, to stand in it during the space of 6 or 7 hours.

In all cases, it is of great importance that the animal be afterwards exposed only to a moderate temperature, be invigorated with proper food, and kept in clean, easy, dry pasture; and the disease will be effectually remedied in the course of a few days.

No. 477.

To cure the Scab in Sheep.

Take 1 pound quicksilver, ½ pound Venice turpentine, 2 pounds hog's lard, and ½ pound oil or spirits of turpentine. A greater or less quantity than this may be mixed up, in the same proportion, according to the number of sheep affected. Put the quicksilver and Venice turpentine into a mortar or small pan, and beat together until not a particle of the quicksilver can be discerned; put in the oil, or spirits of turpentine, with the hog's lard, and work them well together until made into an ointment. The parts of the sheep affected must be rubbed with a piece of this salve, about the size of a nut, or rather less. When the whole flock is affected, the shepherd must be careful in noticing those that show any symptoms of the disorder, by looking back and offering to bite or scratch the spot; and if affected, he must immediately apply the ointment, as it is only by paying early and particular attention that a flock can be cured.

No. 478.

To destroy Maggots in Sheep.

Mix with 1 quart spring-water a tablespoonful spirits of turpentine, and as much of the sublimate powder as will lie upon a shilling. Shake them well together, and cork it up in a bottle, with a quill through the cork, so that the liquid may come out of the bottle in small quantities at once. The bottle must always be well shaken when it is to be used. When the spot is observed where the maggots are, do not disturb them, but pour a little of the mixture upon the spot, as much as will wet the wool and the maggots. In a few minutes after the liquor is applied, the maggots will all creep to the top of the wool, and in a short time drop off dead. The sheep must, however, be inspected next day, and if any of the maggots remain undestroyed, shake them off, or touch them with a little more of the mixture.

No. 479.

To cure Hoven or Blown in Cattle.

This complaint is in general occasioned by the animal feeding for a considerable time upon rich, succulent food, so that the stomach becomes overcharged, and they, through their greediness to eat, forget to lie down to ruminate or chew their cud. Thus the paunch, or first stomach, is rendered incapable of expelling its contents; a concoction and fermentation take place in the stomach, by which a large quantity of confined air is formed in the part that extends nearly to the anus, and, for want of vent at that part, causes the animal to swell even to a state of suffocation, or a rupture of some part of the stomach or intestines ensues. As sudden death is the consequence of this, the greatest caution is necessary in turning cattle into a fresh pasture, if the bite of grass be considerable; nor should they be suffered to stop too long at a time in such pasture before they are removed into a fold-yard, or some close where there is but little to eat, in order that the organs of rumination and digestion may have time to discharge their functions. If this be attended to several times, it will take away that greediness of disposition, and prevent this distressing complaint.

Treatment.—As soon as the beast is discovered to be either hoven or blown, by eating too great a quantity of succulent grasses, let a purging-drink be given: this will, for the most part, check fermentation in the stomach, and in a very short time force a passage through the intestines.

No. 480.

Purging-Drinks.

Take of Glauber's salts, 1 pound; ginger, in powder, 2 ounces; molasses, 4 ounces. Put all the ingredients into a pitcher, and pour 3 pints of boiling water upon them. When new-milk-warm, give the whole for one *dose*.

Another.—Take of Epsom salts, 1 pound; aniseseed and ginger, in powder, each, 2 ounces; molasses, 4 ounces. Let this be given in the same manner as the preceding.

In most cases these drinks will be sufficient to purge a full-grown animal of this kind. By strict attention to the above method of application, a fever may be prevented, and the animal speedily restored.

If the fever continues after the intestines have been evacuated, (which is seldom the case,) it will be proper to take some blood from the animal; and the quantity must be regulated according to the disease and habit of body.

No. 481.

To cure the Yellows, or Jaundice, in Neat Cattle.

As soon as this disease makes its first appearance, it may, for the most part, be removed by administering the following drinks.

Reduce to powder cumin-seeds, anise-seed, and turmeric-root, each, 2 ounces; grains of paradise and salt of tartar, each, 1 ounce.

Now slice 1 ounce Castile soap, and mix it with 2 ounces molasses; put the whole into a pitcher; then pour a quart of boiling ale upon the ingredients, and cover them down till new-milk-warm; then give the drink. It will often be proper to repeat this 2 or 3 times every other day, or oftener, if required. If the beast be in good condition, take away from 2 to 3 quarts of blood; but the animal should not be turned out after bleeding that day, not at night, but the morning following it may go to its pasture as usual. After this has had the desired effect, let the following be given.

Take of balsam copaiva, 1 ounce; salt of tartar, 1 ounce; Castile soap, 2 ounces. Beat them together in a marble mortar; and add valerian-root, in powder, 2 ounces; ginger-root and Peruvian bark, in powder, each, 1 ounce; molasses, 2 ounces. Mix, for 1 drink. Let this drink be given in a quart of warm gruel, and repeated, if necessary, every other day. It will be proper to keep the body sufficiently open through every stage of the disease; for, if costiveness be permitted, the fever will increase; and, if not timely removed, the disorder will terminate fatally.

No. 482.

Frenzy, or Inflammation of the Brain,

Is sometimes occasioned by wounds or contusions in the head, that are attended with violent inflammations of the vessels, and, if not speedily relieved, may terminate in a gangrene or a mortification, which is very often the case, and that in a few days.

No. 483.

Method of Cure.

In the cure of this disease, the following method must be attended to. First, lessen the quantity of blood by frequent bleeding, which may be repeated daily, if required, and by which the great efflux of blood upon the temporal arteries will be lessened and much retarded. The following purgative drink will be found suitable for this disease, and likewise for most fevers of an inflammatory nature.

Take of Glauber's salts, 1 pound; tartarized antimony, 1 drachm; camphor, 2 drachms; molasses, 4 ounces.

Mix, and put the whole into a pitcher, and pour 3 pints of boiling water upon them. When new-milk-warm, add laudanum, ½ ounce, and give it all for one dose. This drink will in general operate briskly in the space of 20 or 30 hours; if not, let one-half of the quantity be given to the beast every night and morning, until the desired effect be obtained.

No. 484.
Paunching.

This is a method frequently resorted to in dangerous cases. The operation is performed in the following manner:—

Take a sharp penknife and gently introduce it into the paunch between the haunch-bone and the last rib on the left side. This will instantly give vent to a large quantity of fetid air; a small tube of a sufficient length may then be introduced into the wound, and remain until the air is sufficiently evacuated; afterward take out the tube and lay a pitch-plaster over the orifice. Wounds of this kind are seldom attended with danger; where it has arisen, it has been occasioned by the injudicious operator introducing his knife into a wrong part. After the wind is expelled and the body has been reduced to its natural state, give the following:—

Cordial Drink.—Take anise-seed, diapente, and elecampane, in powder, each 2 ounces; tincture of rhubarb, 2 ounces; sweet spirits of nitre, 1 ounce; treacle, 4 tablespoonfuls. Mix, and give it in a quart of warm ale or gruel. This drink may be repeated every other day for two or three times.

Another.—Take anise-seed, grains of paradise, and cumin-seed, each 2 ounces, in powder; spirits of turpentine, 2 tablespoonfuls; sweet spirits of nitre, 1 ounce; treacle, 2 tablespoonfuls. Mix, and give them in a quart of warm ale or gruel. This may be repeated once a day for two or three times.

No. 485.

Cure for Sore Backs of Horses.

The best method of curing sore backs is to dissolve half an ounce of blue vitriol in a pint of water, and daub the injured parts with it four or five times a day.

No. 486.

An Infallible Lotion for Blows, Bruises, and Sprains in Horses.

Take of spirits of wine, 8 ounces; dissolve 1 ounce of camphor first in the spirits of wine; then add 1 ounce oil of turpentine, 1 ounce spirit of sal-ammoniac, ½ ounce oil of origanum, and 1 large tablespoonful of liquid laudanum. It must be well rubbed in with the hand, for full a quarter of an hour, every time it is used, which must be four times a day. You will be astonished at its efficacy when you try it.

No. 487.

To make a Horse drink freely.

A horse has a very sweet tooth when he is unwell and will not drink freely. Mix molasses and coarse brown sugar in the water: he will then drink freely.

No. 488.

How to construct a Battery for Gilding and Silver-Plating.

1st. Make five copper cylinders or cups, 4 inches in diameter and 4 inches high, with copper sockets soldered to the top, to receive the conducting-wires.

2d. Construct 5 sheepskin cups, of the same height as the copper ones and 3¼ inches in diameter. Set them inside the copper cups.

3d. Make 5 zinc cylinders, 4½ inches high and 2½ inches in diameter, open at each end, and place them inside the sheepskin cups, with copper sockets attached to them, as with the copper cups.

4th. After placing the cups thus formed in a convenient position, connect them together with copper wires, as follows:—The first copper cylinder with the second zinc; the second copper with the third zinc; the third copper with the fourth zinc; and the fourth copper with the fifth zinc; observing always to connect the copper with the zinc.

How to charge the Battery.—Fill the cups within about half an inch of the top with water; then put 1 teaspoonful of Glauber's salts into each of the sheepskin cups, between the zinc and sheepskin; then put 1 teaspoonful of blue vitriol into each of the copper cups, which, when dissolved, will charge the battery for some days. Introduce the conducting-wires, and it is ready for action.

To prepare the Gold Solution.—Dissolve the gold in two parts of muriatic acid with one of nitric acid. Then evaporate it to dryness, and redissolve the powder in the proportion of 1 gill of pure water to 1 pennyweight of gold. Boil it a few minutes, and then add ½ ounce prussiate of potash: boil it 5 or 10 minutes. Let it cool and settle; then pour it off, and it is ready for use.

N.B.—Dissolve silver in nitric acid, and pursue the same process as with the gold. Prepare a solution by dissolving 1 ounce prussiate of potash in 1 quart water. Put a sufficient quantity of it in a bowl or other earthen vessel, and add to it the gold solution. Bend the conducting wires so that the two poles will be immersed in the solution. Attach a small piece of gold or platina to the positive pole or conducting-wire which is attached to the copper cups, and place the pieces to be gilted on the negative or the one proceeding from the zinc cup.

No. 489.
Galvanism Simplified.—Silver-Plating Fluid.

Dissolve 1 ounce nitrate of silver, in crystal, in 12 ounces soft water. Then dissolve in the water 2 ounces cyanuret of potash. Shake the whole together, and let it stand till it becomes clear. Have ready some half-ounce vials, and fill them half full of Paris white, or fine whiting; then fill up the bottles with the liquid, and it is ready for use. The whiting does not increase the coating-powder; it only helps to clean the articles, and to save the silver-fluid by the bottles.

No. 490.
Silver Solution for Plating Copper, Brass, and German Silver.

Cut into small pieces a twenty-five-cent-piece, and put it into an earthen vessel with ½ ounce of nitric acid. Put the vessel into warm water, uncovered, until it dissolves. Add ½ gill of water and 1 teaspoonful of fine salt: let it settle. Drain off and repeat, adding water to the sediment until the acid taste is all out of the water. Add, finally, about a pint of water to the sediment and 4 scruples cyanide of potassa, and all is ready. Put in bottom of solution a piece of zinc about 2 inches long, 1 wide, and $\frac{1}{8}$ in thickness. After cleaning, immerse the article to be plated in the solution about half a minute, letting it rest on the zinc. Wipe off with a dry cloth and repeat once. Polish with buckskin. Thickness of plate can be increased by repeating.

No. 491.
Gilding the Edges of Paper.

The edges of the leaves of books and letter-paper are gilded while in a horizontal position in the bookbinder's press, by first applying a composition formed of four parts of Armenian bole and one of candied sugar, ground together with water to a proper consistence, and laid on by a brush with the white of an egg. This coating, when nearly dry, is smoothed by the burnisher. It is then slightly moistened by a sponge dipped in clean water and squeezed in the hand. The gold-leaf is now taken up on a piece of cotton from the leather cushion and applied on the moistened surface. When dry, it is to be burnished, by rubbing the burnisher over it repeatedly from end to end, taking care not to wound the surface by the point.

No. 492.
To Silver by Heat.

Dissolve 1 ounce pure silver in aqua-fortis, and precipitate it with common salt; to which add $\frac{1}{2}$ pound sal-ammoniac, sandever, and white vitriol, and $\frac{1}{4}$ ounce sublimate.

Or dissolve 1 ounce pure silver in aqua-fortis and precipitate it with common salt; and add, after washing, 6 ounces common salt, 3 ounces each of sandever and white vitriol, and ¼ ounce of sublimate. These are to be ground into a paste, upon a fine stone, with a muller. The substance to be silvered must be rubbed over with a sufficient quantity of the paste and exposed to a proper degree of heat. When the silver runs, it is taken from the fire and dipped into weak spirits of salts, to clean it.

No. 493.
A method of Washing occupying one hour.

Have a preparation made from 2 tablespoonfuls alcohol, 2 tablespoonfuls turpentine, ½ pound brown soap, cut fine and mixed in 1 quart hot water. Pour the same into a large tub of boiling water, and allow the clothes to soak for 20 minutes. Then take them out and put them in a tub of clean cold water for 20 minutes. Afterward boil them in a like quantity of the above preparation for 20 minutes, and rinse in cold water.

N.B.—In using the above method of washing, all fine clothes should be gone through with first, as coloured, very dirty, or greasy clothes ought not to be boiled with those of finer fabric and containing less dirt, as the water in which they are boiled must of course partake more or less of its contents. The same water that has been used for the finer clothes will likewise do for the coarse and coloured. Should the wristbands of the shirts be very dirty, a little soap may be previously rubbed on.

The above is a very excellent receipt, and may be confided in as particularly effective in labour-saving.

No. 494.

Another Washing-Receipt.

Take 1 pint alcohol, 1 pint spirits of turpentine, and 2 quarts strong soda-water. Manage the clothes as above directed.

Another very good Receipt.—Take 1 pound hard soap, (for 4 dozen clothes,) 7 teaspoonfuls spirits of turpentine, 5 teaspoonfuls hartshorn, and 5 teaspoonfuls vinegar.

Directions.—Dissolve the soap in hot water; mix the ingredients. Then divide the mixture in two parts; put half in the water with the clothes overnight; next morning wring them out. Put them to boil in 5 or 6 gallons of water, and add the rest of the mixture; boil 30 minutes, and rinse out thoroughly in cold water; blue them, and hang out to dry.

This receipt has been found to answer a very valuable purpose, and is worthy of trial.

No. 495.

How to cure the Lockjaw.

The "New York Observer" says:—A young lady ran a rusty nail into her foot recently. The injury produced lockjaw of such a malignant character that her physicians pronounced her recovery hopeless. An old nurse took her in hand, and applied pounded beet-roots to her foot, removing them as often as they became dry. The result was a most complete and astounding cure. Such a simple remedy should be borne in mind.

No. 496.

A Remedy for Rheumatism, &c.   No. 4.

Take 1 raw egg well beaten, ½ pint vinegar, 1 ounce spirits of turpentine, ¼ ounce camphor. These ingredients to be beaten well together, then put in a bottle and shaken for 10 minutes, after which, to be corked down tightly to exclude the air. In half an hour it is fit for use.

Directions.—To be well rubbed in, 2, 3, or 4 times a day. For rheumatism in the head, to be rubbed at the back of the neck and behind the ears.

No. 497.

Cure for Rheumatic Gout.   No. 1.

Take ½ ounce nitre, ½ ounce sulphur, ½ ounce flour of mustard, ½ ounce Turkey rhubarb, and 2 drachms powdered gum guaiacum. Mix. A teaspoonful to be taken every other night for three nights, and omit three nights, in a wineglassful of cold water,—water which has been well boiled.

No. 498.

Ointment for Piles.   No. 2.

Take of hog's lard, 4 ounces; camphor, 2 drachms; powdered galls, 1 ounce; laudanum, ½ ounce. Mix, and make an ointment. To be applied every night, at bedtime.

No. 499.

How to make Tomato Catsup.   No. 1.

Take 1 bushel tomatoes, and boil them until they

are soft; squeeze them through a fine wire sieve, and add ½ gallon vinegar, 1½ pints salt, 2 ounces cloves, ¼ pound allspice, 3 ounces cayenne pepper, 3 tablespoonfuls black pepper, and 5 heads garlic, skinned and separated. Mix together, and boil about 3 hours, or until reduced to about one-half; then bottle without straining.

No. 500.

How to preserve Fruit.

A number of persons who have been putting up fruit in "air-tight cans" have stated to us that they are losing large quantities of it by fermentation, and inquire of us the cause of the difficulty. This we cannot easily explain without first seeing the cans. The cause may be in the imperfect manner of scalding and putting up the fruit; or it may arise from the defective form in which the cans are made.

If the cans are properly constructed, it only remains to scald the fruit sufficiently, and to fill the cans so near the top as to leave the least possible amount of air in them, taking care that the moisture does not rise into the channel formed for the sealing-material, and to close the cans while scalding hot. To do this, as we before stated, the most expeditious and sure method is to first scald the fruit in a kettle, fill the cans, and set them into a vessel of boiling water, there to remain until the sealing is completed.—*Louisville Journal.*

No. 501.

Another method of preserving Fruits and Vegetables.

A great deal of mystery has been made of this simple matter, and it is generally supposed that the process is known only to the initiated.

With a good air-tight can, the simple agent in the work is heat; and it is only necessary to know what degree of heat is required, and how to apply it. The common mode is to fill the can with the fruit, and set it in a vessel of boiling water, letting it remain until the fruit is thoroughly heated through, —say from a half to three-quarters of an hour, and then seal up. This mode is objectionable, on account of the time required and shrinkage of the fruit, leaving the can but about two-thirds full, by which the use of one-third (or four cans of every dozen) is lost.

The most convenient, certain, and expeditious method is to prepare fruit, either with or without sugar, as if for immediate use, put it in a preserving-kettle or open vessel, (with a small quantity of water when necessary to prevent scorching,) and let it remain over the fire until it comes to the boiling-point; then fill the can, and seal it up immediately.

Direction for sealing.—Fill one can at a time with the boiling fruit, put on the cap, press it to its place, until you fill the groove around it with the melted composition; pour a little cold water on the top of the can to chill the wax; then set the can in cold water, and let it remain until cool: when taken out, hold it to the ear, and, if there be any imperfection in the can, the air will be heard forcing itself in.

No. 502.

Another way to make Tomato Catsup. No. 2.

To ½ bushel skinned tomatoes, add 1 quart good vinegar, 1 pound salt, ¼ pound black pepper, 2 ounces African cayenne, ¼ pound allspice, 6 onions, 1 ounce cloves, and 2 pounds brown sugar. Boil this mass for 3 hours, constantly stirring, it to keep it from burning. When cool, strain it through a fine sieve or coarse cloth, and bottle it for use. Many persons omit the vinegar in this preparation.

No. 503.

How to make Cucumber Catsup.

Take 3 dozens full-grown cucumbers and 8 white onions. Peel the onions and cucumbers, and then chop them as fine as possible. Sprinkle on ¾ pint fine salt; put the whole in a sieve, and let it drain 12 hours; then take a teacupful of mustard-seed, ½ teacupful ground black pepper, and mix them well with the cucumbers and onions. Put the whole into a stone jar with the strongest vinegar; close it up tightly for 3 days, and it is fit for use. It will keep for years.

No. 504.

How to destroy a Foul Smell.

Dissolve 1 pound copperas (green) in 1 quart water, and pour down a privy, will effectually concentrate and destroy the foulest smells. For water-closets aboard ships and steamboats, about hotels and other public places, there is nothing so nice to cleanse places as simple green copperas dissolved, under the bed, in any thing that will hold water, and thus render a hospital, or other places for the sick, free from unpleasant smells. For butchers' stalls, fish-markets, slaughter-houses, sinks, and wherever there are offensive putrid gases, dissolve copperas and sprinkle it about, and in a few days the smell will pass away. If a cat, rat, or mouse dies about the house, and sends forth an offensive gas, place some dissolved copperas in an open vessel near the place where the nuisance is, and it will soon purify the atmosphere.

No. 505.

Directions for making good Candles from Lard.

For 12 pounds lard, take 1 pound saltpetre, and 1 pound alum; mix and pulverize them; dissolve the saltpetre and alum in a gill of boiling water; pour the compound into the lard before it is quite all melted; stir the whole until it boils; skim off what rises; let it simmer until the water is boiled out, or until it ceases to throw off steam; pour off the lard as soon as it is done, and clean the boiler while it is hot. If the candles are to be run, you may commence immediately; if to be dipped, let the lard cool to a cake, and then treat it as you would tallow.

No. 506.

How to make a Cement which will get, gradually, as hard as a stone.

Take 20 parts by weight clean sharp sand, 2 parts litharge, and 1 part whiting; mix, and make them into thin putty with linseed-oil. For seams in roofs, a cement may be made of white or red lead, thinned with boiling linseed-oil, into which some sharp, dry white sand is stirred. For the joints of water and gas pipes, white lead cement is the best.

No. 507.
Liquid Cement.

Cut gum-shel-lac in 70 per cent. alcohol; put it in vials, and it is ready for use. Apply it to the edge of the broken dish with a feather, and hold it in a spirit-lamp as long as the cement will simmer; then join together evenly, and, when cold, the dish will break in another place first, and is as strong as new.

No. 508.
Crockery Cement which is transparent.

Take 1 pound white shel-lac, pulverized, 2 ounces clean gum mastic; put them into a bottle, and then add ½ pound pure sulphuric ether. Let it stand half an hour, and then add ½ gallon 90 per cent. alcohol: shake occasionally till it is dissolved. Heat the edges of the article to be mended, and apply the cement with a pencil brush; hold the article firmly together till the cement cools.

No. 509.
Hard Cement for Seams.

Take equal quantities of white lead and white sand, and as much oil as will make it into the consistence of putty. Apply this to the seams in the roofs of houses, &c. It will in a few weeks become as hard as a stone.

No. 510.

Water-Proof and Fire-Proof Cement for Roofs of Houses.

Slake stone-lime in a large tub or barrel with boiling water, covering the tub or barrel to keep in the steam. When thus slaked, pass 6 quarts through a fine sieve: it will then be in a state of fine flour. To this add 1 quart rock-salt, and 1 gallon water. Boil the mixture, add 1 pound alum and ½ pound copperas; by slow degrees add ¾ pound potash, and 4 quarts fine sand or wood-ashes, sifted. Both of the above will admit of any colouring you please. It looks better than paint, and is as durable as slate.

No. 511.

To cure Rancid Butter.

A writer in the "Journal of Industrial Progress" recommends that butter should be kneaded with fresh milk, and then with pure water. He states that by this treatment the butter is rendered as fresh and pure in flavour as when recently made. He ascribes this result to the fact that butyric acid, to which the rancid taste and odour are owing, is readily soluble in fresh milk, and thus removed.

No. 512.

How to improve bad Butter.

Bad butter may be improved greatly by dissolving it thoroughly in hot water; let it cool, then skim it off, and churn again, adding a little salt and sugar. A small quantity can be tried and approved before doing a larger one. The water should be merely hot enough to melt the butter—or it will become oily.

No. 513.

How to cure Butter that will keep for Years.

Take 2 parts good common salt, 1 part sugar, and 1 part saltpetre; beat them up and blend the whole together. Take 1 ounce of this composition for every pound of butter; work it well into the mass, and close it up for use. Butter cured in this way appears of a rich, marrowy consistence and fine colour, and never acquires a brittle hardness nor tastes salt. It will likewise keep good 3 years,—only observing that it must stand 3 weeks or a month before it is used. It ought to be packed in wooden vessels, or in jars vitrified throughout, which do not require glazing, because during the decomposition of the salts they corrode the glazing, and the butter becomes rancid.

No. 514.

How to preserve Eggs. No. 1.

Apply with a brush a solution of gum-arabic to the shells, or immerse the eggs therein; let them dry, and afterward pack them in dry charcoal-dust. This prevents their being affected by any alternations of temperature.

No. 515.

Another method to preserve Eggs.   No. 2.

Mix together, in a tub or vessel, 1 bushel quick-lime, 2 pounds salt, ½ pound cream of tartar, with as much water as will reduce the composition to a sufficient consistence to float an egg. Then put and keep the eggs therein,—which will preserve them perfectly sound for 2 years at least.

No. 516.

Another method to preserve Eggs.   No. 3.

Take a half-inch board of any convenient length or breadth, and pierce it as full of holes (each 1½ inches in diameter) as you can, without risking the breaking of one hole into another. Then take 4 strips of the same board, 2 inches broad, and nail them together edgewise into a rectangular frame of the same size as your board; nail the board upon the frame, and the work is done. Put your eggs in this board as they come in from the poultry-house, the small end down, and they will keep good for 6 months, if you take the following precautions:— Take care that the eggs do not get wet, either in the nest or afterward. If 2 boards are kept, one can be filling and the other emptying at the same time.

No. 517.

A Pickle to cure Hams, Pork, and Beef.

To each gallon of water add 1½ pounds salt, ½ pound sugar, ½ ounce saltpetre; boil all together and skim it off, then rub the meat with salt, and pack it down; pour on your pickle when milk-warm.

No. 518.

T. E. Hamilton's Receipt for Pickling Meat or Hams.

To every 100 pounds of pork take 8 pounds ground alum-salt, 2 ounces saltpetre, 2 pounds brown sugar, 1½ ounces potash, and 4 gallons water. Mix them all together, and pour the brine over the meat after it has lain in the tub some 2 days. Let the hams remain 6 weeks in the brine, and then be dried several days before smoking. He says he has had the meat rubbed with fine salt when it is packed down. The meat should be perfectly cool before packing.

No. 519.

How to cure Pork and Hams dry without Brine.

First rub your hams and pork on the flesh-side with brown sugar thoroughly, and take care that as much sugar will lie on it as you possibly can. Having it covered all over, (from 1 to 2 pounds of sugar to each hog is sufficient,) you can either lay the meat on a table or any kind of vessel that will not hold any pickle; then, when you have one layer laid, cover it all over with fine salt, (of course, the flesh-side,) and squeeze it on with your hand as tight as you can, and so on with each layer. Then leave it so for 8 or 10 days. By this time the salt will nearly all be dissolved, when you have to take it out and pack it again, and cover it all over with fine salt the same as at first. Then let it stand for 3 or 4 weeks longer, according to the size of the hogs, then hang it in smoke. This method is excellent for dried beef.

No. 520.

Blackberry Jam.

Gather the fruit in dry weather; allow half a pound of good brown sugar to every pound of fruit; boil the whole together gently for an hour, or till the blackberries are soft, stirring and mashing them well. Preserve it like any other jam. It will be found very useful in families, particularly for children, regulating their bowels, and enabling you to dispense with cathartics. It may be spread on bread or on puddings, instead of butter; and, even when the blackberries are bought, it is cheaper than butter.

No. 521.

Blackberry Wine.

Gather when ripe, on a dry day. Put into a vessel with the head out, and a tap fitted near the bottom; pour on them boiling water to cover them. Mash the berries with your hands, and let them stand covered till the pulp rises to the top and forms a crust, in 3 or 4 days. Then draw off the fluid into another vessel, and to every gallon add 1 pound sugar; mix well, and put into a cask to work, for 1 week or 10 days, and throw off any remaining lees, keeping the cask well filled, particularly at the commencement. When the working has ceased, bung it down. After 6 to 12 months, it may be bottled.

No. 522.

Green-Corn Omelet.

The following receipt for this delicacy is said to

be excellent:—Grate the corn from 12 ears of corn boiled, beat up 5 eggs, stir them with the corn, season with pepper and salt, and fry the mixture brown, browning the top with a hot shovel. If fried in small cakes, with a little flour and milk stirred in for a batter, it is very nice.

No. 523.

How to keep fresh Fish.

In order to keep fresh fish, draw the fish and remove the gills; then insert a piece of charcoal in their mouths, and 2 or 3 pieces in their bellies. If they are to be conveyed any distance, wrap each fish separately in paper and place them in a box. Fish thus preserved will keep fresh several days.

No. 524.

To varnish Articles of Iron and Steel.

Dissolve 10 parts clear grains of mastic, 5 parts camphor, 15 grains sandarac, and 5 parts elemi, in a sufficient quantity of alcohol, and apply this varnish without heat. The articles will not only be preserved from rust, but the varnish will retain its transparency, and the metallic brilliancy of the articles will not be impaired.

No. 525.

A Turkish Cure for the Gravel.

Take equal parts of small pebble-stones, pulverized very fine, nettle-seed, and honey; mix them well together. *Dose.*—1 teaspoonful morning and evening.

No. 526.
A Cure for Dysentery. No. 2.

Take 1 tablespoonful common salt, mix it with 2 tablespoonfuls of vinegar, and pour upon it a half-pint of water, either hot or cold, (only let it be taken cold.) A wineglassfull of this mixture in the above proportions, taken every half-hour, will be found quite efficacious in curing dysentery. If the stomach be nauseated, a wineglassful taken every hour will suffice. For children, the quantity should be a teaspoonful of salt and one of vinegar, in a teacupful of water.

No. 527.
Another for Dysentery. No. 3.

Take new-churned butter, before it is washed or salted, clarify over the fire and skim off all the milky particles, add brandy to preserve it, and loaf sugar to sweeten: let the patient (an adult) take 2 tablespoonfuls twice a day.

No. 528.
A Cure for Dysentery and Bloody Flux.

Take 2 tablespoonfuls elixir salutis, 1 tablespoonful castor-oil, and 1 tablespoonful loaf sugar; add to these 4 tablespoonfuls boiling water. Skim, and drink hot.

The above is a dose for an adult; for a child 6 to 7 years old, half the quantity; 1 year old, one-quarter the quantity. When this is manufactured for sale, the water is added when used.

No. 529.

A Cure for Rheumatic Gout or Acute Rheumatism. No. 2.

Take ½ ounce saltpetre, ½ ounce sulphur, ½ ounce flour of mustard, ½ ounce Turkey rhubarb, and ¼ ounce powdered gum guaiacum. Mix. A teaspoonful to be taken every other night for three nights, and omit three nights, in a wineglassful of cold water,—water which has been well boiled.

No. 530.

Ointment for Piles. No. 3.

Take of hog's lard, 4 ounces; camphor, 2 drachms; powdered galls, 1 ounce; laudanum, ½ ounce. Mix. Make an ointment, to be applied every night at bedtime.

No. 531.

Ointment for Sore Nipples.

Take of tincture of Tolu, 2 drachms; spermaceti-ointment, ½ ounce; powdered gum, 2 drachms. Mix. Make an ointment.

The white of an egg mixed with brandy is the best application for sore nipples. The person should at the same time use a nipple-shield.

No. 532.
Another Cure for Piles.

Take flour of sulphur, 1 ounce; rosin, 3 ounces; pulverize, and mix well together. *Dose.*—What will lie on a five-cent-piece, night and morning, washing the parts freely in cold water once or twice a day. This is a remedy of great value.

No. 533.
A Cure for Smallpox.

Take 1 grain each of powdered foxglove (digitalis) and sulphate of zinc. Rub together thoroughly in a mortar with 5 or 6 drops of water; this done, add 4 or 5 ounces of water, and sweeten with loaf sugar. *Dose.*—A tablespoonful for an adult, and 1 or 2 teaspoonfuls for a child, every 2 or 3 hours, until symptoms of disease vanish.

No. 534.
A sure Remedy for Inflammatory Rheumatism.

Take 1 ounce pulverized saltpetre and put it into a pint of sweet oil. Bathe the parts affected, and a sound cure will speedily be made.

No. 535.
A certain Cure for Corns.

One teaspoonful tar, 1 teaspoonful coarse brown sugar, and 1 teaspoonful saltpetre; the whole to be warmed together. Spread it on kip leather the size of the corns, and in two days they will be drawn out.

No. 536.
Bedbug-Poison.

Take 1 pint spirits of wine, 2 ounces sal-ammoniac, 1 pint spirits of turpentine, 2 ounces corrosive sublimate, and 2 ounces gum camphor; dissolve the camphor in the alcohol; then pulverize the corrosive sublimate and sal-ammoniac, and add to it; after which put in the spirits of turpentine and shake well together.

No. 537.
Cologne.

Take 1 gallon spirits of wine, and add of the oil of lemon, orange, and bergamot each a spoonful; add also extract of vanilla, 40 drops. Shake until the oils are cut, then add a pint and a half of soft water.

No. 538.
To prevent Hair falling off.

Take ½ pint French brandy, 1 tablespoonful fine salt, and 1 teaspoonful powdered alum. Let these be mixed and well shaken until they are dissolved; then filter, and it is ready for use. If used every day, it may be diluted with soft water.

No. 539.
How to make Extract of Vanilla.

This is made by taking 1 quart pure French brandy, and cutting up fine 1 ounce vanilla beans and 2 ounces Tonqua, bruised. Add these to the brandy, and let it digest for two weeks, frequently shaking; then filter carefully, and it is ready for use. This is excellent for flavouring pies, cakes, and puddings.

No. 540.
How to make Burning-Fluid.

Take 8 gallons 95 per cent. alcohol, and add 2 gallons camphene, 10 grains camphor, and 10 to 15 grains nitre.

No. 541.
A superior article of Cologne.

Take 1 gallon 90 per cent. alcohol, and add to it 1 ounce oil of bergamot, 1 ounce oil of orange, 2 drachms oil of cedrat, 1 drachm oil of Nevoli, and 1 drachm oil of rosemary. Mix well, and it is fit for use.

No. 542.
Ox-Marrow Pomatum.

Take 2 ounces yellow wax and 12 ounces beef-marrow. Melt all together, and, when sufficiently cool, perfume it with the essential oil of almonds. This is an excellent article.

No. 543.
Hair-Restorative.

Take 1 drachm lac-sulphur, 1 drachm sugar of lead, and 4 ounces rose-water. Mix, and shake the vial on using the mixture. Bathe the hair twice a day for a week. This preparation does not dye the hair, but restores its original colour.

No. 544.

A Cure for Salt Rheum or Scurvy.

Take of the pokeweed, any time in summer; pound it, press out the juice, and strain it into a pewter dish. Set it in the sun till it becomes a salve, then put it into an earthen mug. Add to it fresh water and beeswax sufficient to make an ointment of common consistence. Simmer the whole over a fire till thoroughly mixed. When cold, rub the parts affected. The patient will almost immediately experience its good effects, and the most obstinate cases will be cured in three or four months.

N.B.—The juice of the ripe berries may be prepared in the same way.

No. 545.

Cough-Syrup.

Put 1 quart of hoarhound to 1 quart of water, and boil it down to a pint; add 2 or 3 sticks of liquorice and a tablespoonful of essence of lemon.

Dose.—Take a tablespoonful of the syrup three times a day, or as often as the cough may be troublesome.

No. 546.

Toothache-Drops.

Two or three drops of essential oil of cloves, put upon a small piece of lint or cotton-wool and placed in the hollow of the tooth, will be found to have the active power of curing the toothache without destroying the tooth or injuring the gums.

No. 547.
Freckle-Lotion.

Take muriate of ammonia, ½ drachm; lavender-water, 2 drachms; distilled water, ½ pint. Applied with a sponge 2 or 3 times a day.

No. 548.
Tooth-Powder.

Take rose-pink, 2 drachms; precipitated chalk, 12 drachms; carbonate of magnesia, 1 drachm; sulphate of quinine, 6 grains. All to be mixed together.

No. 549.
A certain Cure for the Piles.

Mix 1 ounce ung. gallac, 3 drachms powdered gallac, 1 drachm laudanum, and ½ drachm extract of lead. To be used externally, night and morning.

Then mix 2 ounces confection of senna and 20 grains powdered saltpetre. To be used internally.

Dose.—The size of a hazel-nut to the size of a hickory-nut.

No. 550.
Cough-Drops. No. 2.

Mix 2 ounces syrup of squill, 2 ounces paregoric, ¼ ounce antimonial wine, ½ ounce spirits of nitre, and 1 ounce tinct. benzoin comp. Shake well when two ingredients are in.

Dose.—A teaspoonful an hour before each meal, and 2 teaspoonfuls at going to bed.

No. 551.
How to cure Sun-Stroke.

Immediately bruise horseradish and apply it to the stomach, and give him gin to drink. Never-failing.

No. 552.
Cure for the Quinsy.

Simmer hops in vinegar until their strength is extracted. Strain the liquid, sweeten it with sugar, and give it frequently to the patient until relieved. This is an almost infallible remedy.

No. 553.
Spitting of Blood.

Take 2 spoonfuls of the juice of nettles, at night, or take 3 spoonfuls of sage-juice in a little honey. This presently stops either spitting or vomiting blood. Or give 20 grains of alum, in water, every 2 hours.

No. 554.
To cure the Whitlow.

Steep in distilled vinegar, hot as you can bear it, 4 or 5 times a day, for 2 days successively; then moisten a leaf of tobacco in the vinegar, bind it round the part affected, and a cure follows.

No. 555.

Brilliant White-Wash.

Many have heard of the brilliant stucco white-wash on the east end of the President's house at Washington. The following is a receipt for it: it is gleaned from the "National Intelligencer."

Take ½ bushel nice unslaked lime, slake it with boiling water, cover it during the process to keep in the steam. Strain the liquid through a fine sieve or strainer, and add to it a peck of salt, previously well dissolved in warm water, 3 pounds ground rice, boiled to a thin paste, and stirred in boiling hot, ½ pound powdered Spanish whiting, and a pound of clean glue, which has been previously dissolved by soaking it well, and then hanging it over a slow fire, in a small kettle within a large one filled with water. Add 5 gallons hot water to the mixture, stir it well, and let it stand a few days, covered from the dirt. It should be put on right hot: for this purpose, it can be kept in a kettle on a portable furnace. It is said that about a pint of this mixture will cover a square yard upon the outside of a house, if properly applied. Brushes more or less small may be used, according to the neatness of the job required. It answers as well as oil-paint for wood, brick, or stone, and is cheaper. It retains its brilliancy for many years. There is nothing of the kind that will compare with it, either for inside or outside walls. Colouring-matter may be put in, and made of any shade you like. Spanish brown stirred in will make red pink, more or less deep, according to the quantity. A delicate tinge of this is very pretty for inside walls. Finely pulverized common clay, well mixed with Spanish brown, makes a reddish stone colour. Yellow ochre stirred in makes yellow wash; but crome goes further, and makes a colour generally esteemed prettier. In all these cases the darkness of the shades of course is determined by the quantity of colouring used. It is difficult to make rules, because tastes are different: it would be best to try experiments on a shingle, and let it dry. Green must not be mixed with lime: it destroys the colour, and the colour has an effect on the white-wash which makes it crack and peel. When walls have been badly smoked, and you wish to have them a clean white, it is well to squeeze indigo plentifully through a bag into the water you use, before it is stirred in the whole mixture. If a larger quantity than 5 gallons be wanted, the same proportion should be observed.

No. 556.

An English Cure for Pleuro-Pneumonia in Cattle.

The only chances in this disease are the adoption of very prompt measures,—bleeding early, and repeat if necessary. Then give a drench, composed of 1 pound Epsom salts, 1 ounce powdered saltpetre, $\frac{1}{2}$ drachm tartar-emetic. Give it in 2 pints gruel, and repeat in 6 or 8 hours.

No. 557.

Worms or Bots in Cattle or Horses.

Give $\frac{1}{2}$ pound Epsom salts, with 2 ounces coriander-seed bruised in a quart of water.

No. 558.

Scouring.

Give ½ ounce powdered catechu, and 10 grains powdered opium, in a little gruel.

No. 559.

Flesh-Wounds in Cattle, a Tincture for.

Take Socotrine or Barbadoes aloes, in powder, 4 ounces, myrrh, coarsely powdered, 1 ounce, rectified spirits of wine 1 pint, water 2 pints. Let them stand 14 days, occasionally shaking; then fit for use. Wounds are best without sewing. Cleanse from dirt or gravel. If much inflamed, apply a poultice. If unhealthy fungous granulation arises, wash the part with the following mild caustic wash, previous to applying the tincture:—Blue vitriol (sulphate of copper) 1 ounce, water 1 pint; dissolve.

No. 560.

Blacking for Harness, &c.

Melt 4 ounces mutton-suet with 12 ounces beeswax; add 12 ounces sugar-candy, 4 ounces soft-soap dissolved in water, and 2 ounces indigo, finely powdered. When melted and well mixed, add ¼ pint turpentine. Lay it on the harness with a sponge, and polish off with a brush.

No. 561.

Liniment for Rheumatism.

Take 1 ounce soap liniment, ½ ounce tincture of opium, 2 drachms oil of cajeput, 2 drachms hartshorn. Mix, and rub the parts affected night and morning. Flannel, or chamois leather, should be worn in winter.

No. 562.

A Simple Cure for Rheumatism.

Take 1 drachm hydriodate of potash, distilled water 2 ounces; mix, and give a teaspoonful in a wineglass of water, morning, noon, and night. This seldom fails to afford relief.

No. 563.

To Silver Copper.

Take a small quantity of pure silver, and pour over it twice its weight of nitric acid, and twice as much water as acid. The silver will be quickly dissolved. The solution, if the metal and acid be both pure, will be transparent and colourless. Then precipitate the silver by the immersion of polished plates of copper. Take of the silver 20 grains, cream of tartar 2 drachms, 2 drachms common salt, and ½ drachm alum; mix the whole together. Take then the article to be silvered, clean it well, and rub some of the mixture, previously a little moistened, upon its surface. The silvered surface may be polished with a piece of soft leather. The dial-plates of clocks, scales of barometers, etc. are all plated thus.

No. 564.

A new Pomade against Baldness.

Take of extract of yellow Peruvian bark 15 grains, extract of rhatany-root 8 grains, extract of burdock-root, and oil of nutmegs, (fixed,) of each 2 drachms, camphor (dissolved with spirits of wine) 15 grains, beef-marrow 2 ounces, best olive-oil 1 ounce, citron-juice ½ drachm, aromatic essential oil as much as sufficient to render it fragrant. Mix, and make into an ointment. 2 drachms bergamot and a few drops otto of roses would suffice. This is considered a valuable preparation.

No. 565.

Silvering of Metals.

Cold Silvering.—Mix 1 part chloride of silver with 3 parts pearlash, 1½ parts common salt, and 1 part whiting, and well rub the mixture on the surface of brass or copper, (previously well cleaned,) by means of a piece of soft leather, or a cork moistened with water and dipped into the powder. 1 part precipitate silver powder, mixed with 2 parts each cream of tartar and common salt, may also be used in the same way. When properly silvered, the metal should be well washed in hot water slightly alkalized, and then wiped dry.

No. 566.

To solder Iron or any other Metal without Fire.

Take 1 ounce of sal-ammoniac, and 1 ounce of

common salt, and an equal quantity of calcined tartar, and as much of bell-metal, with 3 ounces of antimony. Pound well all together, and sift it. Put this into a piece of linen, and enclose it well all round with fullers' earth about an inch thick. Let it dry, then put it between two crucibles over a slow fire, to get heat by degrees. Push on the fire till the lump becomes red-hot, and melted all together; let the whole cool gradually, and pound it into powder. When you want to solder any thing, put the two pieces you want to join on a table, approaching their extremities as near as you can to one another, making a crust of fullers' earth, so that holding to each piece and passing under the joint, it should open over it on the top; then throw some of your powder between and over the joint. Have some borax, which put into hot spirits of wine till it is consumed, and with a feather rub your powder at the joint: you will see it immediately boil. As soon as the boiling stops, the consolidation is made. If there be any roughness, grind it off on a stone.

No. 567.

Mild Aperient for Piles.

Take of precipitated sulphur 15 grains, magnesia 1 scruple. Mix. To be taken daily at bedtime, in a glass of milk or of water.

No. 568.

Milk, to Preserve.

When milk contained in wire-corked bottles is heated to the boiling-point in a water-bath, the oxygen of the included small portion of air under the cork seems to be carbonated, and the milk will afterwards keep fresh,—it is said, for a year or two.

No. 569.

Alum for the Hog Cholera.

A writer says,—"Last May my hogs were attacked with hog cholera; and, upon mentioning it to a friend, he spoke of a suggestion published in the Cincinnati papers, advising the use of alum. I procured some, made a strong solution, (all the water would bear,) and drenched all I found with the disease upon them, and gave to the lot (about 100 head) a pound of pulverized alum in some mill-feed each day for two weeks, by which time all remaining seemed healthy. Out of twenty-two drenched with one pint of the solution to each, administered with the assistance of a rope behind the tusks, and a horn with the small end sawed off, I lost five head, and, with the exception of two, the remaining seventeen appear to have entirely recovered to a healthy, thrifty condition. Some of those which have recovered were in the last stage, vomiting, with red blotches on the skin, and bleeding at the nose, which I have always considered the last stage of the disease. The above is but little cost, and, if it is as successful as with me, is well worth the trial."

No. 570.

Green Writing-Ink.

Take 1 ounce verdigris, and, having powdered it, put to it 1 quart vinegar. After it has stood 2 or 3 days, strain off the liquid. Or, instead of this, use the crystals of verdigris dissolved in water; then dissolve in 1 pint water either of the solutions, 5 drachms gum-arabic, and 2 drachms white sugar.

No. 571.

Hooping-Cough.—Dr. Barton's Remedy.

Take of powdered cantharides, powdered camphor, of each 1 scruple, extract of bark 3 drachms. Rub them well together, and divide into powders of 8 grains each. *Dose.*—One every 3 or 4 hours. To be used only in advanced stages of the disease.

No. 572.

How to make Shaving-Soap.

Take 2 pounds best white bar soap, and ½ pound good common bar soap; cut them up fine, so that they will dissolve readily. Put the soap into a copper kettle, with 1 quart of soft water: let it stand over the fire, and, when it is dissolved by boiling, add 1 pint alcohol, 1 gill beef's gall, ½ gill spirits of turpentine; boil all these together for five minutes, stir while boiling; while it is cooling, flavour it with oil of sassafras to suit, and colour it with fine vermilion. This soap makes a rich lather, softens the face, and can be made cheap.

No. 573.

Shaving-Soap,—Best ever Invented.

Take 4½ pounds white bar soap, 1 quart rain-water, 1 gill beef's gall, and 1 gill spirits of turpentine; cut the soap thin, and boil five minutes, stir while boiling, and colour with ½ ounce vermilion. Scent with oil of rose or almond.

No. 574.

Hair-Oil.

Take 1 gallon alcohol 95 per cent., 1 pint castor-oil, or as much as the alcohol will dissolve: add 1 ounce oil of cinnamon, or as much as will bring to the desired flavour.

No. 575.

Cheap Outside Paint.

Take 2 parts (in bulk) of water-lime ground fine, 1 part (in bulk) of white lead ground in oil. Mix them thoroughly, by adding best boiled linseed-oil enough to prepare it to pass through a paint-mill, after which temper with oil till it can be applied with a common paint-brush. Make any colour to suit. It will last three times as long as lead paint, and cost not one-fourth as much. It is superior.

No. 576.

How to clean Silver Articles.

The best way to clean silver articles is to wash them first with warm water and soap, and afterwards polish them with pure London whiting and a piece of leather. As pure whiting, free of grits, cannot always be had, except in London, you may substitute hartshorn-powder for it.

No. 577.

To take Mildew out of Linen.

Wet the linen which contains the mildew with soft water, rub it well with white soap, then scrape some fine chalk to powder and rub it well into the linen, lay it out on the grass in the sunshine, watching to keep it damp with soft water. Repeat the process the next day, and in a few hours the mildew will entirely disappear.

No. 578.

An excellent Powder for Razor-Strops.

Ignite together in a crucible equal parts of well-dried copperas and sea-salt. The heat must be slowly raised and well regulated: otherwise the materials will boil over in a pasty state, and the product will be in a great measure lost. When well made, out of contact with air, it has the brilliant aspect of plumbago. It requires to be ground and elutriated, after which it affords, on drying, an impalpable powder, that may be either rubbed on a strap of smooth buff leather or mixed up with hog's lard or tallow into a stiff cerate.

No. 579.

Cure for Common Diseases of Pigs or Hogs.

For common diseases of pigs, the following receipt may be employed; ½ pound sulphur, ½ pound madder, ¼ pound saltpetre, 2 ounces black antimony; mix these together, and give a tablespoonful night and morning in the food.

No. 580.

Dr. Cullen's treatment of Epilepsy, or Falling Fits.

Take of ammoniate of copper 20 grains, breadcrumbs and mucilage of gum-arabic a sufficient quantity to form it into a mass, which is to be divided into 40 pills. In the beginning, one of these is to be taken three times a day, and gradually increased to 2 or 3 pills, thrice a day.

No. 581.

German Silver. No. 1.

The following are the different receipts for the manufacture of German silver which are adopted by one of the first manufacturers in London; premising that the metals should be as pure as possible.

Common German Silver.—Copper, 8; nickel, 2; zinc, 3½. This is the commonest that can be made with any regard to the quality of the article produced. It might do for common purposes. If the quantity of nickel be reduced much below this, the alloy will be little better than pale brass, and will tarnish rapidly.

No. 582.

German Silver. No. 2.

Good German Silver.—Copper, 8; nickel, 3; zinc, 3½. This is a very beautiful compound. It has the appearance of silver a little below standard; by some persons it is even preferred to the more expensive compound. We strongly recommend manufacturers not to use a metal inferior to this.

No. 583.

German Silver. No. 3.

Electrum.—Copper, 8; nickel, 4; zinc, 3½. This is a compound which, for ease of working and beauty of appearance, is to be preferred to all others by the manufacturer, and is generally preferred by the public. It has a shade of blue like very highly-polished silver; it tarnishes less easily than silver.

No. 584.

German Silver. No. 4.

Copper, 8; nickel, 6; zinc, 3½. This is the richest in nickel that can be made without injuring the mechanical properties of the metal. It is a very beautiful compound, but requires a higher heat for fusion than the preceding, and will be found rather more difficult to work.

No. 585.

German Silver. No. 5.

Tutenag.—Copper, 8; nickel, 3; zinc, 4½. These proportions were obtained by the analysis of a piece of Chinese tutenag of the best ordinary quality; but some of the specimens of Chinese tutenag are equal to the electrum, No. 3; but these are very rare. This alloy is very fusible, but very hard, and not easily rolled: it is the best adapted for casting.

No. 586.
How to Poison Rats.

Mix 2 pounds carbonate of barytes with 1 pound lard, and lay it in their way. It is tasteless, odourless, and impalpable, produces great thirst, and death immediately after drinking. Another way is to mix arsenic and lard together, and spread it on bread, and push a piece in every rat-hole; or some small pieces of sponge may be fried in drippings or honey, and strewed about for them to eat. The sponge will distend their intestines, and will cause their death. Or ½ pint plaster of Paris, mixed with oat-meal, 1 pint, will prove equally fatal to them.

No. 587.
Bilious or Sick Headache.

Headache is in general a symptom of indigestion or deranged general health, or the consequence of a confined state of the bowels. The following alterative pill will be found a valuable medicine. Take of calomel, 10 grains; emetic tartar, 2, 3, or 4 grains; precipitated sulphuret of antimony, 1 scruple; guaiacum, in powder, 1 drachm. Rub them well together in a mortar for 10 minutes; then, with a little conserve of hips, make them into a mass, and divide it into 20 pills. *Dose.*—One pill is given every night, or every other night, for several weeks in succession.

No. 588.

How to make Otto of Roses.

Gather the flowers of the hundred-leaved rose, (rosa centifolia,) put them in a large jar or cask, with just sufficient water to cover them; then put the vessel to stand in the sun, and in about a week afterward the otto (a butyraceous oil) will form a scum on the surface, which should be removed by the aid of a piece of cotton.

No. 589.

Japan for Leather.

1. Boiled linseed-oil, 1 gallon; burnt umber, 8 ounces; asphaltum, 3 ounces; boil, and add oil of turpentine to dilute to a proper consistence.

2. Boiled oil, 1 gallon; the black of Prussian blue to colour. Prussian blue, when heated, turns of a black colour; thus the black japanned cloth used for table-covers is prepared by painting the cloth with Prussian blue and boiled oil, and then drying it by the heat of a stove; when, in the drying, it takes its intense colour.

No. 590.

Jet for Harness and Boots.

Three sticks of the best black sealing-wax dissolved in $\frac{1}{2}$ pint spirits of wine; to be kept in a glass bottle, and well shaken previous to use. Applied with a soft sponge.

No. 591.

To clean French Kid Gloves.

Put the gloves on your hands and wash them, as if you were washing your hands, in some spirits of turpentine, until quite clean; then hang them up in a warm place, or where there is a current of air, and all smell of the turpentine will be removed.

N.B.—This method is practised in Paris, and, since its introduction into this country, thousands of pounds have been saved or gained by it.

No. 592.

How to clean Gloves.

Wash them with soap and water, then stretch them on wooden hands, or pull them into shape without wringing them; next rub them with pipe-clay, or yellow ochre, or a mixture of the two in any required shade, made into a paste with beer; let them dry gradually, and, when about half dry, rub them well, so as to smooth them and put them into shape; then dry them, brush out the superfluous colour, cover them with paper, and smooth them with a warm iron. Other colours may be employed to mix the pipe-clay besides yellow ochre.

No. 593.

Red Sealing-Wax.

Shel-lac, (very pale,) 4 ounces, cautiously melt in a bright copper pan over a clear charcoal fire, and, when fused, add Venice turpentine, $\frac{1}{4}$ ounce; mix, and further add vermilion, 3 ounces; remove the pan from the fire, cool a little, weigh it in pieces, and roll them into circular sticks on a warm stone slab by means of a polished wooden block; or it may be poured into moulds while in a state of fusion.

No. 594.
Black Sealing-Wax. No. 1.

Purchase best black rosin, 3 pounds; beeswax, ½ pound; and finely-powdered ivory-black, 1 pound. Melt the whole together over a slow fire, and pour into sticks. If ¼ pound Venice turpentine is added, it will be fit for letter-use.

No. 595.
Black Sealing-Wax. No. 2.

Take 30 ounces shel-lac, 15 ounces ivory-black, in an impalpable powder, and 10 ounces Venice turpentine. For mode of procedure, see Receipt No. 593.

No. 596.
A Cure for Erysipelas, and all high Inflammation of the Skin.

A simple poultice of cranberries pounded fine, and applied in a raw state.

No. 597.
An excellent Printing-Ink.

Balsam of copaiva, (or Canada balsam,) 9 ounces; lampblack, 3 ounces; indigo and Prussian blue, each

5 drachms; Indian red, ¾ ounce; yellow soap, (dry,) 3 ounces. Grind it to an impalpable smoothness. Mix with old linseed-oil.

No. 598.

How to clean Silk stained by corrosive or sharp Liquor.

We often find that lemon-juice, vinegar, oil of vitriol, and other sharp corrosives, stain dyed garments. Sometimes by adding a little pearlash to a soap-lather, and passing the silks through these, the faded colour will be restored. Pearlash and warm water will sometimes do alone; but it is the most efficacious to use the soap-lather and pearlash together.

No. 599.

How to Write in Silver.

Mix 1 ounce the finest pewter or block tin, and 2 ounces quicksilver, together, till both become fluid; then grind it with gum-water, and write with it. The writing will look as if done with silver.

No. 600.

Toothache Preventive.

A correspondent of the "Monthly Magazine" says:—"Although I am unacquainted with any thing which gives immediate ease in that severe pain, yet I can inform you how the toothache may be prevented. I was much tortured with it about twenty years ago. Since that time, however, by using flour of sulphur as a tooth-powder, I have been wholly free from it. Rub the teeth and gums with a rather hard tooth-brush, using the sulphur every night; if done after dinner, too, all the better. It preserves the teeth, and does not communicate any smell whatever to the mouth.

GAUGING SIMPLIFIED;

OR,

Every Merchant his own Gauger.

GAUGING

REGULAR SHAPED LYING CASKS.

EXPLANATION OF TABLES.

THE chief design in this invention has been to enable any person to ascertain in one minute what number of gallons are contained in a lying cask, regular shaped, of different dimensions, when full or partly full.

RULE I.—FOR TABLE No. 1.

Take the rod with inches and tenths of inches marked on it, put it into the cask diagonally, from the bung-hole to each head, to get the exact centre. Then look at Table No. 1: the first column will show the diagonal inches from centre of bung to each head of cask, and the second column the contents of cask.

RULE II.—FOR TABLE No. 2.

To get the number of gallons when a cask is not full, take the bung diameter and wet inches on rod, and look at Ullage Table No. 2 for full contents of cask.

The 1st column shows the number of gallons in a full cask.
" 2d   "   "   the bung diameter.
" 3d   "   "   wet or dry inches on rod.
" 4th   "   "   what remains, if part be out.

Suppose a cask to contain 135 gallons, and the bung diameter to be 34 inches, and 10 inches wet on the rod, the right-hand, or 4th column will show $30\frac{1}{2}$ gallons remaining. Should the wet inches come above the centre, and only 10 inches be dry, there would be $30\frac{1}{2}$ gallons *out*, leaving $104\frac{1}{2}$ gallons *in*.

Table No. 1.

FOR

WHOLE CONTENTS OF CASKS.

Diagonal inches.	Contents of cask.	Diagonal inches.	Contents of cask.	Diagonal inches.	Contents of cask.	Diagonal inches.	Contents of cask.	Diagonal inches.	Contents of cask.
7.1	1	21.8	28	27.3	55	31.1	82	34.2	109
9.0	2	22.0	29	27.4	56	31.2	83	34.3	110
10.3	3	22.3	30	27.6	57	31.4	84	34.4	111
11.3	4	22.5	31	27.7	58	31.5	85	34.5	112
12.2	5	22.7	32	27.9	59	31.6	86	34.6	113
13.0	6	23.0	33	28.0	60	31.7	87	34.7	114
13.7	7	23.2	34	28.2	61	31.8	88	34.8	115
14.3	8	23.4	35	28.4	62	31.9	89	34.9	116
14.9	9	23.7	36	28.5	63	32.1	90	35.0	117
15.4	10	24.0	37	28.7	64	32.2	91	35.1	118
15.9	11	24.1	38	28.8	65	32.3	92	35.2	119
16.4	12	24.3	39	29.0	66	32.4	93	35.3	120
16.8	13	24.5	40	29.1	67	32.6	94	35.4	121
17.2	14	24.7	41	29.2	68	32.7	95	35.5	122
17.6	15	24.9	42	29.4	69	32.8	96	35.6	123
18.0	16	25.1	43	29.5	70	32.9	97	35.7	124
18.4	17	25.3	44	29.6	71	33.0	98	35.8	125
18.8	18	25.5	45	29.8	72	33.2	99	35.9	126
19.1	19	25.7	46	29.9	73	33.3	100	36.0	127
19.4	20	25.9	47	30.1	74	33.4	101	36.1	128
19.7	21	26.0	48	30.2	75	33.5	102	36.2	129
20.1	22	26.2	49	30.3	76	33.6	103	36.3	130
20.4	23	26.4	50	30.5	77	33.7	104	36.4	131
20.7	24	26.6	51	30.6	78	33.8	105	36.5	132
21.0	25	26.7	52	30.7	79	33.9	106	36.6	133
21.2	26	26.9	53	30.8	80	34.0	107	36.7	134
21.5	27	27.1	54	31.0	81	34.1	108	36.8	135

Diagonal inches.	Contents of cask.	Diagonal inches.	Contents of cask.	Diagonal inches.	Contents of cask.	Diagonal inches.	Contents of cask.	Diagonal inches.	Contents of cask.
36.9	137	38.3	153	39.5	167	40.5	181	41.5	195
37.0	138	38.4	154	39.5	168	40.6	182	41.6	196
37.1	139	38.5	155	39.6	169	40.6	183	41.7	197
37.2	140	38.5	156	39.7	170	40.7	184	41.7	198
37.3	141	38.6	157	39.8	171	40.8	185	41.8	199
37.4	142	38.7	158	39.8	172	40.9	186	41.9	200
37.5	143	38.8	159	39.9	173	40.9	187	42.0	202
37.6	145	38.8	160	40.0	174	41.0	188	42.1	204
37.7	146	38.9	161	40.1	175	41.1	189	42.2	205
37.8	147	39.0	162	40.1	176	41.2	190	42.3	206
37.9	148	39.1	163	40.2	177	41.2	191	42.4	208
38.0	149	39.2	164	40.3	178	41.3	192	42.5	210
38.1	150	39.3	165	40.3	179	41.4	193	42.7	213
38.2	152	39.4	166	40.4	180	41.5	194		

Ullage Table, No. 2.

Whole contents.	Bung diameter.	Wet or dry inches.	Ullage or remainder. galls.	Whole contents.	Bung diameter.	Wet or dry inches.	Ullage or remainder. galls.	Whole contents.	Bung diameter.	Wet or dry inches.	Ullage or remainder. galls.
18	16	2	1			4	$3\frac{1}{4}$			5	$3\frac{1}{4}$
		3	2			5	$4\frac{1}{4}$			6	$4\frac{3}{4}$
		4	3			6	$6\frac{1}{4}$			7	6
		5	$4\frac{1}{2}$			7	$7\frac{3}{4}$			8	$7\frac{3}{4}$
		6	$5\frac{1}{4}$			$7\frac{1}{2}$	$8\frac{1}{2}$			9	$8\frac{3}{4}$
		7	$7\frac{1}{4}$			8	$9\frac{1}{2}$			$9\frac{1}{2}$	$9\frac{1}{2}$
		8	9								
				19	17	2	1	20	16	2	1
18	17	2	1			3	$1\frac{3}{4}$			3	2
		3	$1\frac{3}{4}$			4	3			$3\frac{1}{2}$	$2\frac{3}{4}$
		4	$2\frac{3}{4}$			5	$4\frac{1}{4}$			4	$3\frac{1}{2}$
		5	4			6	$5\frac{3}{4}$			$4\frac{1}{2}$	$4\frac{1}{4}$
		6	$5\frac{1}{2}$			7	$7\frac{1}{4}$			5	5
		7	$6\frac{3}{4}$			8	$8\frac{1}{2}$			$5\frac{1}{2}$	$5\frac{3}{4}$
		8	$8\frac{1}{4}$			$8\frac{1}{2}$	$9\frac{1}{2}$			6	$6\frac{1}{2}$
		$8\frac{1}{2}$	9							$6\frac{1}{2}$	$7\frac{1}{4}$
				19	18	2	1			7	$8\frac{1}{4}$
18	18	2	$\frac{3}{4}$			3	$1\frac{1}{4}$			$7\frac{1}{2}$	9
		3	$1\frac{3}{4}$			4	$2\frac{3}{4}$			8	10
		4	$2\frac{1}{2}$			5	$3\frac{3}{4}$				
		5	$3\frac{3}{4}$			6	5	20	17	2	1
		6	$5\frac{1}{4}$			7	$6\frac{1}{2}$			3	$1\frac{3}{4}$
		7	$6\frac{3}{4}$			8	8			4	$2\frac{1}{2}$
		8	$7\frac{1}{2}$			$8\frac{1}{2}$	$8\frac{3}{4}$			$4\frac{1}{2}$	$3\frac{3}{4}$
		$8\frac{1}{2}$	$8\frac{1}{4}$			9	$9\frac{1}{2}$			5	$4\frac{1}{4}$
		9	9							$5\frac{1}{2}$	$5\frac{1}{4}$
				19	19	2	$\frac{3}{4}$			6	6
19	16	2	1			3	$1\frac{3}{4}$			$6\frac{1}{2}$	$6\frac{3}{4}$
		3	2			4	$2\frac{1}{2}$			7	$7\frac{1}{2}$

Whole contents.	Bung diameter.	Wet or dry inches.	Ullage or remainder. galls.	Whole contents.	Bung diameter.	Wet or dry inches.	Ullage or remainder. galls.	Whole contents.	Bung diameter.	Wet or dry inches.	Ullage or remainder. galls.
		7½	8¼			9	8½			9½	10½
		8	9			9½	9¼				
		8½	10			10	10	22	17	2	1
										3	2
20	18	2	¾	21	17	2	1			4	3
		3	1¾			3	2			5	4¾
		4	2¾			4	3¼			6	6½
		5	4			5	4½			7	8
		6	5¼			6	6			7½	9
		7	6¾			7	7¾			8	10
		7½	7½			7½	8¾			8½	11
		8	8¼			8	9½				
		8½	9			8½	10½	22	18	2	1
		9	10							3	2
				21	18	2	1			4	3
20	19	2	¾			3	1¾			5	4¼
		3	1¾			4	3			6	5¾
		4	2½			5	4¼			6½	6½
		5	3¾			6	5½			7	7½
		6	5			7	7½			7½	8¼
		7	6¼			7½	8			8	9¼
		8	7½			8	8¾			8½	10
		9	9¼			8½	9½			9	11
		9½	10			9	10½				
								22	19	2	1
20	20	2	¾	21	19	2	¾			3	1¾
		3	1½			3	1½			4	2¾
		4	2¼			4	3¼			5	4
		5	3½			5	4¾			6	5½
		6	4½			6	5¼			7	6¾
		7	5¾			7	6½			8	8½
		7½	6½			8	8¼			9	10
		8	7¼			8½	8¾			9½	11
		8½	7¾			9	9½				

Whole contents.	Bung diameter.	Wet or dry inches.	Ullage or remainder. galls.
22	20	2	1
		3	1¾
		4	2¾
		5	3¾
		6	5
		7	6½
		8	7¾
		9	9¼
		10	11
23	17	2	1
		3	2
		4	3½
		5	5½
		6	6½
		7	8½
		8	10½
		8½	11½
23	18	2	1
		3	2
		4	3
		5	4½
		6	6¾
		7	7¾
		8	9½
		9	11½
23	19	2	1
		3	1¾
		4	3
		5	4¼
		6	5¾
		7	6½
		8	8¾
		9	10½
		9½	11½
23	20	2	1
		3	1¾
		4	3
		5	4
		6	5¼
		7	6½
		8	8¼
		9	9¾
		10	11½
24	17	2	1¼
		3	2¼
		4	4
		5	5½
		6	7
		7	9
		8	10¾
		8½	12
24	18	2	1
		3	2¼
		4	3¼
		5	4½
		6	6½
		7	8¼
		8	10¼
		9	12
24	19	2	1
		3	2
		4	3
		5	4½
		6	6
		7	7½
		8	9¾
		9	11
		9½	12
24	20	2	1
		3	2
		4	2¾
		5	3¾
		6	5¾
		7	7
		8	8½
		9	10¼
		10	12
25	17	2	1¼
		3	2¼
		4	4
		5	5½
		6	7¼
		7	8¾
		8	10¼
		8½	12½
25	18	2	1
		3	2
		4	3½
		5	5
		6	6¾
		7	8½
		8	10½

Whole contents.	Bung diameter.	Wet or dry inches.	Ullage or remainder. galls.	Whole contents.	Bung diameter.	Wet or dry inches.	Ullage or remainder. galls.	Whole contents.	Bung diameter.	Wet or dry inches.	Ullage or remainder. galls.
		9	$12\frac{1}{2}$			5	$5\frac{1}{4}$	27	18	2	$1\frac{1}{4}$
						6	7			3	$2\frac{1}{4}$
25	19	2	1			7	$8\frac{3}{4}$			4	$3\frac{1}{4}$
		3	2			8	11			5	$5\frac{1}{2}$
		4	3			9	13			6	$7\frac{1}{2}$
		5	$4\frac{1}{2}$							7	$9\frac{1}{4}$
		6	$6\frac{1}{4}$	26	19	2	1			8	$11\frac{1}{4}$
		7	$7\frac{3}{4}$			3	2			9	$13\frac{1}{2}$
		8	$9\frac{3}{4}$			4	$3\frac{1}{4}$				
		9	$11\frac{3}{4}$			5	$4\frac{3}{4}$	27	19	2	1
		$9\frac{1}{2}$	$12\frac{1}{2}$			6	$6\frac{1}{2}$			3	2
						7	$8\frac{1}{4}$			4	$3\frac{1}{2}$
25	20	2	1			8	$10\frac{1}{4}$			5	5
		3	$1\frac{3}{4}$			9	12			6	$6\frac{3}{4}$
		4	3			$9\frac{1}{2}$	13			7	$8\frac{1}{4}$
		5	$4\frac{1}{4}$							9	$10\frac{1}{2}$
		6	$5\frac{3}{4}$	26	20	2	1			$9\frac{1}{4}$	$12\frac{1}{2}$
		7	$7\frac{1}{4}$			3	$1\frac{3}{4}$			$9\frac{1}{2}$	$13\frac{1}{2}$
		8	9			4	3				
		9	11			5	$4\frac{1}{2}$	27	20	2	1
		10	$12\frac{1}{2}$			6	6			3	2
						7	$7\frac{1}{2}$			4	$3\frac{1}{4}$
26	17	2	$1\frac{1}{4}$			8	$9\frac{3}{4}$			5	$4\frac{3}{4}$
		3	$2\frac{1}{2}$			9	$11\frac{1}{4}$			6	$6\frac{1}{4}$
		4	4			10	13			7	8
		5	$5\frac{3}{4}$							8	$9\frac{1}{2}$
		6	$7\frac{1}{2}$	27	17	2	$1\frac{1}{4}$			9	$11\frac{1}{2}$
		7	$9\frac{3}{4}$			3	$2\frac{1}{2}$			10	$13\frac{1}{2}$
		8	$11\frac{3}{4}$			4	$4\frac{1}{4}$				
		$8\frac{1}{2}$	13			5	$5\frac{3}{4}$	28	17	2	$1\frac{1}{4}$
						6	8			3	$2\frac{1}{4}$
26	18	2	1			7	10			4	$4\frac{1}{2}$
		3	$2\frac{1}{4}$			8	$12\frac{1}{4}$			5	$6\frac{1}{4}$
		4	$3\frac{1}{2}$			$8\frac{1}{2}$	$13\frac{1}{2}$			6	$8\frac{1}{4}$

Whole contents.	Bung diameter.	Wet or dry inches.	Ullage or remainder. galls.
		7	10½
		8	12¾
		8½	14
28	18	2	1¼
		3	2½
		4	4
		5	5¾
		6	7½
		7	9½
		8	11¾
		9	14
28	19	2	1¼
		3	2
		4	3½
		5	5¼
		6	7
		7	8¾
		8	10¾
		9	12¾
		9¼	13¼
		9½	14
28	20	2	1
		3	2
		4	3¼
		5	4¾
		6	6½
		7	8¼
		8	9¾
		9	12
		10	14

Whole contents.	Bung diameter.	Wet or dry inches.	Ullage or remainder. galls.
29	17	2	1¼
		3	2¾
		4	4½
		5	6½
		6	8½
		7	10¾
		8	13¼
		8½	14½
29	18	2	1¼
		3	2½
		4	4
		5	6
		6	7¾
		7	10
		8	12¼
		9	14½
29	19	2	1
		3	2¼
		4	3¾
		5	5½
		6	7¼
		7	9
		8	10¼
		9	13¼
		9½	14½
29	20	2	1
		3	2
		4	3½
		5	5
		6	6¾
		7	8½

Whole contents.	Bung diameter.	Wet or dry inches.	Ullage or remainder. galls.
		8	10¼
		9	12¼
		10	14½
30	17	2	1½
		3	2¾
		4	4¾
		5	6¾
		6	8¾
		7	11¼
		8	13½
		8½	15
30	18	2	1¼
		3	2½
		4	4
		5	6
		6	8
		7	10¼
		8	12½
		9	15
30	19	2	1¼
		3	2¼
		4	3¾
		5	5½
		6	7½
		7	9½
		8	11¾
		9	13¾
		9½	15
30	20	2	1
		3	2

Whole contents.	Bung diameter.	Wet or dry inches.	Ullage or remainder. galls.	Whole contents.	Bung diameter.	Wet or dry inches.	Ullage or remainder. galls.	Whole contents.	Bung diameter.	Wet or dry inches.	Ullage or remainder. galls.
		4	$3\frac{1}{2}$			6	6			7	$8\frac{1}{4}$
		5	$5\frac{1}{4}$			7	$7\frac{3}{4}$			8	$9\frac{3}{4}$
		6	7			8	$9\frac{1}{2}$			9	12
		7	$8\frac{3}{4}$			9	$11\frac{1}{2}$			10	14
		8	$10\frac{3}{4}$			10	$13\frac{1}{2}$			11	16
		9	$12\frac{3}{4}$			11	$15\frac{1}{2}$	33	20	2	$1\frac{1}{4}$
		10	15	32	20	2	$1\frac{1}{4}$			3	$2\frac{1}{2}$
31	20	2	$1\frac{1}{4}$			3	$2\frac{1}{4}$			4	$3\frac{3}{4}$
		3	$2\frac{1}{4}$			4	$3\frac{3}{4}$			5	$5\frac{3}{4}$
		4	$3\frac{1}{2}$			5	$5\frac{1}{2}$			6	$7\frac{3}{4}$
		5	$5\frac{1}{2}$			6	$7\frac{1}{2}$			7	$9\frac{3}{4}$
		6	$7\frac{1}{4}$			7	$9\frac{1}{4}$			8	$11\frac{3}{4}$
		7	9			8	$11\frac{1}{2}$			9	14
		8	11			9	$13\frac{3}{4}$			$9\frac{1}{2}$	$15\frac{1}{2}$
		9	$12\frac{1}{4}$			$9\frac{1}{2}$	$14\frac{3}{4}$			10	$16\frac{1}{2}$
		$9\frac{1}{2}$	$14\frac{1}{4}$			10	16	33	21	2	1
		10	$15\frac{1}{2}$	32	21	2	1			3	$2\frac{1}{4}$
31	21	2	1			3	2			4	$3\frac{1}{2}$
		3	2			4	$3\frac{1}{2}$			5	5
		4	$3\frac{1}{4}$			5	$4\frac{3}{4}$			6	7
		5	$4\frac{3}{4}$			6	$6\frac{3}{4}$			7	$8\frac{3}{4}$
		6	$6\frac{1}{2}$			7	$8\frac{1}{2}$			8	$10\frac{3}{4}$
		7	$8\frac{1}{4}$			8	$10\frac{1}{2}$			9	13
		8	$10\frac{1}{4}$			9	$12\frac{1}{2}$			10	$15\frac{1}{4}$
		9	$12\frac{1}{4}$			10	$14\frac{3}{4}$			$10\frac{1}{2}$	$16\frac{1}{2}$
		10	$14\frac{1}{4}$			$10\frac{1}{2}$	16	33	22	2	1
		$10\frac{1}{2}$	$15\frac{1}{2}$	32	22	2	1			3	2
31	22	2	1			3	2			4	$3\frac{1}{4}$
		3	2			4	$3\frac{1}{4}$			5	$4\frac{3}{4}$
		4	3			5	$4\frac{3}{4}$			6	$6\frac{1}{2}$
		5	$4\frac{1}{2}$			6	$6\frac{1}{4}$			7	$8\frac{1}{4}$

Whole contents.	Bung diameter.	Wet or dry inches.	Ullage or remainder. galls.	Whole contents.	Bung diameter.	Wet or dry inches.	Ullage or remainder. galls.	Whole contents.	Bung diameter.	Wet or dry inches.	Ullage or remainder. galls.
		8	10			9	$12\frac{1}{2}$			10	$14\frac{3}{4}$
		9	$12\frac{1}{4}$			10	$14\frac{3}{4}$			10	$16\frac{1}{4}$
		10	$14\frac{1}{4}$			11	17			11	$17\frac{1}{2}$
		11	$16\frac{1}{2}$								
				35	21	2	1	36	21	2	$1\frac{1}{4}$
34	20	2	$1\frac{1}{4}$			3	$2\frac{1}{4}$			3	$2\frac{1}{2}$
		3	$2\frac{3}{4}$			4	$3\frac{3}{4}$			4	$3\frac{3}{4}$
		4	4			5	$5\frac{1}{2}$			5	$5\frac{3}{4}$
		5	$5\frac{3}{4}$			6	$7\frac{1}{2}$			6	$7\frac{3}{4}$
		6	$7\frac{3}{4}$			7	$9\frac{1}{4}$			7	$9\frac{3}{4}$
		7	10			8	$11\frac{1}{2}$			8	$11\frac{3}{4}$
		8	$12\frac{1}{4}$			9	$13\frac{3}{4}$			9	$14\frac{1}{4}$
		9	$14\frac{1}{2}$			10	$16\frac{1}{4}$			10	$16\frac{1}{2}$
		$9\frac{1}{2}$	15			$10\frac{1}{2}$	$17\frac{1}{2}$			$10\frac{1}{2}$	18
		10	17								
				35	$21\frac{1}{2}$	2	1	36	$21\frac{1}{2}$	2	$1\frac{1}{4}$
34	21	2	1			3	$2\frac{1}{2}$			3	$2\frac{1}{4}$
		3	$2\frac{1}{4}$			4	$3\frac{1}{2}$			4	$3\frac{3}{4}$
		4	$3\frac{1}{2}$			5	$5\frac{1}{4}$			5	$5\frac{1}{2}$
		5	5			6	$7\frac{1}{4}$			6	$7\frac{1}{2}$
		6	$7\frac{1}{4}$			7	9			7	$9\frac{1}{2}$
		7	9			8	$11\frac{1}{4}$			8	$11\frac{1}{2}$
		8	$11\frac{1}{4}$			9	$13\frac{1}{4}$			9	$13\frac{3}{4}$
		9	$13\frac{1}{2}$			10	$15\frac{1}{4}$			10	$15\frac{3}{4}$
		10	$15\frac{1}{2}$			$10\frac{3}{4}$	$17\frac{1}{2}$			$10\frac{3}{4}$	18
		$10\frac{1}{2}$	17								
				35	22	2	1	36	22	2	1
34	22	2	1			3	2			3	$2\frac{1}{4}$
		3	2			4	$3\frac{1}{4}$			4	$3\frac{1}{2}$
		4	$3\frac{1}{4}$			5	5			5	$5\frac{1}{2}$
		5	$4\frac{3}{4}$			6	$6\frac{3}{4}$			6	7
		6	$6\frac{1}{4}$			7	$8\frac{3}{4}$			7	9
		7	$8\frac{1}{2}$			8	$10\frac{1}{2}$			8	11
		8	$10\frac{1}{4}$			9	$12\frac{3}{4}$			9	$13\frac{1}{4}$

Whole contents.	Bung diameter.	Wet or dry inches.	Ullage or remainder. galls.	Whole contents.	Bung diameter.	Wet or dry inches.	Ullage or remainder. galls.	Whole contents.	Bung diameter.	Wet or dry inches.	Ullage or remainder. galls.
		10	15½			10½	17			10½	17½
		11	18			11	18½			11	19
37	21	2	1¼	38	21	2	1¼	39	21	2	1¼
		3	2½			3	2½			3	2½
		4	4			4	4			4	4¼
		5	5¾			5	6			5	6
		6	7¾			6	8			6	8
		7	9¾			7	10			7	10½
		8	12			8	12½			8	12¾
		9	14			9	15			9	15½
		10	16¾			10	17½			10	18
		10½	18½			10½	19			10½	19½
37	21½	2	1¼	38	21½	2	1¼	39	21½	2	1¼
		3	2¼			3	2½			3	2½
		4	3¾			4	3¾			4	4
		5	5½			5	5¾			5	6
		6	7½			6	7¾			6	8
		7	9½			7	10			7	10¼
		8	11¾			8	12			8	12½
		9	14			9	14½			9	14¾
		10	16½			10	17			10	17½
		10¾	18½			10¾	19			10¾	19½
37	22	2	1	38	22	2	1¼	39	22	2	1¼
		3	2¼			3	2¼			3	2½
		4	3½			4	3¾			4	4
		5	5¼			5	5½			5	5¾
		6	7¼			6	7½			6	7¾
		7	9¼			7	9½			7	9¾
		8	11¼			8	11½			8	11¾
		9	13½			9	14			9	14¼
		10	16			10	16¼			10	16¾

Whole contents.	Bung diameter.	Wet or dry inches.	Ullage or remainder. galls.	Whole contents.	Bung diameter.	Wet or dry inches.	Ullage or remainder. galls.	Whole contents.	Bung diameter.	Wet or dry inches.	Ullage or remainder. galls.
		10½	18			10½	18½			10½	19
		11	19½			11	20			11	20½
40	21	2	1¼	41	21	2	1½	42	22	2	1¼
		3	2½			3	2¾			3	2½
		4	4¼			4	4½			4	4¼
		5	6¼			5	6½			5	6¼
		6	8½			6	8¾			6	8¼
		7	10¾			7	11			7	10½
		8	13			8	13½			8	12¾
		9	15¾			9	16¼			9	15½
		10	18½			10	19			10	18¼
		10½	20			10½	20½			11	21
40	21½	2	1¼	41	21½	2	1½	42	22½	2	1¼
		3	2½			3	2¾			3	2½
		4	4			4	4¼			4	4
		5	6			5	6¼			5	6
		6	8¼			6	8½			6	8
		7	10½			7	10¾			7	10¼
		8	12¾			8	13			8	12½
		9	15¼			9	15¾			9	15
		10	18			10	18½			10	17¾
		10¾	20			10¾	20½			11	20
										11¼	21
40	22	2	1¼	41	22	2	1¼				
		3	2½			3	2½	42	23	2	1¼
		4	4			4	4			3	2¼
		5	6			5	6			4	4
		6	7¾			6	8			5	5¾
		7	10			7	10½			6	7¾
		8	12			8	12½			7	10
		9	14¾			9	15			8	12
		10	17¼			10	17¾			9	14¼

Whole contents	Bung diameter	Wet or dry inches	Ullage or remainder galls.	Whole contents	Bung diameter	Wet or dry inches	Ullage or remainder galls.	Whole contents	Bung diameter	Wet or dry inches	Ullage or remainder galls.
		10	17			9	14¾			8	12¾
		11	19½			10	17½			9	15
		11¼	21			11	20			10	17¾
						11½	21½			11	20½
43	22	2	1¼							11½	22
		3	2¾	44	22	2	1½				
		4	4¼			3	2¾	45	22	2	1½
		5	6½			4	4½			3	2¾
		6	8½			5	6½			4	4½
		7	10¾			6	8¾			5	6¾
		8	13			7	11¼			6	9
		9	15¾			8	13¼			7	11½
		10	18¼			9	16¼			8	13½
		11	21½			10	19			9	16½
						11	22			10	19½
43	22½	2	1¼							11	22¼
		3	2½	44	22½	2	1½				
		4	4			3	2¾	45	22½	2	1½
		5	6			4	4			3	2¾
		6	8¼			5	6¼			4	4½
		7	10½			6	8½			5	6¼
		8	12¾			7	10¾			7	11
		9	15¼			8	13			8	13¼
		10	18¼			9	15¾			9	16
		11	20½			10	18½			10	18¾
		11¼	21½			11	21			11¼	22½
						11¼	22				
43	23	2	1¼					45	23	2	1¼
		3	2½	44	23	2	1¼			3	2½
		4	4			3	2½			4	4½
		5	6			4	4			5	6¼
		6	8			5	6			6	8¼
		7	10			6	8			7	10¾
		8	12¼			7	10½			8	13

Whole contents.	Bung diameter.	Wet or dry inches.	Ullage or remainder. galls.	Whole contents.	Bung diameter.	Wet or dry inches.	Ullage or remainder. galls.	Whole contents.	Bung diameter.	Wet or dry inches.	Ullage or remainder. galls.
		9	15½			8	13¼			7	11
		10	18¼			9	15¾			8	13½
		11	20¾			10	19			9	16
		11½	22¼			11	21¼			10	19½
						11½	23			11	21¾
46	22	2	1½							11½	23½
		3	3	47	22	2	1½				
		4	4¾			3	3	48	23	2	1¼
		5	6¾			4	4¾			3	2¾
		6	9			5	7			4	4½
		7	11¾			6	9½			5	6¾
		8	14			7	12			6	9
		9	16¾			8	14¼			7	11¼
		10	20			9	17¼			8	13¾
		11	23			10	20½			9	16¼
						11	23½			10	19½
46	22½	2	1¼							11	22¼
		3	3	47	22½	2	1¼			11½	24
		4	4½			3	3				
		5	6½			4	4½	48	23½	2	1¼
		6	8¾			5	6¾			3	2¾
		7	11¼			6	9			4	4¼
		8	13¾			7	11¾			5	6¼
		9	16½			8	14			6	8¼
		10	19¼			9	16¾			7	11
		11	22			10	19¾			8	13½
		11¼	23			11	22½			9	16¾
						11¼	23½			10	18¼
46	23	2	1¼							11	21½
		3	2¾	47	23	2	1¼			11¾	24
		4	4¼			3	2¾				
		5	6¼			4	4¼	48	24	2	1¼
		6	8½			5	6¼			3	2½
		7	10¾			6	8¾			4	4¼

282

Whole contents.	Bung diameter.	Wet or dry inches.	Ullage or remainder. galls.	Whole contents.	Bung diameter.	Wet or dry inches.	Ullage or remainder. galls.	Whole contents.	Bung diameter.	Wet or dry inches.	Ullage or remainder. galls.
		5	6			3	$2\frac{3}{4}$	51	24	2	$1\frac{1}{4}$
		6	$8\frac{1}{4}$			4	$4\frac{1}{2}$			3	$2\frac{3}{4}$
		7	$10\frac{1}{2}$			5	7			4	$4\frac{1}{4}$
		8	13			6	$9\frac{1}{2}$			5	$6\frac{1}{4}$
		9	$15\frac{1}{2}$			7	$11\frac{3}{4}$			6	$8\frac{1}{2}$
		10	18			8	15			7	$11\frac{1}{4}$
		11	$21\frac{1}{2}$			9	$17\frac{1}{2}$			8	$13\frac{3}{4}$
		12	24			10	$21\frac{1}{4}$			9	$16\frac{1}{4}$
						11	$23\frac{1}{4}$			10	$19\frac{1}{4}$
49	23	2	$1\frac{1}{2}$			$11\frac{1}{2}$	25			11	$22\frac{1}{2}$
		3	$2\frac{3}{4}$							12	$25\frac{1}{2}$
		4	$4\frac{1}{2}$	50	24	2	$1\frac{1}{4}$				
		5	$6\frac{3}{4}$			3	$2\frac{3}{4}$	52	23	2	$1\frac{1}{2}$
		6	9			4	4			3	3
		7	$11\frac{3}{4}$			5	6			4	5
		8	$14\frac{1}{4}$			6	$8\frac{1}{2}$			5	7
		9	$16\frac{3}{4}$			7	$10\frac{1}{2}$			6	$9\frac{1}{2}$
		10	20			8	$13\frac{1}{2}$			7	$12\frac{1}{4}$
		11	$22\frac{3}{4}$			9	16			8	$15\frac{1}{4}$
		$11\frac{1}{2}$	$24\frac{1}{2}$			10	$18\frac{3}{4}$			9	$17\frac{3}{4}$
						11	$21\frac{3}{4}$			10	21
49	24	2	$1\frac{1}{4}$			12	25			11	$24\frac{1}{4}$
		3	$2\frac{1}{2}$							$11\frac{1}{2}$	26
		4	4	51	23	2	$1\frac{1}{2}$				
		5	6			3	3	52	24	2	$1\frac{1}{2}$
		6	$8\frac{1}{2}$			4	$4\frac{3}{4}$			3	$2\frac{3}{4}$
		7	$9\frac{3}{4}$			5	7			4	$4\frac{1}{4}$
		8	$13\frac{1}{4}$			6	$9\frac{1}{2}$			5	$6\frac{1}{2}$
		9	$15\frac{3}{4}$			7	12			6	9
		10	$18\frac{1}{2}$			8	$14\frac{1}{2}$			7	$11\frac{1}{2}$
		11	21			9	$17\frac{1}{2}$			8	14
		12	$24\frac{1}{2}$			10	$19\frac{3}{4}$			9	$16\frac{3}{4}$
						11	$22\frac{3}{4}$			10	$19\frac{3}{4}$
50	23	2	$1\frac{1}{4}$			$11\frac{1}{2}$	$25\frac{1}{2}$			11	$22\frac{3}{4}$

Whole contents.	Bung diameter.	Wet or dry inches.	Ullage or remainder. galls.	Whole contents.	Bung diameter.	Wet or dry inches.	Ullage or remainder. galls.	Whole contents.	Bung diameter.	Wet or dry inches.	Ullage or remainder. galls.
		12	26			10	22			8	14½
						11	25			9	16¼
53	23	2	1½			11½	26			10	19½
		3	3							11	22½
		4	5	54	24	2	1½			12	26
		5	7			3	3			12½	27½
		6	9¾			4	4½				
		7	12½			5	6¾	56	24	2	1½
		8	15¾			6	9¼			3	3
		9	18¼			7	12			4	4¾
		10	20½			8	14½			5	7
		11	24½			9	17¼			6	9¾
		11½	26			10	20½			7	12¼
						11	23½			8	15
53	24	2	1¼			12	26			9	18
		3	3							10	21¼
		4	4½	55	24	2	1½			11	24½
		5	6½			3	3			12	28
		6	9½			4	4¾				
		7	11½			5	6¾	56	25	2	1¼
		8	14¼			6	9½			3	3
		9	17			7	12			4	4½
		10	20			8	15			5	6½
		11	23¼			9	17¾			6	9
		12	26			10	20¾			7	11¾
						11	24			8	14¾
54	23	2	1½			12	27½			9	17
		3	3							10	20
		4	5½	55	25	2	1¼			11	23
		5	7½			3	2¾			12	26
		6	10			4	4½			12½	28
		7	12¾			5	6¼				
		8	16			6	9	57	24	2	1½
		9	18½			7	11½			3	3

Whole contents.	Bung diameter.	Wet or dry inches.	Ullage or remainder. galls.
		4	4¾
		5	7
		6	9¾
		7	12½
		8	15¼
		9	18¼
		10	21½
		11	24¾
		12	28½
57	25	2	1½
		3	2¾
		4	4½
		5	6½
		6	9¼
		7	11¾
		8	15
		9	17¼
		10	20
		11	23½
		12	26½
		12½	28½
58	24	2	1½
		3	3¼
		4	5
		5	7¼
		6	10
		7	12¾
		8	15¾
		9	18¾
		10	22
		11	25½
		12	29
58	25	2	1½
		3	3
		4	4¾
		5	6¾
		6	9½
		7	12
		8	14¾
		9	17½
		10	20¾
		11	24
		12	27
		12½	29
59	24	2	1½
		3	3¼
		4	5
		5	7¼
		6	10¼
		7	13
		8	16
		9	19½
		10	22¼
		11	25¾
		12	29½
59	25	2	1½
		3	3
		4	4½
		5	6¾
		6	9½
		7	12¼
		8	15½
		9	17¾
		10	21
		11	24¼
		12	27½
		12½	29½
60	24	2	1½
		3	3¼
		4	5
		5	7½
		6	10¼
		7	13¼
		8	16¼
		9	19¼
		10	22¾
		11	26¼
		12	30
60	25	2	1½
		3	3
		4	4¾
		5	7
		6	9¾
		7	12½
		8	15¼
		9	18
		10	21½
		11	24¾
		12	28
		12½	30
61	24	2	1½
		3	3¼
		4	5
		5	7½
		6	10½

Whole contents.	Bung diameter.	Wet or dry inches.	Ullage or remainder. galls.	Whole contents.	Bung diameter.	Wet or dry inches.	Ullage or remainder. galls.	Whole contents.	Bung diameter.	Wet or dry inches.	Ullage or remainder. galls.
		7	13¼			4	4¾			12½	31½
		8	16¼			5	7				
		9	19½			6	10	64	24	2	1¾
		10	23			7	12¾			3	3½
		11	26¾			8	15¾			4	5¼
		12	30½			9	18¾			5	8
						10	22			6	11
61	25	2	1½			11	25½			7	14¼
		3	3			12	28¾			8	17½
		4	4¾			12½	31			9	20½
		5	7							10	24
		6	10	63	24	2	1½			11	28
		7	12½			3	3½			12	32
		8	15½			4	5¼				
		9	18½			5	7¾	64	25	2	1½
		10	21¼			6	10¾			3	3¼
		11	25¼			7	13¾			4	5
		12	28½			8	17			5	7¼
		12½	30½			9	20¼			6	10½
						10	23¾			7	14
62	24	2	1½			11	27½			8	17
		3	3¼			12	31½			9	19¼
		4	5							10	22¾
		5	7½	63	25	2	1½			11	26½
		6	10½			3	3¼			12	30
		7	13½			4	4¾			12½	32
		8	16½			5	7				
		9	20			6	10¼	65	25	2	1¾
		10	23½			7	13			3	3½
		11	27			8	16			4	5
		12	31			9	19			5	7¼
						10	22½			6	10½
62	25	2	1½			11	26			7	13½
		3	3			12	29½			8	16¾

Whole contents.	Bung diameter.	Wet or dry inches.	Ullage or remainder. galls.	Whole contents.	Bung diameter.	Wet or dry inches.	Ullage or remainder. galls.	Whole contents.	Bung diameter.	Wet or dry inches.	Ullage or remainder. galls.
		9	19¾			4	5			12	29½
		10	23¼			5	7			13	33½
		11	26¾			6	9¾				
		12	30¼			7	12¾	68	25	2	1¾
		12½	32½			8	16			3	3½
						9	19½			4	5½
65	26	2	1½			10	22			5	7¾
		3	3¾			11	25			6	11
		4	4¾			12	29			7	14¼
		5	7			13	33			8	17½
		6	9¾							9	20½
		7	12½	67	25	2	1½			10	24¼
		8	15¾			3	3½			11	28¼
		9	19¼			4	5½			12	31¾
		10	21¾			5	7½			12½	34
		11	25¼			6	11				
		12	28½			7	14	68	26	2	1½
		13	32½			8	17¼			3	3¼
						9	20¼			4	5¼
66	25	2	1¾			10	24			5	7¼
		3	3½			11	27¾			6	10
		4	5¼			12	31¼			7	13
		5	7½			12½	33½			8	16¼
		6	10¾							9	20
		7	13¾	67	26	2	1½			10	22¾
		8	17			3	3¾			11	26
		9	20			4	4¾			12	29¾
		10	23¾			5	7¼			13	33
		11	26½			6	10				
		12	30¾			7	13	69	25	2	1¾
		12½	33			8	16			3	3½
						9	19¼			4	5½
66	26	2	1½			10	22¼			5	8
		3	3¼			11	26			6	11¼

Whole contents.	Bung diameter.	Wet or dry inches.	Ullage or remainder. galls.
		7	14¼
		8	17¾
		9	20¾
		10	24¾
		11	28½
		12	32¼
		12½	34½
69	26	2	1½
		3	3¼
		4	5
		5	7½
		6	10¼
		7	13¼
		8	16½
		9	20¼
		10	23
		11	26¾
		12	30¼
		13	34½
70	25	2	1¾
		3	3½
		4	5¼
		5	8
		6	11½
		7	14½
		8	17¾
		9	21
		10	25
		11	28¾
		12	32¾
		12½	35

Whole contents.	Bung diameter.	Wet or dry inches.	Ullage or remainder. galls.
70	26	2	1½
		3	3¼
		4	5
		5	7½
		6	10¼
		7	13¼
		8	16¾
		9	20½
		10	23¼
		11	27
		12	30¾
		13	35
71	25	2	1¾
		3	3½
		4	5½
		5	8¼
		6	11½
		7	14¾
		8	18
		9	21½
		10	25¼
		11	29¼
		12	33¼
		12½	35½
71	26	2	1¾
		3	3¼
		4	5¼
		5	7¾
		6	10½
		7	13½
		8	17
		9	21

Whole contents.	Bung diameter.	Wet or dry inches.	Ullage or remainder. galls.
		10	24
		11	27½
		12	31¼
		13	35½
72	25	2	1¾
		3	3¾
		4	5¾
		5	8¼
		6	11¾
		7	15
		8	18
		9	21¾
		10	25¾
		11	29¾
		12	31¾
		12½	36
72	26	2	1¾
		3	3½
		4	5¼
		5	7¾
		6	10¾
		7	13¾
		8	17¼
		9	21¾
		10	24
		11	28
		12	31¼
		13	36
73	25	2	1¾
		3	3¾
		4	6

Whole contents.	Bung diameter.	Wet or dry inches.	Ullage or remainder. galls.	Whole contents.	Bung diameter.	Wet or dry inches.	Ullage or remainder. galls.	Whole contents.	Bung diameter.	Wet or dry inches.	Ullage or remainder. galls.
		5	$8\frac{1}{4}$			$12\frac{1}{2}$	37			8	18
		6	12							9	$22\frac{1}{4}$
		7	$15\frac{1}{4}$	74	26	2	$1\frac{3}{4}$			10	$25\frac{1}{2}$
		8	$18\frac{3}{4}$			3	$3\frac{3}{4}$			11	29
		9	22			4	$5\frac{1}{2}$			12	33
		10	26			5	8			13	$37\frac{1}{2}$
		11	$30\frac{1}{4}$			6	11				
		12	34			7	$14\frac{1}{4}$	76	26	2	$1\frac{3}{4}$
		$12\frac{1}{2}$	$36\frac{1}{2}$			8	$17\frac{3}{4}$			3	$3\frac{3}{4}$
						9	$21\frac{3}{4}$			4	6
73	26	2	$1\frac{3}{4}$			10	25			5	$8\frac{1}{4}$
		3	$3\frac{1}{2}$			11	$28\frac{3}{4}$			6	$11\frac{1}{4}$
		4	$5\frac{1}{4}$			12	$32\frac{1}{2}$			7	$14\frac{3}{4}$
		5	$7\frac{3}{4}$			13	37			8	18
		6	11							9	$21\frac{1}{2}$
		7	14	75	25	2	$1\frac{3}{4}$			10	$25\frac{1}{2}$
		8	$17\frac{1}{2}$			3	4			11	$29\frac{1}{2}$
		9	$21\frac{1}{2}$			4	$6\frac{3}{4}$			12	$33\frac{1}{2}$
		10	$24\frac{3}{4}$			5	$8\frac{1}{2}$			13	38
		11	$28\frac{1}{4}$			6	$12\frac{1}{4}$				
		12	32			7	$15\frac{3}{4}$	76	27	2	$1\frac{3}{4}$
		13	$36\frac{1}{2}$			8	$19\frac{1}{4}$			3	$3\frac{1}{2}$
						9	$22\frac{3}{4}$			4	6
74	25	2	$1\frac{3}{4}$			10	27			5	$7\frac{3}{4}$
		3	4			11	31			6	$10\frac{3}{4}$
		4	6			12	35			7	$14\frac{1}{2}$
		5	$8\frac{1}{2}$			$12\frac{1}{2}$	$37\frac{1}{2}$			8	17
		6	$12\frac{1}{4}$							9	$20\frac{1}{2}$
		7	$15\frac{1}{2}$	75	26	2	$1\frac{3}{4}$			10	24
		8	19			3	$3\frac{3}{4}$			11	$27\frac{3}{4}$
		9	$22\frac{1}{2}$			4	$5\frac{3}{4}$			12	$31\frac{3}{4}$
		10	$26\frac{1}{2}$			5	$8\frac{1}{4}$			13	$35\frac{1}{2}$
		11	$30\frac{3}{4}$			6	$11\frac{1}{4}$			$13\frac{1}{2}$	38
		12	$34\frac{1}{2}$			7	$14\frac{1}{2}$				

289

Whole contents.	Bung diameter.	Wet or dry inches.	Ullage or remainder. galls.	Whole contents.	Bung diameter.	Wet or dry inches.	Ullage or remainder. galls.	Whole contents.	Bung diameter.	Wet or dry inches.	Ullage or remainder. galls.
77	26	2	1¾			9	22½			3	3½
		3	3¾			10	26			4	5½
		4	5¾			11	30			5	8
		5	8¼			12	34¼			6	11¼
		6	11½			13	39			7	14¼
		7	15							8	17¾
		8	18½	78	27	2	1¾			9	21¼
		9	22			3	3¼			10	25
		10	25¾			4	6			11	29
		11	29¾			5	8			12	33
		12	33¾			6	11			13	37
		13	38½			7	14			13½	39½
						8	17½				
77	27	2	1¾			9	21	80	26	2	2
		3	3½			10	24½			3	3¾
		4	5¼			11	28½			4	6
		5	7¾			12	32½			5	8½
		6	11			13	36½			6	11¾
		7	14			13½	39			7	15½
		8	17¼							8	19
		9	20¾	79	26	2	2			9	22¾
		10	24¼			3	3¼			10	26¾
		11	28			4	6			11	31
		12	32¼			5	8½			12	35
		13	36			6	11¾			13	40
		13½	38½			7	15¼				
						8	19	80	27	2	1¾
78	26	2	1¾			9	22½			3	3½
		3	3½			10	26½			4	5½
		4	6			11	30½			6	11¼
		5	8½			12	34¾			7	14½
		6	11½			13	39½			8	18
		7	15							9	21½
		8	18½	79	27	2	1¾			10	25

Whole contents.	Bung diameter.	Wet or dry inches.	Ullage or remainder. galls.	Whole contents.	Bung diameter.	Wet or dry inches.	Ullage or remainder. galls.	Whole contents.	Bung diameter.	Wet or dry inches.	Ullage or remainder. galls.
		11	29¼			5	8¾			12	36½
		12	33½			6	12¼			13	41½
		13	37½			7	15¾				
		13½	40			8	19¾	83	27	2	2
						9	23¼			3	3¾
81	26	2	1¾			10	27¼			4	5¾
		3	3¾			11	31¾			5	8¼
		4	6			12	36			6	11¼
		5	8¾			13	41			7	15
		6	12							8	18¾
		7	15½	82	27	2	2			9	22½
		8	19½			3	3¾			10	26
		9	23			4	5¾			11	30¼
		10	27			5	8¼			12	34¼
		11	31½			6	11¼			13	38¾
		12	35½			7	14¾			13½	41½
		13	40½			8	18½				
						9	22	84	26	2	2
81	27	2	1¾			10	25¾			3	4
		3	3½			11	30¾			4	6¼
		4	5½			12	34¼			5	9
		6	11½			13	38¼			6	12½
		7	14½			13½	41			7	16
		8	18¼							8	20
		9	21¾	83	26	2	2			9	24
		10	25½			3	4			10	28
		11	29½			4	6¼			11	32½
		12	33¾			5	9			12	36¾
		13	37¼			6	12¼			13	42
		13½	40¼			7	16				
						8	20	84	27	2	2
82	26	2	2			9	23½			3	4
		3	4			10	27¾			4	6
		4	6¼			11	32¼			5	8½

Whole contents.	Bung diameter.	Wet or dry inches.	Ullage or remainder. galls.
		6	12
		7	15¼
		8	19
		9	22¾
		10	25¾
		11	30¾
		12	35¼
		13	39¼
		13½	42
85	26	2	2
		3	4¼
		4	6½
		5	9¼
		6	12¾
		7	16½
		8	20½
		9	24¼
		10	28½
		11	33
		12	37¼
		13	42½
85	27	2	2
		3	4
		4	6¼
		5	8¾
		6	12¼
		7	15½
		8	19¼
		9	23
		10	26¾
		11	31
		12	35¾

Whole contents.	Bung diameter.	Wet or dry inches.	Ullage or remainder. galls.
		13	39¾
		13½	42½
86	27	2	2
		3	4
		4	6
		5	8¾
		6	12
		7	15¼
		8	19¼
		9	23¼
		10	27
		11	31½
		12	36
		13	40
		13½	43
86	28	2	2
		3	3¾
		4	5¾
		5	8
		6	11
		7	14¾
		8	18¼
		9	22
		10	25½
		11	29¾
		12	34
		13	38¾
		14	43
87	27	2	2
		3	4
		4	6

Whole contents.	Bung diameter.	Wet or dry inches.	Ullage or remainder. galls.
		5	8¾
		6	12
		7	15½
		8	19½
		9	23½
		10	27¼
		11	31¾
		12	36½
		13	40½
		13½	43½
87	28	2	1¾
		3	3¾
		4	5¾
		5	8¼
		6	12
		7	15
		8	18¼
		9	22
		10	26
		11	30
		12	34½
		13	38½
		14	43½
88	27	2	2
		3	4
		4	6
		5	8¾
		6	12¼
		7	15¾
		8	19¾
		9	23½
		10	27¾

Whole contents.	Bung diameter.	Wet or dry inches.	Ullage or remainder. galls.	Whole contents.	Bung diameter.	Wet or dry inches.	Ullage or remainder. galls.	Whole contents.	Bung diameter.	Wet or dry inches.	Ullage or remainder. galls.
		11	32			3	3¾			9	23
		12	36¾			4	6			10	27
		13	41			5	8½			11	31
		13½	44			6	11½			12	35¾
88	28	2	1¾			7	15¼			13	40
		3	3½			8	18¾			14	45
		4	5¾			9	22¼				
		5	8¼			10	26	91	27	2	2¼
		6	11¼			11	30¾			3	4¼
		7	15			12	35¼			4	6½
		8	18½			13	39½			5	9½
		9	22¼			14	44½			6	13
		10	26	90	27	2	2			7	16½
		11	30¼			3	4			8	20½
		12	34¾			4	6¼			9	24½
		13	39			5	9¼			10	28½
		13½	44			6	12¾			11	33¼
89	27	2	2			7	16¼			12	38¼
		3	4			8	20			13	42½
		4	6¼			9	24¼			13½	45½
		5	9			10	28¾	91	28	2	2
		6	12½			11	32¾			3	4
		7	16			12	37¾			4	6
		8	20			13	42			5	8¾
		9	23			13½	45			6	11¾
		10	28	90	28	2	2			7	15½
		11	32½			3	3¾			8	19¼
		12	37¼			4	6			9	23¼
		13	41½			5	8¾			10	27
		13½	44½			6	11¾			11	31½
						7	15¼			12	36
										13	40½
89	28	2	2			8	19			14	45½

Whole contents.	Bung diameter.	Wet or dry inches.	Ullage or remainder. galls.	Whole contents.	Bung diameter.	Wet or dry inches.	Ullage or remainder. galls.	Whole contents.	Bung diameter.	Wet or dry inches.	Ullage or remainder. galls.
92	27	2	2			8	21	94	28	2	2
		3	4¼			9	25			3	4
		4	6¼			10	29½			4	6¼
		5	9¼			11	34			5	9
		6	12¾			12	39			6	12¼
		7	16¼			13½	46½			7	16¼
		8	20¾							8	19¾
		9	24¾	93	28	2	2			9	24
		10	29			3	4			10	28
		11	33½			4	6¼			11	32½
		12	38½			5	8¾			12	37¼
		13	42¾			6	12			13	41¾
		13½	46			7	16			14	47
						8	19¾				
92	28	2	2			9	23¾	95	27	2	2¼
		3	4			10	27½			3	4¼
		4	6			11	32¼			4	6¾
		5	8¾			12	36¾			5	9¾
		6	12			13	41¼			6	13½
		7	15¾			14	46½			7	17¼
		8	19½							8	21½
		9	23½	94	27	2	2¼			9	25¾
		10	27¼			3	4¼			10	30
		11	31¾			4	6¼			11	34½
		12	36¼			5	9¾			12	39¾
		13	42¾			6	13¼			13	44½
		14	46			7	17			13½	47½
						8	21¼				
93	27	2	2			9	25½	95	28	2	2
		3	4¼			10	29¾			3	4
		4	6½			11	34¼			4	6½
		5	9½			12	39½			5	9
		6	13			13	44			6	12½
		7	16¾			13½	47			7	16½

294

Whole contents.	Bung diameter.	Wet or dry inches.	Ullage or remainder. galls.	Whole contents.	Bung diameter.	Wet or dry inches.	Ullage or remainder. galls.	Whole contents.	Bung diameter.	Wet or dry inches.	Ullage or remainder. galls.
		8	20			14	45			4	6¼
		9	24¼			14½	48			5	9¼
		10	28¼							6	12¾
		11	33	97	28	2	2			7	17
		12	37½			3	4			8	20½
		13	42¼			4	6¼			9	25½
		14	47½			5	9¼			10	29¼
						6	12½			11	34
96	28	2	2			7	16¾			12	38¾
		3	4			8	20¼			13	43¾
		4	6¼			9	25			14	49
		5	9			10	28¾				
		6	12¼			11	33½	98	29	2	2
		7	16½			12	38¼			3	4
		8	20			13	43			4	6¼
		9	24¾			14	48½			5	9
		10	28½							6	12
		11	33	97	29	2	1¾			7	16
		12	37¾			3	3¾			8	19¾
		13	42½			4	6			9	23¾
		14	48			5	9			10	28
						6	11¾			11	32
96	29	2	2			7	16			12	36¾
		3	3¾			8	19½			13	41½
		4	6			9	23½			14	46
		5	8¾			10	27½			14½	49
		6	11½			11	31¾				
		7	15¾			12	36½	99	28	2	2¼
		8	19¼			13	41			3	4¼
		9	23¼			14	45½			4	6¾
		10	27			14½	48½			5	9½
		11	31¼							6	13
		12	36	98	28	2	2			7	17
		13	40¾			3	4			8	21

Whole contents.	Bung diameter.	Wet or dry inches.	Ullage or remainder (galls.)	Whole contents.	Bung diameter.	Wet or dry inches.	Ullage or remainder (galls.)	Whole contents.	Bung diameter.	Wet or dry inches.	Ullage or remainder (galls.)
		9	25¾			14	50			5	9½
		10	29½							6	12½
		11	34¼	100	29	2	2			7	16½
		12	39¼			3	4			8	20½
		13	44			4	6½			9	24¼
		14	49½			5	9¼			10	28½
						6	12½			11	33
99	29	2	2¼			7	16½			12	39¼
		3	4			8	20			13	42¾
		4	6½			9	24¼			14	47½
		5	9¼			10	28¼			14½	50¼
		6	12¼			11	32¼				
		7	16¼			12	37½	102	28	2	2
		8	20			13	42½			3	4½
		9	23¾			14	47			4	6¾
		10	28			14½	50			5	9¾
		11	32½							6	13½
		12	37¼	101	28	2	2			7	17½
		13	42			3	4½			8	21½
		14	46½			4	6¾			9	26½
		14½	49½			5	9½			10	30¼
						6	12¼			11	35¼
100	28	2	2			7	17½			12	40½
		3	4¼			8	21¼			13	45
		4	6¾			9	26			14	51
		5	9½			10	30				
		6	13			11	34¾	102	29	2	2
		7	17¼			12	40			3	4¼
		8	21			13	44¾			4	6½
		9	25¾			14	50½			5	9¼
		10	29¾							6	12¾
		11	34¼	101	29	2	2			7	16¾
		12	39½			3	4¼			8	20¾
		13	44½			4	6½			9	24¾

Whole contents.	Bung diameter.	Wet or dry inches.	Ullage or remainder. galls.	Whole contents.	Bung diameter.	Wet or dry inches.	Ullage or remainder. galls.	Whole contents.	Bung diameter.	Wet or dry inches.	Ullage or remainder. galls.
		10	29			14½	51½			5	10¼
		11	33½							6	13¾
		12	38¼	104	28	2	2¼			7	18¼
		13	43¼			3	4½			8	22¼
		14	48			4	7¼			9	27½
		14½	51			5	10			10	31¼
						6	13½			11	36½
103	28	2	2¼			7	18			12	41¾
		3	4½			8	22			13	46¾
		4	7			9	27			14	52½
		5	10			10	31				
		6	13½			11	36	105	29	2	2¼
		7	17¾			12	41¼			3	4½
		8	21¾			13	46¼			4	6¾
		9	26¾			14	52			5	9¾
		10	30¾							6	13
		11	35¾	104	29	2	2¼			7	17½
		12	40¾			3	4¼			8	21¼
		13	45¾			4	6¾			9	25½
		14	51½			5	9¾			10	29¾
						6	12¾			11	34½
103	29	2	2			7	17¼			12	39½
		3	4¼			8	21			13	44¾
		4	6¾			9	25¼			14	49½
		5	9¾			10	29½			14½	52½
		6	12¾			11	34¼				
		7	17			12	39	106	29	2	2¼
		8	21			13	44¼			3	4¼
		9	25			14	49			4	6¾
		10	30¼			14½	52			5	9¾
		11	33							6	13
		12	38¾	105	28	2	2¼			7	18½
		13	43¾			3	4¾			8	21½
		14	48			4	7¼			9	24¾

Whole contents.	Bung diameter.	Wet or dry inches.	Ullage or remainder. galls.
		10	30¼
		11	34¾
		12	39¾
		13	45
		14	50
		14½	53
106	30	2	2
		3	4
		4	6¼
		5	9½
		6	12½
		7	16½
		8	20½
		9	24¾
		10	28¾
		11	32¾
		12	38
		13	43
		14	47½
		15	53
107	29	2	2¼
		3	4½
		4	7
		5	10
		6	13¼
		7	17¾
		8	21¾
		9	26
		10	30½
		11	35¼
		12	40¼
		13	45½
		14	50½
		14½	53½
107	30	2	2
		3	4¼
		4	6¾
		5	9½
		6	12¾
		7	16¾
		8	20¾
		9	25
		10	29
		11	33¼
		12	38¼
		13	43½
		14	48
		15	53½
108	29	2	2¼
		3	4½
		4	7
		5	10
		6	13¼
		7	18
		8	21¾
		9	26¼
		10	30¾
		11	35½
		12	40¾
		13	46
		14	51
		14½	54
108	30	2	2
		3	4¼
		4	6¾
		5	9½
		6	12¾
		7	16¾
		8	21
		9	25¼
		10	29
		11	33½
		12	38½
		13	43¾
		14	48½
		15	54
109	29	2	2¼
		3	3¼
		4	7
		5	10
		6	13½
		7	19
		8	22¼
		9	26½
		10	31
		11	36
		12	41
		13	46½
		14	51½
		14½	54½
109	30	2	2¼
		3	4¼
		4	6¾
		5	9½
		6	13

Whole contents.	Bung diameter.	Wet or dry inches.	Ullage or remainder. galls.
		7	17
		8	21¼
		9	25½
		10	29½
		11	33¾
		12	39
		13	44¼
		14	49
		15	54½
110	29	2	2¼
		3	4¼
		4	7
		5	10
		6	13¾
		7	18¼
		8	22½
		9	26¾
		10	31½
		11	36¼
		12	41½
		13	47
		14	51¾
		14½	55
110	30	2	2¼
		3	4¼
		4	6¾
		5	9¾
		6	13¼
		7	17
		8	21¼
		9	25½
		10	29¾
		11	34¼
		12	39¼
		13	44½
		14	49½
		15	55
111	29	2	2¼
		3	4¼
		4	7
		5	11
		6	13¾
		7	18½
		8	22½
		9	27
		10	31¾
		11	36¼
		12	41¾
		13	47¼
		14	52¼
		14½	55½
111	30	2	2
		3	4¼
		4	6¼
		5	10¾
		6	13
		7	17
		8	21¼
		9	25¾
		10	30
		11	34½
		12	39½
		13	45
		14	49¾
		15	55½
112	29	2	2
		3	4¼
		4	7
		5	10
		6	13½
		7	18½
		8	22¾
		9	27
		10	32
		11	36¾
		12	42
		13	47½
		14	52¾
		14½	56
112	30	2	2
		3	4¼
		4	6¾
		5	9¾
		6	13
		7	17¼
		8	21¼
		9	26
		10	30¼
		11	34¾
		12	40
		13	45
		14	50¼
		15	56
113	29	2	2¼
		3	4½

299

Whole contents.	Bung diameter.	Wet or dry inches.	Ullage or remainder. galls.	Whole contents.	Bung diameter.	Wet or dry inches.	Ullage or remainder. galls.	Whole contents.	Bung diameter.	Wet or dry inches.	Ullage or remainder. galls.
		4	7			8	23			12	$43\frac{1}{4}$
		5	10			9	$27\frac{1}{2}$			13	$48\frac{3}{4}$
		6	$13\frac{3}{4}$			10	$31\frac{1}{4}$			14	$54\frac{1}{4}$
		7	$18\frac{1}{2}$			11	$37\frac{1}{2}$			$14\frac{1}{2}$	$57\frac{1}{2}$
		8	23			12	$42\frac{3}{4}$				
		9	$27\frac{1}{4}$			13	$47\frac{3}{4}$	115	30	2	$2\frac{1}{4}$
		10	33			14	$53\frac{1}{4}$			3	$4\frac{1}{4}$
		11	$37\frac{1}{2}$			$14\frac{1}{2}$	57			4	7
		12	$42\frac{1}{2}$							5	10
		13	48	114	30	2	$2\frac{1}{4}$			6	$13\frac{1}{2}$
		14	$53\frac{1}{4}$			3	$4\frac{1}{4}$			7	$17\frac{3}{4}$
		$14\frac{1}{2}$	$56\frac{1}{2}$			4	$6\frac{3}{4}$			8	22
						5	$9\frac{3}{4}$			9	$26\frac{3}{4}$
113	30	2	$2\frac{1}{4}$			6	$13\frac{1}{4}$			10	31
		3	$4\frac{1}{4}$			7	$17\frac{1}{2}$			11	$35\frac{3}{4}$
		4	$6\frac{3}{4}$			8	22			12	41
		5	$9\frac{3}{4}$			9	$26\frac{1}{2}$			13	$46\frac{3}{4}$
		6	$13\frac{1}{4}$			10	$30\frac{3}{4}$			14	$51\frac{3}{4}$
		7	$17\frac{1}{2}$			11	$35\frac{1}{4}$			15	$57\frac{1}{2}$
		8	$21\frac{1}{2}$			12	$40\frac{3}{4}$				
		9	$26\frac{1}{4}$			13	$46\frac{1}{4}$	116	30	2	$2\frac{1}{4}$
		10	$30\frac{1}{2}$			14	$51\frac{1}{4}$			3	$4\frac{1}{2}$
		11	35			15	57			4	7
		12	$40\frac{1}{4}$							5	10
		13	$45\frac{3}{4}$	115	29	2	$2\frac{3}{4}$			6	$13\frac{1}{2}$
		14	$50\frac{3}{4}$			3	$4\frac{1}{2}$			7	18
		15	$56\frac{1}{2}$			4	$7\frac{1}{4}$			8	$22\frac{1}{2}$
						5	$10\frac{1}{4}$			9	27
114	29	2	$2\frac{1}{4}$			6	14			10	$31\frac{1}{4}$
		3	$4\frac{1}{4}$			7	19			11	36
		4	7			8	$23\frac{1}{4}$			12	41
		5	10			9	28			13	47
		6	14			10	$32\frac{3}{4}$			14	$52\frac{1}{4}$
		7	$18\frac{3}{4}$			11	$37\frac{3}{4}$			15	58

Whole contents.	Bung diameter.	Wet or dry inches.	Ullage or remainder. galls.	Whole contents.	Bung diameter.	Wet or dry inches.	Ullage or remainder. galls.	Whole contents.	Bung diameter.	Wet or dry inches.	Ullage or remainder. galls.
116	31	2	2			5	$9\frac{3}{4}$			8	$21\frac{1}{2}$
		3	$4\frac{1}{4}$			6	$12\frac{3}{4}$			9	26
		4	$6\frac{1}{2}$			7	17			10	$30\frac{1}{2}$
		5	$10\frac{1}{2}$			8	$21\frac{1}{4}$			11	$34\frac{3}{4}$
		6	$12\frac{3}{4}$			9	$25\frac{3}{4}$			12	40
		7	17			10	$30\frac{1}{4}$			13	$45\frac{1}{4}$
		8	21			11	$34\frac{1}{2}$			14	$50\frac{1}{2}$
		9	$25\frac{1}{2}$			12	$39\frac{1}{2}$			15	$55\frac{3}{4}$
		10	30			13	$44\frac{3}{4}$			$15\frac{1}{2}$	59
		11	$34\frac{1}{4}$			14	50				
		12	$39\frac{1}{4}$			15	$55\frac{1}{4}$	119	30	2	$2\frac{1}{2}$
		13	$44\frac{1}{2}$			$15\frac{1}{2}$	$58\frac{1}{2}$			3	$4\frac{3}{4}$
		14	$49\frac{1}{2}$							4	$7\frac{1}{4}$
		15	$54\frac{3}{4}$	118	30	2	$2\frac{1}{2}$			5	10
		$15\frac{1}{2}$	58			3	$4\frac{3}{4}$			6	$13\frac{3}{4}$
						4	$7\frac{1}{4}$			7	$18\frac{1}{2}$
117	30	2	$2\frac{1}{4}$			5	10			8	$22\frac{1}{2}$
		3	$4\frac{3}{4}$			6	$13\frac{3}{4}$			9	$27\frac{1}{2}$
		4	7			7	$18\frac{1}{4}$			10	$32\frac{1}{4}$
		5	10			8	23			11	37
		6	$13\frac{3}{4}$			9	$27\frac{1}{2}$			12	$42\frac{1}{2}$
		7	18			10	$31\frac{3}{4}$			13	$48\frac{1}{4}$
		8	$22\frac{1}{4}$			11	$36\frac{3}{4}$			14	$53\frac{1}{2}$
		9	$27\frac{1}{4}$			12	$42\frac{1}{4}$			15	$59\frac{1}{2}$
		10	$31\frac{1}{2}$			13	$47\frac{3}{4}$				
		11	$36\frac{1}{2}$			14	$53\frac{1}{4}$	119	31	2	2
		12	$41\frac{3}{4}$			15	59			3	$4\frac{1}{4}$
		13	$47\frac{1}{2}$							4	$6\frac{3}{4}$
		14	$52\frac{3}{4}$	118	31	2	2			5	$9\frac{3}{4}$
		15	$58\frac{1}{2}$			3	$4\frac{1}{4}$			6	13
						4	$6\frac{3}{4}$			7	$17\frac{1}{4}$
117	31	2	$2\frac{1}{4}$			5	$9\frac{1}{2}$			8	$21\frac{3}{4}$
		3	$4\frac{1}{4}$			6	13			9	$26\frac{1}{4}$
		4	$6\frac{3}{4}$			7	$17\frac{1}{4}$			10	$30\frac{3}{4}$

301

Whole contents.	Bung diameter.	Wet or dry inches.	Ullage or remainder. galls.	Whole contents.	Bung diameter.	Wet or dry inches.	Ullage or remainder. galls.	Whole contents.	Bung diameter.	Wet or dry inches.	Ullage or remainder. galls.
		11	35¼			14	51¼			15	50
		12	40¼			15	56¾			16	55
		13	45¾			15½	60			17	61½
		14	51								
		14	56¼	121	33	2	1¾	122	31	2	2
		15½	59½			3	3¾			3	4¼
						4	6¼			4	7
120	30	2	2¼			5	8¾			5	10
		3	4¾			6	12			6	13
		4	7½			7	15½			7	17¾
		5	10			8	20			8	22
		6	13¾			9	24¼			9	26¾
		7	18½			10	28¼			10	31½
		8	23¾			11	32¾			11	36
		9	27¾			12	36¾			12	39½
		10	32½			13	42			13	46¾
		11	37¼			14	47			14	52½
		12	42¾			15	52½			15	58
		13	48¼			16	57½			15½	61
		14	54			16½	61½				
		15	60					122	32	2	2
				121	34	2	1¾			3	3
120	31	2	2			3	2¾			4	6¾
		3	4¼			4	6			5	9½
		4	6¾			5	9½			6	12¾
		5	9½			6	11¾			7	16¾
		6	13			7	15			8	21
		7	17¼			8	18¼			9	25½
		8	21¾			9	22¾			10	30¼
		9	26¼			10	27¼			11	34¾
		10	31			11	30½			12	39¼
		11	35¼			12	34¼			13	44¾
		12	40½			13	40¼			14	50
		13	46			14	45			15	55½

Whole contents.	Bung diameter.	Wet or dry inches.	Ullage or remainder. galls.
		16	61
123	31	2	2¼
		3	4½
		4	7
		5	10
		6	13¼
		7	17¾
		8	22¼
		9	27¼
		10	31¼
		11	36¼
		12	42
		13	47
		14	53
		15	58¼
		15½	61½
124	31	2	2¼
		3	4½
		4	7
		5	10¼
		6	13½
		7	18
		8	22¼
		9	27½
		10	32
		11	36¾
		12	42¼
		13	47½
		14	52
		15	58¾
		15½	62

Whole contents.	Bung diameter.	Wet or dry inches.	Ullage or remainder. galls.
125	31	2	2¼
		3	4¾
		4	7¼
		5	10½
		6	13¾
		7	18
		8	22½
		9	27½
		10	32½
		11	37
		12	42½
		13	48
		14	52½
		15	59¼
		15½	62½
126	31	2	2¼
		3	4¾
		4	7
		5	10½
		6	13¾
		7	17¼
		8	22½
		9	27¾
		10	32¾
		11	37½
		12	42¾
		13	49¾
		14	54¼
		15	59¾
		15½	63
126	33	2	2
		3	4

Whole contents.	Bung diameter.	Wet or dry inches.	Ullage or remainder. galls.
		4	6¾
		5	9¼
		6	12¾
		7	16½
		8	20¾
		9	25
		10	30
		11	34¼
		12	39
		13	44¼
		14	49¼
		15	54¾
		16	59¾
		16½	63
127	31	2	2
		3	4¾
		4	7¼
		5	10½
		6	14
		7	18¼
		8	22¾
		9	27¾
		10	32¾
		11	37½
		12	43¼
		13	48¾
		14	54½
		15	60¼
		15½	63½
128	31	2	2¼
		3	4¾
		4	7¼

Whole contents.	Bung diameter.	Wet or dry inches.	Ullage or remainder. galls.	Whole contents.	Bung diameter.	Wet or dry inches.	Ullage or remainder. galls.	Whole contents.	Bung diameter.	Wet or dry inches.	Ullage or remainder. galls.
		5	9¼			6	14			8	23½
		6	14			7	18¾			9	27¼
		7	18½			8	23			10	32¼
		8	23			9	28¼			11	37¼
		9	28			10	33½			12	41
		10	33			11	38¼			13	47¾
		11	38			12	43¾			14	55
		12	43½			13	49½			15	59
		13	49½			14	54¼			16	65½
		14	53¾			15	61				
		15	60¾			15½	64½	132	32	2	2
		15½	64							3	4½
				130	31	2	2½			4	7¼
128	33	2	2			3	4¾			5	10¼
		3	4			4	7¾			6	13
		4	7			5	10¾			7	18¼
		5	9½			6	14¼			8	22¾
		6	13			7	19			9	27½
		7	16¾			8	23¼			10	32¼
		8	21			9	28¼			11	37½
		9	25½			10	33¾			12	42½
		10	30¼			11	38½			13	48¼
		11	34¾			12	44¼			14	55½
		12	39¾			13	50			15	59
		13	44¾			14	54½			16	66
		14	50			15	61¾				
		15	55½			15½	65	133	32	2	2¼
		16	60¾							3	4½
		16½	64	131	32	2	2			4	7½
						3	4½			5	10½
129	31	2	2¼			4	7¼			6	14
		3	4¾			5	10¼			7	18½
		4	7½			6	13¾			8	23
		5	10¾			7	19			9	27¾

Whole contents.	Bung diameter.	Wet or dry inches.	Ullage or remainder. galls.	Whole contents.	Bung diameter.	Wet or dry inches.	Ullage or remainder. galls.	Whole contents.	Bung diameter.	Wet or dry inches.	Ullage or remainder. galls.
		10	33			11	34½			11	34¾
		11	37¾			12	39			12	38¾
		12	42¾			13	44½			13	42¾
		13	48½			14	49¾			14	49¾
		14	56			15	55¼			15	55¾
		15	60			16	60½			16	61
		16	66½			17	66½			17	67
133	33	2	2¼	134	33	2	2¼	135	33	2	2¼
		3	4¼			3	4¼			3	4½
		4	7¼			4	7			4	7½
		5	11¼			5	10			5	10
		6	13½			6	13½			6	13¾
		7	17½			7	16¾			7	17¾
		8	22			8	22¼			8	22½
		9	26½			9	26¾			9	27
		10	31¼			10	31½			10	31¼
		11	36¼			11	36¼			11	36½
		12	41¼			12	41½			12	41¾
		13	46½			13	47			13	47¼
		14	52			14	52½			14	51½
		15	57½			15	58			15	61½
		16	63½			16	63¾			16	64¼
		16½	66½			16½	67			16½	67½
133	34	2	2¼	134	34	2	2¼	135	34	2	2¼
		3	4			3	4			3	4
		4	6¾			4	6½			4	6
		5	9¼			5	9¼			5	9½
		6	13			6	13			6	13¼
		7	16½			7	16½			7	16¾
		8	21			8	21¼			8	21½
		9	25			9	25¼			9	25½
		10	30			10	30			10	30½

305

Whole contents.	Bung diameter.	Wet or dry inches.	Ullage or remainder. galls.	Whole contents.	Bung diameter.	Wet or dry inches.	Ullage or remainder. galls.	Whole contents.	Bung diameter.	Wet or dry inches.	Ullage or remainder. galls.
		11	35			11	35¼			11	35½
		12	39¾			12	40			12	40½
		13	45¾			13	45¼			13	45¾
		14	50			14	50¾			14	51¼
		15	56			15	56½			15	57
		16	61½			16	61¾			16	62½
		17	67½			17	68			17	68½
136	33	2	2¼	137	33	2	2	138	33	2	2
		3	4¼			3	4¼			3	4¼
		4	7¼			4	7¼			4	7¼
		5	10			5	10¼			5	10¼
		6	13¾			6	13¾			6	13¾
		7	17¾			7	17¾			7	18¼
		8	22½			8	22¾			8	22¾
		9	27			9	27			9	27½
		10	32			10	32			10	32¼
		11	36¾			11	37			11	37¼
		12	42			12	42¼			12	42½
		13	47¾			13	48			13	48¼
		14	53¼			14	53½			14	54
		15	60¼			15	59¼			15	59¾
		16	64½			16	65			16	65½
		16½	68			16½	68½			16½	69
136	34	2	2	137	34	2	2	138	34	2	2
		3	4			3	4			3	4
		4	6¾			4	6¾			4	6¾
		5	9¾			5	9½			5	9½
		6	13¼			6	13¼			6	13¼
		7	16¾			7	17			7	17¼
		8	21½			8	21¾			8	21¾
		9	25½			9	25¾			9	26
		10	30½			10	30¾			10	30¾

Whole contents.	Bung diameter.	Wet or dry inches.	Ullage or remainder. galls.	Whole contents.	Bung diameter.	Wet or dry inches.	Ullage or remainder. galls.	Whole contents.	Bung diameter.	Wet or dry inches.	Ullage or remainder. galls.
		11	35¾			11	35¾			11	36
		12	40¾			12	40¾			12	41
		13	46			13	46¼			13	46½
		14	51½			14	52			14	52¼
		15	57½			15	56¾			15	58
		16	62½			16	62			16	63½
		17	69			17	69½			17	70
139	33	2	2	140	33	2	2¼	141	32	2	2
		3	4¼			3	4¼			3	4½
		4	7¼			4	7¼			4	7¾
		5	10¼			5	10¼			5	10¾
		6	13¾			6	14			6	14¾
		7	18			7	18¼			7	19¼
		8	22¾			8	23			8	24
		9	27¾			9	27¾			9	29
		10	32½			10	32¾			10	34¼
		11	37½			11	37¾			11	39¾
		12	43			12	43¼			12	44¾
		13	48½			13	48¾			13	51
		14	54¼			14	54¾			14	58¾
		15	60¼			15	60½			15	63
		16	66			16	66½			16	70
		16½	69½			16½	70				
								141	33	2	2¼
139	34	2	2	140	34	2	2			3	4½
		3	4			3	4			4	7¼
		4	6¾			4	6¾			5	10½
		5	9½			5	9½			6	14¼
		6	13¼			6	13½			7	18½
		7	17¼			7	17¼			8	23
		8	21¾			8	22			9	28
		9	26¼			9	26¼			10	33
		10	31			10	31¼			11	38

Whole contents.	Bung diameter.	Wet or dry inches.	Ullage or remainder. galls.	Whole contents.	Bung diameter.	Wet or dry inches.	Ullage or remainder. galls.	Whole contents.	Bung diameter.	Wet or dry inches.	Ullage or remainder. galls.
		12	43¾			12	43¾			12	44
		13	49¼			13	49¾			13	50
		14	55			14	55½			14	56
		15	61¼			15	61¾			15	62½
		16	67			16	67¼			16	67¾
		16½	70½			16½	71			16½	71½
141	34	2	2¼	142	34	2	2¼	143	34	2	2¼
		3	4			3	4¼			3	4½
		4	7			4	6¾			4	7
		5	9¾			5	10			5	10
		6	13¾			6	13¾			6	13¾
		7	17¼			7	17½			7	17¾
		8	22			8	22¼			8	22¾
		9	26			9	27			9	27
		10	31½			10	31¾			10	32¼
		11	36¼			11	36¾			11	36¾
		12	41			12	41½			12	41¾
		13	46¾			13	46¼			13	47¾
		14	52½			14	53			14	53¼
		15	57			15	59			15	57¾
		16	64			16	64¾			16	65
		17	70½			17	71			17	71½
142	33	2	2	143	33	2	2½	144	33	2	2¼
		3	4¾			3	4¾			3	4¾
		4	7½			4	7½			4	7¾
		5	10½			5	10¾			5	10¾
		6	14¼			6	14½			6	14½
		7	18¾			7	18¾			7	19
		8	23¼			8	23½			8	23¾
		9	28¼			9	29½			9	28¾
		10	33			10	33½			10	33¾
		11	38¼			11	38¾			11	39

Whole contents.	Bung diameter.	Wet or dry inches.	Ullage or remainder. galls.	Whole contents.	Bung diameter.	Wet or dry inches.	Ullage or remainder. galls.	Whole contents.	Bung diameter.	Wet or dry inches.	Ullage or remainder. galls.
		12	44¼			12	44¾			12	42¾
		13	50¼			13	50¾			13	48¾
		14	56½			14	57			14	54½
		15	62¾			15	63			15	60½
		16	68¼			16	69			16	66½
		16½	72			16½	72½			17	73
144	34	2	2½	145	34	2	2½	147	34	2	2¼
		3	4½			3	4¾			3	4½
		4	7			4	7½			4	7½
		5	10			5	10			5	10½
		6	14			6	14			6	14¼
		7	18			7	18			7	18¼
		8	22¾			8	23			8	23¼
		9	27			9	27½			9	27¾
		10	32½			10	32½			10	33¼
		11	37¼			11	37½			11	38
		12	42½			12	42½			12	43¼
		13	47½			13	48½			13	49
		14	53¾			14	54			14	54¾
		15	59¾			15	60¼			15	61
		16	65½			16	66			16	67
		17	72			17	72½			17	73½
145	33	2	2½	146	34	2	2½	148	34	2	2¼
		3	5			3	4¾			3	4½
		4	8			4	7½			4	7½
		5	11			5	10¼			5	10½
		6	14½			6	14¼			6	14½
		7	19			7	18¼			7	18¼
		8	24			8	23¼			8	23½
		9	29			9	27¾			9	28
		10	34			10	33			10	33¼
		11	39			11	37¾			11	38¼

309

Whole contents.	Bung diameter.	Wet or dry inches.	Ullage or remainder. galls.	Whole contents.	Bung diameter.	Wet or dry inches.	Ullage or remainder. galls.	Whole contents.	Bung diameter.	Wet or dry inches.	Ullage or remainder. galls.
		12	43¼			12	43½			11	37
		13	49¼			13	49¼			12	42½
		14	55			14	55½			13	48½
		15	61½			15	62			14	54½
		16	67¾			16	68			15	60¼
		17	74			17	75			16	66¼
										17	72½
149	34	2	2½	151	35	2	2¼			17½	76
		3	4½			3	4½				
		4	7½			4	7½	153	35	2	2¼
		5	10½			5	10¼			3	4½
		6	14½			6	14			4	7½
		7	18½			7	19¾			5	10½
		8	23¾			8	24¾			6	14¼
		9	28¼			9	27¾			7	18¼
		10	33½			10	32½			8	23
		11	38½			11	37¾			9	28
		12	43¾			12	42¼			10	33
		13	49½			13	48¾			11	38¼
		14	55½			14	54¾			12	43
		15	66			15	60			13	48½
		16	67¾			16	65¾			14	54¾
		17	74½			17	72			15	60¾
						17½	75½			16	66¾
150	34	2	2½							17	73
		3	4½	152	35	2	2¼			17½	76
		4	7½			3	4½				
		5	11			4	7½	154	33	2	2¼
		6	14½			5	10½			3	5
		7	18½			6	14¼			4	8
		8	23¾			7	18¼			5	11¾
		9	28½			8	23			6	15¾
		10	33½			9	27¾			7	20
		11	38½			10	32¼			8	25½

Whole contents.	Bung diameter.	Wet or dry inches.	Ullage or remainder. galls.	Whole contents.	Bung diameter.	Wet or dry inches.	Ullage or remainder. galls.	Whole contents.	Bung diameter.	Wet or dry inches.	Ullage or remainder. galls.
		9	30¾			8	23½			6	14
		10	35¾			9	28½			7	18
		11	41¾			10	33½			9	27½
		12	49¾			11	38¾			10	32¼
		13	56			12	43½			11	37½
		14	60			13	49½			12	42½
		15	67½			14	55½			13	47½
		16	73¼			15	61½			14	53½
		16½	77			16	67¾			15	59¾
154	35	2	2¼			17	74			16	65½
		3	4½			17½	77½			17	71¼
		4	7½	156	36	2	2			18	78½
		5	10½			3	4½	158	36	2	2¼
		6	14½			4	7¾			3	4¾
		7	18½			5	10¼			4	7½
		8	23¼			6	13¾			5	10½
		9	28¼			7	18			6	14
		10	33¼			8	22¾			7	18¼
		11	38½			9	27½			8	22¾
		12	43¼			10	32¼			9	27½
		13	48¾			11	37¼			10	32¾
		14	55			12	42¼			11	37¾
		15	61			13	47¼			12	42¾
		16	67¾			14	53¼			13	47¾
		17	73½			15	59½			14	50
		17½	77			16	65½			15	54
155	35	2	2½			17	71¼			16	56¼
		3	4½			18	78			17	72¼
		4	7¾	157	36	2	2			18	79
		5	10¾			3	4½	158	37	2	2
		6	14½			4	7½			3	4¼
		7	18½			5	10¼			4	7¼

Whole contents.	Bung diameter.	Wet or dry inches.	Ullage or remainder. galls.	Whole contents.	Bung diameter.	Wet or dry inches.	Ullage or remainder. galls.	Whole contents.	Bung diameter.	Wet or dry inches.	Ullage or remainder. galls.
		5	10			10	32			16	$64\frac{1}{4}$
		6	$13\frac{1}{4}$			11	38			17	70
		7	$17\frac{1}{2}$			12	43			18	76
		8	$21\frac{3}{4}$			13	$48\frac{1}{4}$			$18\frac{1}{2}$	$79\frac{1}{2}$
		9	$26\frac{3}{4}$			14	$54\frac{1}{4}$				
		10	$31\frac{1}{2}$			15	$60\frac{1}{2}$	160	37	2	$2\frac{1}{2}$
		11	$36\frac{1}{2}$			16	67			3	$4\frac{1}{2}$
		12	$41\frac{1}{4}$			17	$72\frac{3}{4}$			4	$7\frac{1}{4}$
		13	$46\frac{1}{4}$			18	$79\frac{1}{2}$			5	10
		14	$51\frac{3}{4}$							6	$13\frac{3}{4}$
		15	$57\frac{3}{4}$	159	37	2	2			7	$17\frac{1}{2}$
		16	$63\frac{3}{4}$			3	$4\frac{1}{2}$			8	$22\frac{1}{4}$
		17	69			4	$7\frac{1}{4}$			9	27
		18	$75\frac{1}{2}$			5	$10\frac{1}{4}$			10	$31\frac{3}{4}$
		$18\frac{1}{2}$	79			6	$13\frac{1}{2}$			11	$36\frac{3}{4}$
						7	$17\frac{1}{4}$			12	$41\frac{3}{4}$
159	36	2	2			8	22			13	47
		3	$4\frac{1}{4}$			9	27			14	$52\frac{1}{4}$
		4	$7\frac{1}{4}$			10	$31\frac{3}{4}$			15	$58\frac{1}{4}$
		5	$10\frac{1}{2}$			11	$36\frac{3}{4}$			16	$64\frac{3}{4}$
		6	$14\frac{1}{4}$			12	$41\frac{1}{4}$			17	$70\frac{1}{2}$
		7	$18\frac{1}{4}$			13	$46\frac{3}{4}$			18	$76\frac{1}{2}$
		8	23			14	$52\frac{1}{4}$			$18\frac{1}{2}$	80
		9	28			15	$58\frac{1}{4}$				

THE END.

www.ingramcontent.com/pod-product-compliance
Lightning Source LLC
Chambersburg PA
CBHW030757230426
43667CB00007B/1001